DISPUTE RESOLUTION

David Sixsmith

Series editors: Amy Sixsmith and David Sixsmith

First published in 2022 by Fink Publishing Ltd

Apart from any fair dealing for the purposes of research, private study, or criticism or review, as permitted under the Copyright, Designs and Patents Act, 1988, this publication may not be reproduced, stored or transmitted in any form, or by any means, without the prior permission in writing of the publisher, or in the case of reprographic reproduction, in accordance with the terms of licences issued by the Copyright Licensing Agency. Enquiries concerning reproduction outside those terms should be sent to the publisher.

Crown Copyright material is published with the permission of the controller of the Stationery Office.

© 2022 David Sixsmith

British Library Cataloguing in Publication Data
A catalogue record for this book is available from the British Library
ISBN: 9781914213168

This book is also available in various ebook formats.
Ebook ISBN: 9781914213236

The right of David Sixsmith to be identified as the author of this work has been asserted by him in accordance with sections 77 and 78 of the Copyright, Designs and Patents Act 1988.

Multiple-choice questions advisor: Mark Thomas
Cover and text design by BMLD (bmld.uk)
Production by River Editorial
Typeset by Westchester Publishing Services
Commissioning by R Taylor Publishing Services
Development Editing by Peter Hooper and Sonya Barker
Indexing by Terence Halliday

Fink Publishing Ltd
E-mail: hello@revise4law.co.uk
www.revise4law.co.uk

Contents

About the author	iv
Series editors	iv
Introduction to Revise SQE	v
SQE1 table of legal authorities	xiv
Table of cases	xiv
Table of statutes	xiv
1 Different options for dispute resolution	1
2 Resolving a dispute through a civil claim	20
3 Commencing proceedings	35
4 Responding to a claim	53
5 Statements of case	70
6 Interim applications	86
7 Case management	103
8 Evidence	121
9 Disclosure and inspection	138
10 Costs and funding	153
11 Trial, appeals and enforcement of money judgments	175
Index	193

About the author

David Sixsmith is a senior lecturer in law and programme leader for the Legal Practice Course and postgraduate SQE provision at the University of Sunderland. Previously a partner at a high-street law firm, he is now a non-practising solicitor and a senior fellow of the Higher Education Academy. He is heavily involved with the development of the profession-facing legal education provision at the University of Sunderland and teaches dispute resolution, wills and administration of estates, as well as land and property law and practice, at both undergraduate and postgraduate level as part of their SQE offering.

Series editors

Amy Sixsmith is a senior lecturer in law and programme leader for LLB at the University of Sunderland, and a senior fellow of the Higher Education Academy.

David Sixsmith is a senior lecturer in law and programme leader for LPC at the University of Sunderland, and a senior fellow of the Higher Education Academy.

Introduction to Revise SQE

Welcome to *Revise SQE*, a new series of revision guides designed to help you in your preparation for, and achievement in, the Solicitors Qualifying Examination 1 (SQE1) assessment. SQE1 is designed to assess what the Solicitors Regulation Authority (SRA) refer to as 'functioning legal knowledge' (FLK); this is the legal knowledge and competencies required of a newly qualified solicitor in England and Wales. The SRA has chosen single best answer multiple-choice questions (MCQs) to test this knowledge, and *Revise SQE* is here to help.

PREPARING YOURSELF FOR SQE

The SQE is the new route to qualification for aspiring solicitors introduced in September 2021 as one of the final stages towards qualification as a solicitor. The SQE consists of two parts:

SQE1
- **Functioning legal knowledge (FLK)**
- two x 180 MCQs
- closed book; assessed by two sittings, over 10 hours in total.

SQE2
- **Practical legal skills**
- 16 written and oral assessments
- assesses six practical legal skills, over 14 hours in total.

In addition to the above, any candidate will have to undertake two years' qualifying work experience. More information on the SQE assessments can be found on the SRA website; this revision guide series will focus on FLK and preparation for SQE1.

It is important to note that the SQE can be perceived to be a 'harder' set of assessments than the Legal Practice Course (LPC). The reason for this, explained by the SRA, is that the LPC is designed to prepare candidates for 'day one' of their training contract; the SQE, on the other hand, is designed to prepare candidates for 'day one' of being a newly qualified solicitor. Indeed, the SRA has chosen the SQE1 assessment to be 'closed book' (ie without permitting use of any materials) on the basis that a newly qualified solicitor would know all of the information tested, without having to refer to books or other sources.

With that in mind, and a different style of assessments in place, it is understandable that many readers may feel nervous or wary of the SQE. This is especially so given that this style of assessment is likely to be different from what readers will have experienced before. In this *Introduction* and revision guide series, we hope to alleviate some of those concerns with guidance on preparing for the SQE assessment, tips on how to approach single best answer MCQs and expertly written guides to aid in your revision.

What does SQE1 entail?

SQE1 consists of two assessments, containing 180 single best answer MCQs each (360 MCQs in total). The table below breaks down what is featured in each of these assessments.

Assessment	Contents of assessment ('functioning legal knowledge')
FLK assessment 1	• Business law and practice • Dispute resolution • Contract • Tort • The legal system (the legal system of England and Wales and sources of law, constitutional and administrative law and European Union law and legal services)
FLK assessment 2	• Property practice • Wills and the administration of estates • Solicitors accounts • Land law • Trusts • Criminal law and practice

Please be aware that in addition to the above, ethics and professional conduct will be examined pervasively across the two assessments (ie it could crop up anywhere).

Each substantive topic is allocated a percentage of the assessment paper (eg 'legal services' will form 12–16% of the FLK1 assessment) and is broken down further into 'core principles'. Candidates are advised to read the SQE1 Assessment Specification in full (available on the SRA website). We have also provided a *Revise SQE checklist* to help you in your preparation and revision for SQE1 (see below).

HOW DO I PREPARE FOR SQE1?

Given the vastly different nature of SQE1 compared to anything you may have done previously, it can be quite daunting to consider how you could possibly prepare for 360 single best answer MCQs, spanning 11 different substantive topics (especially given that it is 'closed book'). The *Revise SQE FAQ* below, however, will set you off on the right path to success.

Revise SQE FAQ

Question	Answer
1. Where do I start?	We would advise that you begin by reviewing the assessment specification for SQE1. You need to identify what subject matter can be assessed under each substantive topic. For each topic, you should honestly ask yourself whether you would be prepared to answer an MCQ on that topic in SQE1.
	We have helped you in this process by providing a *Revise SQE checklist* on our website (revise4law.co.uk) that allows you to read the subject matter of each topic and identify where you consider your knowledge to be at any given time. We have also helpfully cross-referenced each topic to a chapter and page of our *Revise SQE* revision guides.
2. Do I need to know legal authorities, such as case law?	In the majority of circumstances, candidates are not required to know or use legal authorities. This includes statutory provisions, case law or procedural rules. Of course, candidates will need to be aware of legal principles deriving from common law and statute.
	There may be occasions, however, where the assessment specification does identify a legal authority (such as *Rylands v Fletcher* in tort law). In this case, candidates will be required to know the name of that case, the principles of that case and how to apply that case to the facts of an MCQ. These circumstances are clearly highlighted in the assessment specification and candidates are advised to ensure they engage with those legal authorities in full.

Revise SQE FAQ (continued)

Question	Answer
3. Do I need to know the history behind a certain area of law?	While understanding the history and development of a certain area of law is beneficial, there is no requirement for you to know or prepare for any questions relating to the development of the law (eg in criminal law, candidates will not need to be aware of the development from objective to subjective recklessness). SQE1 will be testing a candidate's knowledge of the law as it stands four calendar months prior to the date of the first assessment in an assessment window.
4. Do I need to be aware of academic opinion or proposed reforms to the law?	Candidates preparing for SQE1 do not need to focus on critical evaluation of the law, or proposed reforms to the law either.
5. How do I prepare for single best answer MCQs?	See our separate *Revise SQE* guide on preparing for single best answer MCQs below.

Where does *Revise SQE* come into it?

The *Revise SQE* series of revision guides is designed to aid your revision and consolidate your understanding; the series is not designed to replace your substantive learning of the SQE1 topics. We hope that this series will provide clarity as to assessment focus, useful tips for sitting SQE1 and act as a general revision aid.

There are also materials on our website to help you prepare and revise for the SQE1, such as a *Revise SQE checklist*. This *checklist* is designed to help you identify which substantive topics you feel confident about heading into the exam – see below for an example.

Revise SQE checklist

Dispute Resolution

SQE content	Corresponding chapter	*Revise SQE checklist*		
Different options for dispute resolution	Chapter 1, Pages 1–19	I do not know this subject and I am not ready for SQE1 ☐	I partially know this subject, but I am not ready for SQE1 ☐	I know this subject and I am ready for SQE1 ☐

Dispute Resolution (continued)

SQE content	Corresponding chapter	*Revise SQE checklist*		
Responding to a claim	Chapter 4, Pages 53-69	I do not know this subject and I am not ready for SQE1 ☐	I partially know this subject, but I am not ready for SQE1 ☐	I know this subject and I am ready for SQE1 ☐
Case management	Chapter 7, Pages 103-120	I do not know this subject and I am not ready for SQE1 ☐	I partially know this subject, but I am not ready for SQE1 ☐	I know this subject and I am ready for SQE1 ☐

PREPARING FOR SINGLE BEST ANSWER MCQS

As discussed above, SQE1 will be a challenging assessment for all candidates. This is partly due to the quantity of information a candidate must be aware of in two separate sittings. In addition, however, an extra complexity is added due to the nature of the assessment itself: MCQs.

The SRA has identified that MCQs are the most appropriate way to test a candidate's knowledge and understanding of fundamental legal principles. While this may be the case, it is likely that many candidates have little, if any, experience of MCQs as part of their previous study. Even if a candidate does have experience of MCQs, SQE1 will feature a special form of MCQs known as 'single best answer' questions.

What are single best answer MCQs and what do they look like?

Single best answer MCQs are a specialised form of question, used extensively in other fields such as in training medical professionals. The idea behind single best answer MCQs is that the multitude of options available to a candidate may each bear merit, sharing commonalities and correct statements of law or principle, but only one option is absolutely correct (in the sense that it is the 'best' answer). In this regard, single best answer MCQs are different from traditional MCQs. A traditional MCQ will feature answers that are implausible in the sense that the distractors are 'obviously wrong'. Indeed, distractors in a traditional MCQ are often very dissimilar, resulting in a candidate being able to spot answers that are clearly wrong with greater ease.

x   Introduction to Revise SQE

In a well-constructed single best answer MCQ, on the other hand, each option should look equally attractive given their similarities and subtle differences. The skill of the candidate will be identifying which, out of the options provided, is the single best answer. This requires a much greater level of engagement with the question than a traditional MCQ would require; candidates must take the time to read the questions carefully in the exam.

For SQE1, single best answer MCQs will be structured as follows:

A woman is charged with battery, having thrown a rock towards another person intending to scare them. The rock hits the person in the head, causing no injury. The woman claims that she never intended that the rock hit the person, but the prosecution allege that the woman was reckless as to whether the rock would hit the other person.	**The factual scenario.** First, the candidate will be provided with a factual scenario that sets the scene for the question to be asked.
Which of the following is the most accurate statement regarding the test for recklessness in relation to a battery? A. There must have been a risk that force would be applied by the rock, and that the reasonable person would have foreseen that risk and unjustifiably taken it. B. There must have been a risk that force would be applied by the rock, and that the woman should have foreseen that risk and unjustifiably taken it. C. There must have been a risk that force would be applied by the rock, and that the woman must have foreseen that risk and unjustifiably taken it. D. There must have been a risk that force would be applied by the rock, and that both the woman and the reasonable person should have foreseen that risk and unjustifiably taken it. E. There must have been a risk that force would be applied by the rock, but there is no requirement that the risk be foreseen.	**The question.** Next, the candidate will be provided with the question (known as the 'stem') that they must find the single best answer to. **The possible answers.** Finally, the candidate will be provided with **five** possible answers. There is only one single best answer that must be chosen. The other answers, known as 'distractors', are not the 'best' answer available.

Now that you know what the MCQs will look like on SQE1, let us talk about how you may go about tackling an MCQ.

How do I tackle single best answer MCQs?
No exact art exists in terms of answering single best answer MCQs; your success depends on your subject knowledge and understanding of how that subject knowledge can be applied. Despite this, there are tips and tricks that may be helpful for you to consider when confronted with a single best answer MCQ.

| 1. Read the question twice | 2. Understand the question being asked | 3. If you know the answer outright | 4. If not, employ a process of elimination | 5. Take an educated and reasoned guess | 6. Skip and come back to it later |

1. Read the entire question at least twice
This sounds obvious but is so often overlooked. You are advised to read the entire question once, taking in all relevant pieces of information, understanding what the question is asking you and being aware of the options available. Once you have done that, read the entire question again and this time pay careful attention to the wording that is used.
- **In the factual scenario:** Does it use any words that stand out? Do any words used have legal bearing? What are you told and what are you not told?
- **In the stem:** What are you being asked? Are there certain words to look out for (eg 'should', 'must', 'will', 'shall')?
- **In the answers:** What are the differences between each option? Are they substantial differences or subtle differences? Do any differences turn on a word or a phrase?

You should be prepared to give each question at least two viewings to mitigate any misunderstandings or oversights.

2. Understand the question being asked
It is important first that you understand what the question is asking of you. The SRA has identified that the FLK assessments may consist of single best answer MCQs that, for example,
- require the candidate to simply identify a correct legal principle or rule
- require the candidate to not only identify the correct legal principle or rule, but also apply that principle or rule to the factual scenario
- provide the candidate with the correct legal principle or rule, but require the candidate to identify how it should be properly applied and/or the outcome of that proper application.

By first identifying what the question is seeking you to do, you can then understand what the creators of that question are seeking to test and how to approach the answers available.

3. If you know the answer outright

You may feel as though a particular answer 'jumps out' at you, and that you are certain it is correct. It is very likely that the answer is correct. While you should be confident in your answers, do not allow your confidence (and perhaps overconfidence) to rush you into making a decision. Review all of your options one final time before you move on to the next question.

4. If you do not know the answer outright, employ a process of elimination

There may be situations in which the answer is not obvious from the outset. This may be due to the close similarities between different answers. Remember, it is the 'single best answer' that you are looking for. If you keep this in your mind, it will thereafter be easier to employ a process of elimination. Identify which answers you are sure are not correct (or not the 'best') and whittle down your options. Once you have only two options remaining, carefully scrutinise the wording used in both answers and look back to the question being asked. Identify what you consider to be the best answer, in light of that question. Review your answer and move on to the next question.

5. Take an educated and reasoned guess

There may be circumstances, quite commonly, in which you do not know the answer to the question. In this circumstance, you should try as hard as possible to eliminate any distractors that you are positive are incorrect and then take an educated and reasoned guess based on the options available.

6. Skip and come back to it later

If time permits, you may think it appropriate to skip a question that you are unsure of and return to it before the end of the assessment. If you do so, we would advise

- that you make a note of what question you have skipped (for ease of navigation later on), and
- ensure you leave sufficient time for you to go back to that question before the end of the assessment.

The same advice is applicable to any question that you have answered but for which you remain unsure.

We hope that this brief guide will assist you in your preparation towards, and engagement with, single best answer MCQs.

GUIDED TOUR

Each chapter contains a number of features to help you revise, apply and test your knowledge.

Make sure you know Each chapter begins with an overview of the main topics covered and why you need to understand them for the purpose of the SQE1 assessments.

SQE assessment advice This identifies what you need to pay particular attention to in your revision as you work through the chapter.

What do you know already? These questions help you to assess which topics you feel confident with and which topics you may need to spend more time on (and where to find them in the chapter).

Key term Key terms are highlighted in bold where they first appear and defined in a separate box.

Exam warning This feature offers advice on where it is possible to go wrong in the assessments.

Revision tip Throughout the chapters are ideas to help you revise effectively and be best prepared for the assessment.

Summary This handy box brings together key information in an easy to revise and remember form.

Practice example These examples take a similar format to SQE-type questions and provide an opportunity to see how content might be applied to a scenario.

Procedural link Where relevant, this element shows how a concept might apply to another procedural topic in the series.

Key point checklist At the end of each chapter there is a bullet-point summary of its most important content.

Key terms and concepts These are listed at the end of each chapter to help ensure you know, or can revise, terms and concepts you will need to be familiar with for the assessments.

SQE-style questions Five SQE-style questions on the chapter topic give you an opportunity to test your knowledge.

Answers to questions Check how you did with answers to both the quick knowledge test from the start of the chapter and the SQE questions at the end of the chapter.

Key cases, rules, statutes and instruments These list the key sources candidates need to be familiar with for the SQE assessment.

SQE1 TABLE OF LEGAL AUTHORITIES

The SQE1 Assessment Specification states the following in respect of legal authorities and their relevance to SQE1:

> On occasion in legal practice a case name or statutory provision, for example, is the term normally used to describe a legal principle or an area of law, or a rule or procedural step (eg *Rylands v Fletcher*, CPR Part 36, Section 25 notice). In such circumstances, candidates are required to know and be able to use such case names, statutory provisions etc. In all other circumstances candidates are not required to recall specific case names, or cite statutory or regulatory authorities.

This *SQE1 table of legal authorities* identifies the legal authorities you are required to know for the purpose of the SQE1 Functioning Legal Knowledge assessments for *Dispute Resolution*.

Legal authority	Corresponding *Revise SQE* chapter/pages
Halsey v Milton Keynes General NHS Trust [2004] EWCA Civ 576 – whether refusal to consider ADR is justified	Chapter 1: Different options for dispute resolution, page 3
CPR 1.1 (overriding objective)	Chapter 7: Case management and the overriding objective, page 105
CPR 36	Chapter 10: Costs and funding, page 153

TABLE OF CASES

Halsey v Milton Keynes General NHS Trust [2004] EWCA Civ 576... 3–4

TABLE OF STATUTES

Administration of Justice Act 1920 (AJA 1920) 185
Arbitration Act 1996... 8, 9, 19
   s 66... 9
   s 68... 9, 19

Civil Evidence Act 1972... 122, 123–4
Civil Evidence Act 1995... 122, 125

Civil Procedure Rules 1998 (CPR) 1-2, 8-15, 18, 21, 25-7, 36-44, 51, 57-9, 64-9, 73, 77-81, 84, 90-4, 103-22, 130-1, 136-7, 141-2, 150-5, 160-75, 181, 185-6
CPR 1.1... 105-6, 118
CPR 3.8... 113, 114
CPR 3.9... 113, 115, 119
CPR 6.3... 40
CPR 6.9... 41, 44
CPR 16.3(6)... 37
CPR 16.4(1)... 73
CPR 18... 79, 80
CPR 20... 70-1, 77-81, 84-5, 108
CPR 24... 90-2
CPR 25... 94
CPR 26.8(1)... 108
CPR 26.8(2)... 108
CPR 27... 109, 119
CPR 28... 109, 119, 141, 150
CPR 29... 110, 119
CPR 31... 141-2
CPR 36... 153-4, 162, 163-9, 172, 173, 174
CPR 44.4... 160, 172
CPR 45... 155
CPR 74... 185
County Courts Act 1984... 75

Foreign Judgment (Reciprocal Enforcement) Act 1933 (FJ(RE)A 1933) 185

Limitation Act 1980... 20

Mental Capacity Act 2005... 26

Supreme Courts Act 1981... 75

1

Different options for dispute resolution

■ MAKE SURE YOU KNOW

This chapter will cover the different options for dispute resolution. It will explore mediation, arbitration and litigation, the advantages and disadvantages of each of these processes, and the ways in which they can be used to resolve a dispute. You are required to be able to apply these methods of dispute resolution appropriately and effectively to realistic client-based and ethical problems and situations for your SQE1 assessment.

■ SQE ASSESSMENT ADVICE

As you work through this chapter, remember to pay particular attention in your revision to:
- the features of mediation, arbitration and litigation, and their respective advantages and disadvantages when you would recommend alternative methods of dispute resolution;
- the requirement under the Civil Procedure Rules to consider and explore alternative methods of dispute resolution;
- how a litigated claim would proceed if alternative dispute resolution methods were unsuccessful.

■ WHAT DO YOU KNOW ALREADY?

Have a go at these questions before reading this chapter. If you find some difficult or cannot remember the answers, make a note to look more closely at that subtopic during your revision.
1) Fill in the blank: 'Litigation should be the _____ .'
   [Litigation, page 10]
2) Would the court impose a costs penalty on a party for ignoring an offer to mediate from their opponent?
   [In what circumstances is it reasonable to refuse alternative dispute resolution (ADR)?, page 3]
3) After arbitration has concluded, a party who is dissatisfied with the outcome:
   a) Is bound by the determination.
   b) May refer the matter to the court to decide instead.
   c) May use another form of alternative dispute resolution.
   [Arbitration, page 7]

2   Different options for dispute resolution

4) True or false? Litigation is the quickest and most cost-effective way of resolving a dispute.
[Litigation, page 10]

5) Which of the following is not a method of alternative dispute resolution?
   a) Litigation
   b) Mediation
   c) Early Neutral Evaluation

[Introduction to general principles of alternative dispute resolution, page 2]

INTRODUCTION TO GENERAL PRINCIPLES OF ALTERNATIVE DISPUTE RESOLUTION

Alternative dispute resolution (ADR) is an umbrella term that covers methods of resolving a dispute between parties outside of the civil court process. Although parties enter the ADR process voluntarily, the procedural code which governs civil litigation in England and Wales, the Civil Procedure Rules 1998 (CPR; see **page 10**), makes it clear that **litigation** should be a last resort and that an offer to engage in a form of ADR by one party should not be unreasonably refused by the other. In situations where the court considers that a party has unreasonably refused ADR, or that the party has been silent in the face of an invitation to participate, the court is entitled to impose sanctions or penalties on that party. Such sanctions are generally in the form of an unfavourable costs order against the refusing or silent party. All forms of ADR are confidential, or 'without prejudice'. This means that parties cannot disclose any information used as part of the ADR process if a resolution is not reached, and the matter is subsequently referred back to court for determination.

There are many forms of alternative dispute resolution. The SQE only requires you to be aware of two: **mediation** and **arbitration**.

Key term: litigation
The formal process by which disputes are resolved through the courts. At the conclusion of the process, a trial will be held and a judge will make a determination on the claim which is binding on the parties.

Key term: mediation
A form of ADR that involves the agreed instruction of an independent third party (mediator) to facilitate discussions between disputing parties with the aim of reaching an agreed settlement.

> **Key term: arbitration**
> A form of ADR that involves the appointment of an arbitrator, or panel of arbitrators, by the disputing parties. The decision made by the arbitrator(s) at the conclusion of the procedure is binding on the parties, and they are not entitled to subsequently seek a judgment on the matter from the court.

It is likely that any questions you will be asked in your SQE assessment on this topic will centre around three themes:
- In what circumstances is it reasonable to refuse ADR?
- If it is determined that ADR has been refused unreasonably, what sanctions are available for the court to impose?
- Which type of dispute resolution mechanism is most suitable to a particular dispute?

Each of these questions will now be considered in turn.

IN WHAT CIRCUMSTANCES IS IT REASONABLE TO REFUSE ADR?

The court places a duty on the parties to *consider* ADR. A party's reasons to refuse it must be justifiable under scrutiny from the court. The Court of Appeal set out a list of criteria to determine whether refusal to consider ADR is justified (*Halsey v Milton Keynes General NHS Trust* [2004] EWCA Civ 576). When considering an SQE question on this topic, make sure you have these in mind. They are as follows:

(a) the nature of the dispute;

(b) the merits of the case;

(c) the extent to which other settlement methods have been attempted;

(d) whether the costs of the ADR would be disproportionately high;

(e) whether any delay in setting up and attending the ADR would have been prejudicial;

(f) whether the ADR had a reasonable prospect of success.

> **Exam warning**
> Be aware that it has been held by the Court of Appeal since *Halsey* that *failing to respond* to an invitation to ADR is unreasonable in and of itself. Even if a party refuses, they must at least engage with the proposal. Therefore, if you come across a question where a party has simply not responded to an invitation, it is likely that the court will find this conduct unreasonable and impose a sanction or penalty against the refusing party.

4 Different options for dispute resolution

> **Revision tip**
>
> When faced with a scenario where ADR has been refused by a party, consider what you could use from the facts of the case to justify refusal of ADR in front of a judge. Would you be able to argue convincingly that one or more of the *Halsey* considerations applied? If the answer is yes, then there may not be sanctions applied. If the answer is no, then it is likely that the court would impose sanctions.

IF IT IS DETERMINED THAT ADR HAS BEEN REFUSED UNREASONABLY, WHAT SANCTIONS ARE AVAILABLE FOR THE COURT TO IMPOSE?

The court can issue penalties to parties who unreasonably refuse to either comply with a court order requiring the parties to attempt ADR or accept an offer made by the other side to attempt to reach settlement using ADR. This is the case even when that party has been successful in the action overall. The penalties, or sanctions, that are available for the court to impose are known as **adverse costs orders**, and they include:

- depriving a party of being awarded their costs even if they are successful in the litigation;
- ordering the party to pay some or all of the losing side's costs as well as their own, even if the party is successful in the litigation;
- ordering a higher rate of interest to be paid on damages awarded by the court;
- depriving a party of interest on damages awarded by the court.

> **Key term: adverse costs order**
>
> A court order that requires a party to proceedings to pay some or all of the other party's costs associated with the legal action.

The SQE is likely to ask you to identify the most likely penalty in a given set of circumstances. **Practice example 1.1** tests your ability to identify the type of penalty a court may impose.

> **Practice example 1.1**
>
> Annie has issued proceedings against Joshua for breach of contract. During the course of litigation proceedings, the court orders on two occasions that the matter be stayed (paused) for a 28-day period for the parties to explore ADR. During the 28-day stay period, Annie writes to Joshua on seven occasions to ask that he engage in mediation. Joshua writes back refusing, on the basis that there is no realistic possibility of it succeeding; however, he offers no reasons as to why. The matter proceeds to court and Joshua is successful in defending all of the claim. Joshua requests the court to order that Annie pays all of his legal costs

associated with the action. However, when questioned by the judge about his refusal to mediate, he simply says, 'I didn't see why I should.' What order is the court likely to make?

The court is likely to order that Joshua pays Annie's legal costs of the action as well as being responsible for his own, despite Joshua being successful in defending the claim. Where the court has specifically directed that the matter be stayed to allow the parties to attempt mediation and there is clear evidence that a party has refused with no grounds, the court has discretion to impose a costs sanction on that party.

Exam warning
Rapidly developing case law has shown that objections raised to ADR at the time the discussions are taking place are much more likely to be accepted as arguments for justifiably refusing it. Parties who raise objections having simply refused or ignored an invitation at the time are much more likely to be found to have acted unreasonably, and therefore have sanctions imposed upon them.

WHICH TYPE OF DISPUTE RESOLUTION MECHANISM IS MOST SUITABLE FOR A PARTICULAR DISPUTE?

For you to be able to answer this question, you must know and understand how the processes of mediation, arbitration and litigation work, as well as their key advantages and disadvantages. We will therefore consider each of these in turn.

Mediation

Mediation involves settlement by agreement between the parties, with discussions and negotiations facilitated by a mediator.

Once parties to a dispute have consented to mediate in principle, they will nominate and agree on the appointment of an independent mediator. Following this, both parties will send written position statements to the mediator, which set out a background to the case, the points in dispute and any proposals they may have for settlement. The mediator will use this document to prepare for the face-to-face meeting.

A date and place for the mediation to take place will then be agreed between the parties and the mediator. On the day, each party will generally occupy a separate room, and the mediator will 'shuttle' between them. It is the mediator's job to isolate the areas of genuine legal and practical disagreement between the parties and to direct the parties towards a personalised settlement that is to both of their satisfactions.

6 Different options for dispute resolution

It is important to note that any documents or representations made or relied upon by any parties to mediation are 'without prejudice', meaning they are confidential and are not to be used in the context of any subsequent court proceedings should the mediation be unsuccessful.

Advantages and disadvantages of mediation

Tables 1.1 and 1.2 outline the key advantages and disadvantages of mediation.

Table 1.1: Advantages of mediation

Advantage	Explanation
Flexible	There is no set process – it can be set to suit the individual circumstances of the case (including keeping parties entirely separate if the relationship has disintegrated to that extent). Mediation also allows issues to be 'unbundled' (ie broken down into smaller issues that can be resolved more easily).
Cost-effective	Mediation is often much cheaper than litigation.
Speedy	Mediations can be arranged reasonably quickly and can result in swifter resolution of the dispute compared with litigation.
Confidential	Mediation is a private process, and therefore is useful to commercial entities who may find their reputation damaged at trial or wish to protect trade secrets or confidential information from competitors.
Preserves relationships	As a mediated settlement requires agreement from both parties, it is more likely to preserve commercial or personal relationships than an adversarial trial followed by a win/lose court determination.
Settlement terms can be more creative	The court is only able to award a remedy that has been claimed and is legally within their discretion. Mediation allows parties to be creative in the terms of settlement (eg apologising or agreeing to continue trading with each other on renewed terms).
Increases the likelihood of a later negotiated settlement, even if unsuccessful	Even if an agreement is not reached, it helps parties to understand each other's position to the point that settlement could take place via negotiations between party solicitors after the mediation.
Parties can return to court if a settlement is not reached	If it is clear that an agreed settlement will not be reached, parties can be safe in the knowledge that they can still commence or continue with proceedings through the court.

Table 1.2: Disadvantages of mediation

Disadvantage	Explanation
Enforceability of verbal agreements	Unless there is a written agreement (essentially a contract) between the parties, then it is not enforceable through the courts.
All parties must agree to a proposed resolution	If one party has already shown rigid unwillingness to negotiate, mediation could prove to be a futile exercise.
Can increase costs if parties are unwilling to cooperate	If one or both parties are unwilling to even consider settlement, then mediation will likely fail and just increase the costs to the parties overall.
Parties are not required to disclose documentation	There are no formal rules in mediation, and therefore parties can deliberately withhold information if they think it will be damaging to their case. The risk, therefore, is that parties settle without having the full facts, and this can hinder settlement in disputes where trust between the parties has completely disintegrated or there is a history of dishonesty between them.
Ability to withdraw	Parties can withdraw from mediation at any time, risking the exercise being expensive and causing unnecessary delay to court proceedings without a resolution being reached.
No 'day in court'	A party who is seeking vindication or validation of their conduct or looking for the conduct of the opposing party to be penalised will likely not achieve this through mediation.

Arbitration

This is a more formal type of ADR than mediation. It involves an appointed arbitrator, or a panel of three arbitrators, hearing both sides of a dispute before coming to a decision that is binding on the parties.

Arbitration as a form of dispute resolution is most often selected in two ways, either due to a business agreement containing a clause that requires parties to arbitrate in the event of a dispute, or by an agreement in writing between the parties to arbitrate once a dispute has arisen. In either of those situations, the parties contractually agree with each other to: first, engage in arbitration; and second, be bound by the arbitrator's decision at the conclusion of the proceedings. The arbitrator(s) will typically be selected because they have been specifically identified in the original contract between the parties or by subsequent written agreement.

8 Different options for dispute resolution

Arbitration proceedings in England and Wales are governed by the Arbitration Act 1996, provided the agreement is in writing. The arbitrator will decide on the relevant procedural and evidential matters, often require disclosure of key documents, and allow for witnesses to be examined and cross-examined. In this way, arbitration is similar to the court process. The key difference is that arbitration is quicker as it does not need to comply with the formal requirements and timetables laid out in the CPR.

The parties are not entitled to refer the matter to court if they are not satisfied with the outcome; this is an important distinction between arbitration and mediation. The decision taken by the arbitrator is legally binding on the parties, in the same way that a court judgment would be.

Advantages and disadvantages of arbitration

Tables **1.3** and **1.4** outline the key advantages and disadvantages of arbitration.

Table 1.3: Advantages of arbitration

Advantage	Explanation
Expertise of the arbitrator	Often the appointed arbitrator will have significant professional expertise in the area that is the subject of the dispute. This sometimes means that they can be more pragmatic than a judge, who may have only minimal experience by comparison.
Speed	Arbitration can be arranged more swiftly than parties could expect a full trial to take place, and the parties can put a time limit on the length of the overall process.
Flexible	The procedure that is laid down by the arbitrator can be tailored to suit the dispute. The solution that is reached by the arbitrator is often more practical and pragmatic than any order which the parties could receive from the court.
Confidential	Proceedings and awards are confidential, unlike court judgments. This is particularly attractive in commercial actions where the parties do not want their clients or competitors to be aware that a dispute has arisen.
Preserves relationships	As with mediation, arbitration is more likely to preserve commercial or personal relationships since it is entirely confidential. Neither party need lose face publicly, and it is more likely that a pragmatic solution will be reached and imposed by the arbitrator which takes account of the parties' need or desire to maintain a working relationship.

Which mechanism is most suitable for a particular dispute? 9

Table 1.3: (continued)

Advantage	Explanation
Binding decision	The parties contractually agree that they will both abide by the arbitrator's decision prior to the arbitration hearing. This means that an outcome is certain, whereas with mediation it is not.
Enforcement	Under section 66 Arbitration Act 1996, a party can apply to the High Court to enforce a final arbitral award in the same way as a party is free to return to the court to enforce a judgment.

Table 1.4: Disadvantages of arbitration

Disadvantage	Explanation
Powers are more limited	The powers that the arbitrator has to deal with obstructive or awkward parties are significantly less than those of the court. Therefore, the process requires a degree of good faith between the parties.
Cost advantage over litigation is potentially small	The arbitrator (or panel of arbitrators), legal representatives of both sides and any experts involved will all need to be paid, much in the same way as court proceedings. This therefore erodes any potential financial advantage over litigation.
Limited scope to challenge a decision	Section 68 (2) Arbitration Act 1996 provides that a challenge to a decision will only be successful where the applicant can prove that there is a serious irregularity in the proceedings, the tribunal or the award which caused substantial injustice to the applicant. The application must be made within 28 days of the award being made. The criteria are therefore very narrow. A serious irregularity can include where the arbitrator has erred on the particular point of law.
Disclosure and remedies available	Depending on the process, rules relating to disclosure of key documents are not as prescriptive in arbitration, leaving open the possibility that information could be withheld. The legal remedies available to the arbitrator are also slightly more limited than those of the court (eg the arbitrator could not make an order imposing an injunction on one of the parties).

Exam warning

Read the question carefully to identify the client's personal objectives if you are asked what type of ADR would be most suited to a particular dispute. If one of the client's key objectives is flexibility to return to court if ADR does not work out, disregard arbitration as an option. If, however, the client would just like the matter to be settled quickly, however that is achieved, then arbitration would be most suitable.

Practice example 1.2 tests your ability to identify which type of dispute resolution mechanism is most suitable for a particular dispute.

Practice example 1.2

John consults you regarding a dispute that has arisen between him and his neighbour, Barry, over the location of a boundary fence. John informs you that he previously got on well with Barry, that he does not wish to move house in the future and that he would prefer a swift settlement. Which type of ADR would best suit John's situation?

Mediation would be John's best option. It allows him the opportunity to reach a negotiated settlement with Barry that both of them have worked towards and leaves him with the best chance of preserving a reasonable relationship with Barry once the dispute is over.

Litigation

Litigation is referred to in the CPR as the 'last resort' for parties who have been unable to resolve their dispute through ADR. It is the process through which parties ask the court to impose a solution on them after having presented their case through documents and oral representations to a judge. The litigation process is governed by a set of rules, the **Civil Procedure Rules 1998 (CPR)**.

Entering into litigation must be carefully considered by the parties involved. Once proceedings are issued and defended, withdrawing without an agreement will likely result in the withdrawing party being ordered to pay the other side's costs.

Key term: Civil Procedure Rules 1998 (CPR)

The CPR are the set of rules that govern how a civil court claim is conducted. There are 89 rules in total, each of which is accompanied by a Practice Direction that explains how the rule is to operate. It is essential that the CPR are complied with by litigating parties or their representatives. Failure to comply with a rule could result in a sanction, or penalty, being imposed by the court on the offending party.

There are a number of key litigation terms and definitions that the SQE requires you to be familiar with. These are contained in **Table 1.5**.

Which mechanism is most suitable for a particular dispute? 11

Table 1.5: Key litigation terms

Key term	Definition
claimant	A person who makes a claim.
defendant	A person against whom a claim is made.
proceedings	An action taken through the court to settle a dispute.
direction	Instructions given to parties by the court on how they are to prepare or conduct a case (not to be confused with a Practice Direction).
disclosure	The process by which a party makes documents and evidence available to the other party as part of the 'cards on the table' approach encouraged by the CPR.
expert	A person who has been instructed to give or prepare expert evidence for the purpose of proceedings.
case management	The process by which the court actively manages the timetable and requirements of a particular claim/case.
costs	Reference to costs typically means the costs that are associated with the litigation incurred by the parties. This can include court fees, expert fees and solicitor/barrister fees.
leave	'Leave', in the context of civil litigation, is another word for 'permission'. For example, a judge will give 'leave to appeal', which means permission for a party to appeal a decision that has gone against them.
listed	The process by which the court arranges the date for a hearing or trial.
file	Where a party sends a formal document to court for placement on the court file, they are said to 'file' that document with the court.
serve	Where a party sends a formal document to their opponent, they are said to 'serve' that document on the other party.
sanction	A penalty that is imposed by the court on a party for failing to comply with a particular rule, order or direction.
statement of case	A document that sets out a party's case in court proceedings.
the other side	This is a colloquial expression used commonly in practice to describe the solicitors on the opposing side of a dispute.
enforcement	The process by which a party asks the court to force their opponent to comply with an order made by the court at trial.

12 Different options for dispute resolution

Advantages and disadvantages of litigation

The SQE requires you to be familiar with the advantages and disadvantages of litigation, as well as knowing the content of the rules that relate to conducting litigation on behalf of a client. These are covered in **Tables 1.6** and **1.7**.

Table 1.6: Advantages of litigation

Advantage	Explanation
Strict rules that govern the behaviour of parties	The CPR provide a rigid framework of rules that the court expects parties to comply with. If one party does not conduct themselves within the confines of these rules, the court can impose sanctions. These rules also contain guidance on pre-action conduct (ie how parties behave before a claim is issued) to ensure that litigation is only used where there is no other alternative.
Disclosure	Parties are required to put their 'cards on the table' and produce all available evidence that relates to the claim (including that which adversely affects a party's claim) at as early a stage as possible. Failure to disclose a key piece of evidence by the deadline for disclosure will result in that piece being excluded unless the court specifically gives permission for it to be used.
Outcome may be easier to predict if there are similar previously decided cases	Due to the rules surrounding precedent, a lower court is bound to follow the ruling of a higher court in the event that a decision on a point of law has been taken previously.
Binding decision	Once the trial has concluded, the judge or judges will make a decision, enshrined into an order, that is binding on the parties.
Appeal	The parties have the right to apply for leave, or permission, to appeal a decision that has been taken.
Enforcement	In the event that the losing party fails to comply with a court order, the successful party can apply to the court to enforce the terms of that order.

Table 1.7: Disadvantages of litigation

Disadvantage	Explanation
Time-consuming	Litigation is time-consuming for a variety of different reasons. First, in order to be thorough and ensure the proper administration of justice, the court sets a full timetable for the case to follow, which is designed to allow for exploration of all the legal and evidential issues between the parties. Second, the court is almost constantly dealing with a huge backlog of cases, and listing takes place on a first come, first served basis. Parties could therefore be waiting months before a future trial date is set.
Complex to conduct without legal representation	Despite there being helpful Practice Directions, the CPR were drafted for lawyers by lawyers and are very difficult to follow for a layperson without the benefit of any legal advice or representation.
Costly	Litigation is notoriously expensive for parties. Due to its complexity, parties typically instruct legal representation; and given the volume of work that is required to prepare a matter for trial, legal fees are often very high indeed. Other fees are also potentially payable, such as expert fees, barrister fees or court fees.
Adversarial	The way in which litigation is conducted is naturally adversarial. There will be a winner and a loser, and typically there is very little chance of preservation of the relationship between parties after litigation has concluded.

Exam warning

Bear in mind that even if the client in your SQE question desires all the advantages of litigation, they are still required to consider ADR. Simply stating to the court that litigation fits better with the aims of a client will not be sufficient reason to not engage in ADR before issuing proceedings.

The litigation process

The litigation process can be divided into five stages, which are summarised below:

1. Pre-court involvement

    This is commonly referred to as the 'pre-action conduct' stage. The CPR contain a number of pre-action protocols and a Practice Direction on Pre-Action Conduct, which guide parties on the steps to take prior to issuing proceedings. These are explained in more detail in **Chapter 2**.

2. Commencing and defending formal proceedings

    The claimant will commence proceedings by filing a claim form with the court, which will include particulars of the claim (ie a document that sets out the facts, the legal basis on which the claim is made and the remedy sought). If the defendant wishes to defend the action, they will file a defence with the court and serve it on the claimant. This is explained in more detail in **Chapters 3** and **4**.

3. Case management by the court

    Once the claim and defence have been filed with the court, a judge will allocate the claim to one of three 'tracks'. The court will also issue directions to the parties on how they are to conduct the case and set deadlines to meet for each stage. Stages include dates by which disclosure must take place, by which witness statements must be exchanged and, if the parties have the court's permission to rely on expert evidence, when that evidence must be filed with the court. This is explained in more detail in **Chapter 7**.

4. Trial

    A judge will hear all of the evidence and make an order that sets out who is liable to whom (liability) and for how much (quantum). Once the judge has made their decision on liability and quantum, they will then make an order on who will pay the legal costs of the matter, and in what percentage. This is explained in further detail in **Chapter 11**.

5. Post-trial

    This stage is only necessary if one party disagrees with the decision, and therefore appeals it, or if one party fails to pay some or all of the judgment debt or associated legal costs, and therefore needs to enforce the judgment. This is explained in further detail in **Chapter 11**.

■ KEY POINT CHECKLIST

This chapter has covered the following key knowledge points. You can use these to structure your revision, ensuring you recall the key details for each point, as covered in this chapter.

- The Civil Procedure Rules 1998 are clear that parties are expected to engage in ADR to attempt to resolve matters outside of the court.
- Mediation is a form of ADR that involves the parties to a dispute negotiating through an independent mediator to try to reach an agreed settlement.
- Arbitration is a form of ADR that involves the parties to a dispute presenting their arguments to an independent arbitrator, or panel of arbitrators, who will then impose a final determination on the parties.
- The court may impose a range of sanctions or penalties on a party who refuses or ignores an invitation to engage in ADR. The most common sanction is an adverse costs order.
- Litigation is considered a last resort.
- There are five stages of the litigation process.

■ KEY TERMS AND CONCEPTS
- litigation (**page 2**)
- mediation (**page 2**)
- arbitration (**page 3**)
- adverse costs order (**page 4**)
- Civil Procedure Rules 1998 (CPR) (**page 10**)

■ SQE1-STYLE QUESTIONS

QUESTION 1

A client has a dispute with a builder. The builder carried out some remedial work on the client's roof two months ago. The roof subsequently leaked, causing £20,000 of damage to the client's property. The builder has written to the client requesting that he agrees to mediate and offering £2,000 to settle the dispute; however, the client simply wants his day in court and to expose the builder for his poor workmanship.

Which of the following responses best explains the advice that the solicitor should give to the client?

A. The client should engage in mediation with the builder. If he fails to do so, the court will impose costs sanctions on him.

B. The client should ignore the invitation to mediate on the basis that he has not technically refused. This means that no costs sanctions will be imposed on him.

C. The client should write back to the builder refusing to mediate and informing him that he wants his day in court. However, the solicitor should warn him that the court will likely impose sanctions on him for failing to engage in alternative forms of dispute resolution.

D. The client should write back to the builder refusing to mediate on the basis that the offer made is unreasonable and significantly below the overall value of the claim. The court will be unlikely to impose sanctions if it feels that the refusal is justified.

E. The client should write back to the builder refusing to mediate on the basis that their commercial relationship has broken down and is unsalvageable, and that mediation will therefore not work. The court will be unlikely to impose sanctions if it feels that the refusal is justified.

QUESTION 2

A client is a car dealer specialising in selling luxury vintage cars to collectors. A customer who purchased a 1975 vintage car three weeks ago has contacted the client with a complaint, saying that the car is not as described and is

16 Different options for dispute resolution

therefore not worth the amount the customer paid for it. The customer generally purchases between four and six vehicles a year from the client and is widely known in the vintage car collecting community.

Which of the following is the client's best option for resolving the dispute, and why?

A. Mediation, as it is quicker and more likely to result in a better settlement for the client.
B. Mediation, as it is confidential, and therefore no other customers can find out about any settlement reached.
C. Mediation, as it is most likely to result in a preservation of the existing business relationship between the parties.
D. Arbitration, as the parties can involve witnesses and experts in the proceedings.
E. Arbitration, as it is best that a confidential decision is imposed on the parties.

QUESTION 3

A client writes to their opponent offering to mediate on seven separate occasions: three before proceedings were issued and four while proceedings were ongoing. The opponent writes back on two occasions refusing mediation and ignores the remaining invitations. The client is the defendant in the action, and at trial the judge finds in the claimant's favour and awards the full value of the claimant's claim.

Which of the following best describes how the court will deal with the legal costs of the action, and why?

A. The court will order that the client pay their opponent's legal costs as well as their own, as the client has lost the case.
B. The court will order that the client only pay a proportion of their opponent's legal fees as well as their own, as even though the client has lost the case overall they did attempt to engage in alternative dispute resolution.
C. The court will order that the client's opponent pays their own legal costs by way of sanction for refusing to mediate.
D. The court will order that the opponent pays the client's full legal costs as well as their own by way of sanction for refusing to mediate.
E. The court will order that the opponent pays a percentage of the client's legal costs as well as their own by way of sanction for refusing to mediate.

QUESTION 4

A company enters into a written agreement with a customer to appoint an arbitrator to resolve a dispute. The matter proceeds to arbitration and the customer is successful. However, upon taking legal advice immediately after the award is made, the company believes that the arbitrator may have misunderstood the law and applied it incorrectly.

Which of the following best reflects the legal position?

A. The company can refer the matter back to the arbitrator with an explanation of why they feel the law was wrongly applied. The arbitrator will then reconsider.
B. The company can appeal to the High Court on the basis that the arbitrator has wrongly applied the law.
C. The company can seek the permission of the High Court to challenge the decision of the arbitrator on the basis that they have wrongly applied the law.
D. The company can request that the matter be heard by a different arbitrator with specific knowledge of the law in the relevant area.
E. The company is bound by the decision and award made by the arbitrator, and therefore must comply with its terms.

QUESTION 5

A client has repeatedly attempted to settle a dispute by mediation with their opponent. The opponent has attended mediation, but this failed as the opponent left the meeting after 25 minutes, saying that it was a waste of time. The client has since written again to the opponent offering to rearrange mediation, but the opponent has not responded. It is now six weeks since the opponent last responded to correspondence.

Which of the following responses best explains the advice the solicitor should give to the client, and why?

A. The client should issue proceedings against their opponent. Mediation has been unsuccessful and it is clear that the opponent does not wish to engage any further in pre-action negotiations.
B. The client should issue proceedings against their opponent. It is most appropriate for the court to deal with the matter from this point.
C. The client should issue proceedings against their opponent. After a six-week lapse in time, parties are automatically entitled to apply to the court for resolution.
D. The client should keep trying to arrange mediation. The opponent is clearly willing to mediate in principle as they attended the original

18 Different options for dispute resolution

mediation, and the court could impose costs sanctions on the client if they are shown to have issued proceedings too quickly.
E. The client should try to arrange arbitration. This would clearly be a better method of alternative dispute resolution.

■ ANSWERS TO QUESTIONS

Answers to 'What do you know already?' questions at the start of the chapter

1) Litigation should be the last resort. The CPR make it clear that parties should only resort to litigation once alternative methods of dispute resolution have been explored.
2) Yes, it is very likely that the court would impose a costs sanction in this case. Case law has made clear that if a party refuses to engage in mediation following an offer from their opponent, they should communicate this clearly and give reasons for their refusal.
3) The correct answer was (a). Parties who agree to arbitration are not able to refer their matter to the court if they are dissatisfied with the outcome.
4) False. Litigation is arguably the slowest and most expensive method of dispute resolution.
5) The correct answer was (a). Litigation is not a form of ADR.

Answers to end-of-chapter SQE1-style questions

Question 1:
 The correct answer was C. The instructions the client has given is that he does not wish for mediation to go ahead because he wants his day in court, but the solicitor ought to advise him it is likely that costs sanctions will be applied to him as this is not a potentially justifiable reason for failing to mediate. Option D is not correct as basing a refusal on the fact that the opening offer is low would be too premature, and option E can be disregarded as preservation of a commercial relationship is an advantage of mediation, as opposed to a reason for not engaging in it. Mediation is not compulsory, so option A is incorrect, and parties should never simply ignore an offer to mediate, making option B incorrect as well.

Question 2:
 The correct answer was C. Given the long-standing business relationship between the parties and its regularity, a mediated settlement is most likely to result in a preservation of that relationship, and therefore be the best option. Arbitration is more adversarial, and therefore not suitable for a dispute such as this, which discards options D and E. Options A and B are both good reasons for pursuing mediation, but do not reflect

the commercial reality of the relationship between the parties in this scenario, and are therefore incorrect.

Question 3:
The correct answer was E. Due to the opponent failing to acknowledge repeated attempts to mediate, the court would almost certainly impose a costs sanction by ordering them to pay their own legal costs and fees as well as a percentage of the client's. Options A and B are incorrect as, even though the opponent has won the case overall, the courts would not follow the general rule of loser pays winner's costs on account of the invitations to mediation being ignored. Option C is not likely as it would not be regarded as a sufficient penalty, and option D is unlikely as it would be viewed as too harsh.

Question 4:
The correct answer was B. Under section 68 Arbitration Act 1996, parties have a right to refer a matter to the court where they feel that the arbitrator has misapplied the law. Option A is incorrect as the arbitrator would not reconsider a decision already taken, option C is not correct as the parties do not need to seek permission of the court to appeal an arbitral decision, and option D is incorrect as there is no mechanism by which this is possible. Finally, option E is incorrect as the ground for appeal under section 68 seems to be met, and therefore the party is not simply stuck with the decision as they would be if they simply disagreed with it.

Question 5:
The correct answer was A. It is quite clear that mediation has failed and that the opponent is no longer willing to engage in it. Litigation is treated as a last resort, but in this case the client can evidence to the court that attempts at alternative dispute resolution (ADR) have been made and have failed. Option B is not correct as the justification is not as strong as option A, and option C is incorrect as there is no time frame contained in either the Civil Procedure Rules or case law to indicate that after six weeks of no communication, parties are justified in issuing proceedings. Option D is not correct as the court does recognise that some parties are simply unwilling to engage in ADR, and therefore the court is the right place to go in that situation. Finally, option E is not correct as ADR has already failed; there is no reason to think that the opponent would engage with arbitration, and the client is under no obligation to pursue other forms of ADR once one has failed.

■ KEY CASES, RULES, STATUTES AND INSTRUMENTS

The SQE1 Assessment Specification does not require you to know any case names or statutory materials for the topic of different options for dispute resolution.

Resolving a dispute through a civil claim

■ MAKE SURE YOU KNOW

This chapter will cover the initial stages of resolving a dispute through a civil claim. It will cover the preliminary considerations a solicitor and a client must take into account before a claim is commenced, limitation and pre-action protocols, and how to calculate limitation periods for claims in contract and tort. You are required to be able to apply the steps outlined in this chapter appropriately and effectively to realistic client-based and ethical problems and situations for your SQE1 assessment.

■ SQE ASSESSMENT ADVICE

As you work through this chapter, remember to pay particular attention in your revision to:
- what a client should consider before issuing proceedings;
- the provisions of the Limitation Act 1980 and how they relate to claims in contract and tort;
- how pre-action protocols and the Practice Direction on Pre-Action Conduct and Protocols regulate how parties behave prior to issuing proceedings.

■ WHAT DO YOU KNOW ALREADY?

Have a go at these questions before reading this chapter. If you find some difficult or cannot remember the answers, make a note to look more closely at that subtopic during your revision.
1) True or false? Once the limitation period for a claim has expired, there is nothing a party can do to enable the court to hear the claim.
   [Limitation, page 23]
2) How should a defendant respond if a claimant issues proceedings against them outside of the limitation period?
   [Limitation, page 23]
3) Under what circumstances can a claimant with a contractual dispute with a company based in the EU issue proceedings in a court of England and Wales?
   [Jurisdiction and governing law, page 22]

4) True or false? The Practice Direction on Pre-Action Conduct and Protocols (PDPACP) is advisory and can therefore be ignored without penalty.
   [Pre-action protocols and Practice Direction on Pre-Action Conduct and Protocols, page 26]
5) What can the court do to punish a party who fails to comply with a pre-action protocol?
   [Consequences for failing to follow a pre-action protocol or PDPACP without good reason, page 29]

INTRODUCTION TO GENERAL PRINCIPLES OF PRE-ACTION CONDUCT

As we know, parties are encouraged by the court to make attempts to settle their dispute prior to the court being involved. To assist with this further, the Civil Procedure Rules 1998 (CPR; see **Chapter 1**) have a series of **pre-action protocols** and a **Practice Direction on Pre-Action Conduct and Protocols (PDPACP)** embedded within them. Between them, they provide a framework or checklist of things that should be done by the parties before commencing court proceedings.

For the SQE, you must know and understand the preliminary considerations that a solicitor must make their client aware of before issuing proceedings, as well as the purpose and broad principles of the pre-action protocols and Practice Direction on Pre-Action Conduct and Protocols. This section is therefore divided into two parts: the practical considerations that a solicitor must take into account before advising a client to issue proceedings and the steps that the CPR require the parties to take before a dispute is referred to court.

> **Key term: pre-action protocol**
> Pre-action protocols explain the conduct and set out the steps that the court would normally expect parties to take before commencing proceedings for particular types of civil claims.

> **Key term: Practice Direction on Pre-Action Conduct and Protocols (PDPACP)**
> This is a safety net provision. For any matter type that does not have an associated pre-action protocol, parties are expected to follow the guidance in this Practice Direction instead.

PRELIMINARY CONSIDERATIONS

When a client first instructs a solicitor in connection with a dispute, aside from emphasising the benefits of ADR (see **Chapter 1**), the solicitor must explore

and give consideration to the following matters before advising the client to issue proceedings:
- jurisdiction and governing law;
- limitation;
- whether there is a legal cause of action, and if so the merits of the client's claim;
- who the claimant and defendant are, and the nature of their financial circumstances.

Each of these will now be explored in turn.

Jurisdiction and governing law

You must first ensure that the dispute is governed by the law of England and Wales, and second be sure that you can commence proceedings in a court of England and Wales.

Which country's laws apply?

If there is an express declaration in a contract that the law of England and Wales applies to its terms, this will be the position. However, where this express declaration is absent, parties must follow specific rules to determine this jurisdiction. Different rules exist for whether the dispute is inside or outside the EU and whether it is a contractual or tortious dispute. **Figure 2.1** shows the way in which you would establish the correct jurisdiction for a claim that has arisen in the EU.

Contracts in EU ↓
- Country where the seller/supplier has their habitual residence
- For property disputes, where the property in dispute is located

Torts in EU ↓
- Country in which the damage has occurred/is likely to occur

Figure 2.1: Establishing the correct jurisdiction for a claim that has arisen in the EU

For claims outside the EU, there are no specific 'default rules' to cover a situation where there is no express declaration of governing law. This would have to be settled by the court by way of a preliminary issue, before proceedings were commenced.

Where can proceedings be commenced?

Where the defendant is located in the EU, if there is a specific clause in the contract that specifies the location of the court in which a dispute will be heard, then proceedings will be commenced there. Where no express declaration exists, the basic rule is that proceedings will be issued in the local court to where the defendant is domiciled, if they are an individual, or where the registered office is located, if they are a company. An alternative does exist for contract and tort cases, however. The claimant can elect that the case is heard in the state in which the contract was due to be performed or the damages resulting from the tort were incurred, if they so wish.

Where the defendant is habitually resident outside the EU but spends time in England and Wales for whatever reason, provided the claim form can be served on the defendant while they are present in England and Wales, then the claim can be heard here. The court's view is that by allowing proceedings to be served here, the defendant accepts the court's jurisdiction over them.

Now attempt **Practice example 2.1** and test your understanding of jurisdiction.

> **Practice example 2.1**
>
> Pierre, a French resident, negligently crashes into Martha while he is driving in England, causing Martha injury. Martha wishes to know what the governing law is and whether she needs to issue proceedings against Pierre in England and Wales or in France. How would you advise Martha?
>
> **The governing law would be England and Wales, as this is where the damage flowing from the negligent act took place. Martha would have the option of issuing proceedings in France (as the defendant is habitually resident there) or in England and Wales (as the damages resulting from the negligent act were incurred here).**

Limitation

The limitation date is the last date on which a claimant can issue proceedings against a defendant. It is crucial to get right, as issuing a claim that is outside of its limitation period will give the defendant an absolute defence to that action. For instance, if the limitation date of a contractual dispute was on 17 March, issuing proceedings on 20 March would mean that the defendant would not need to defend the claim on the facts. They would simply need to state that the claim has been brought out of time and is therefore **statute barred**.

> **Key term: statute barred**
>
> Where a claim is no longer legally enforceable as it has not been issued in the prescribed limitation period.

How to calculate limitation periods

To calculate the correct limitation date, follow this formula:
1. Work out the type of matter that you are dealing with.
2. Establish when the limitation period began.
3. Apply the relevant statutory limitation period.

For the SQE, you are only required to know limitation periods in relation to claims in contract and tort. **Table 2.1** sets out the relevant considerations.

Table 2.1: Limitation periods in contract and tort

Type of claim	Start date of limitation period	Limitation period
Contract	Date of breach of contract	Six years
Tort (excluding personal injury and **latent damage** cases)	Date the damage occurs	Six years
Tort (personal injury claims)	Date the cause of action occurs or date of knowledge of the person injured, whichever is later	Three years
Tort (latent damage cases)	The date when damage occurs or the date on which the claimant first knew about the cause of action, whichever is later	Six years from the date when damage occurred Three years from the date of knowledge (but the claim must be brought within 15 years after the negligent act or omission)

> **Key term: latent damage**
>
> Damage that is not immediately obvious (eg where a chimney is designed, built and installed by a defendant company which transpires several years after installation to be defective, causing damage to the rest of the building).

> **Revision tip**
>
> Remember in the tort of negligence that the date the cause of action arose is the date on which damages occurred, not necessarily the date on which the original breach took place. Negligence has three composite elements – duty, breach and damage – all of which must occur before the cause of action arises.

Extending the limitation period

As highlighted above, a defendant will have an absolute defence to a claim made outside of the relevant limitation period. In that instance, the claim will not proceed. In exceptional circumstances, however, the court may allow a party an extension of the limitation period (eg where the parties are engaged in alternative dispute resolution that has not concluded by the limitation date, or in limited personal injury cases where the prejudice to the claimant in not being able to bring the claim substantially outweighs the detriment to the defendant). The party requiring the extension would need to apply to the court for it, setting out its reasons and any available evidence to support those reasons in the application. The court would then make a decision.

Exam warning

If the scenario of an SQE question involves a solicitor being instructed by a client on the day that limitation is due to expire where there is no good reason to apply for an extension of the limitation period, the CPR do allow a party to 'issue protectively'. This means that a claim would be lodged with the court but not served on the defendant, up to a maximum of four months after proceedings are issued. This is to enable solicitors to protect their client's interests while at the same time conducting preliminary investigations and exploring ADR with the defendant before the formal court process commences.

The SQE is likely to assess your knowledge of limitation periods. See **Practice example 2.2** for an illustration of how to identify the correct limitation period.

Practice example 2.2

Twelve years ago, Great Borders Limited instructed Final Design Limited to design, build and install a fireplace in their great hall. Two years ago, John, a director of Great Borders Limited, noticed cracking around the brickwork surrounding the fireplace, but initially put it down to the age of the building. The cracking worsened in the last six months, causing Great Borders Limited to instruct an expert to inspect it. The expert has concluded that the fireplace was designed and installed defectively, which has led to around £600,000 of remedial work to the building structure in the great hall. Are Great Borders Limited statute barred from issuing proceedings against Final Design Limited?

No. This is a clear example of a latent damage claim in tort. The start date for Great Borders Limited's limitation period would be two years ago, when they are first deemed to have had knowledge of the damage. Furthermore, they are issuing a claim within 15 years of when the negligent act was carried out (we are told the work was done 12 years ago), so Great Borders Limited will be entitled to issue proceedings without running into limitation issues.

Whether there is a legal cause of action, and if so, the merits of the client's claim

A solicitor will be required to establish, before considering any procedural points, whether there is a legal cause of action for the client's claim. A legal cause of action is the legal basis on which a claimant issues proceedings. If no legal cause of action can be brought, then no claim exists.

Relevant legal causes of action and how to identify them are set out in the *Revise SQE: Contract Law* and *Tort Law* revision guides.

Who the claimant and defendant are, and the nature of their financial circumstances

It is of crucial importance to the claim to identify the claimant and the defendant properly, as well as establishing their circumstances. Some questions to ask are as follows:
- Is the claimant an individual, a company or another legal entity?
- Is the defendant an individual, a company or another legal entity?
- Is there more than one defendant? For instance, in claims where a tort has been committed by an employee of a company in the course of their employment, any court action should be against both the employee and the company as the company is vicariously liable for the actions of their employee.
- Does the claimant or defendant lack the requisite mental capacity under the Mental Capacity Act 2005 to conduct court proceedings? Are they a minor? If so, they may need a **litigation friend** to assist them with the proceedings. Commonly, an appropriate person would be a parent or guardian, a solicitor, or a close friend of the family.
- If the claim is successful, does the defendant have the assets or finances to be able to pay any judgment or not? Conducting investigations such as a bankruptcy or company search could reveal that the defendant would not be able to meet any liabilities arising from a court order in any event, making it a very expensive procedure for very little reward.

> **Key term: litigation friend**
>
> A person who conducts court proceedings on behalf of a child or protected party (eg somebody who by reason of a mental disorder is incapable of conducting proceedings on their own behalf).

PRE-ACTION PROTOCOLS, AND PRACTICE DIRECTION ON PRE-ACTION CONDUCT AND PROTOCOLS (PDPACP)

Having discussed above the practical preliminary considerations that you must deal with after you have been instructed to act for a client, we must now consider how the CPR expect parties to behave before issuing proceedings. These are called 'pre-action rules'. Non-compliance with these pre-action rules can result in a party being penalised by the court at a later stage in the proceedings.

Pre-action rules are therefore designed to encourage early resolution, thereby ensuring that litigation is only ever a last resort for the parties.

The objectives of pre-action conduct are set out in the PDPACP, and are as follows:
(a) Understand each other's position.
(b) Make decisions about how to proceed.
(c) Try to settle the issues without proceedings.
(d) Consider a form of alternative dispute resolution (ADR) to assist with settlement.
(e) Support the efficient management of proceedings.
(f) Reduce the costs of resolving the dispute.

The rules relating to pre-action conduct are found in two areas of the CPR:
- pre-action protocols;
- Practice Direction on Pre-Action Conduct and Protocols (PDPACP).

Both the pre-action protocols and the PDPACP set out a common series of steps that should be taken prior to proceedings being issued. They are as follows:
- The claimant should write to the defendant with concise details of the claim. The letter should include the basis on which the claim is made, a summary of the facts, what the claimant wants from the defendant, and – if money – how the amount is calculated.
- The defendant should respond to the claimant's letter within a reasonable time – 14 days in a straightforward case and no more than three months in a very complex one. The reply should include confirmation as to whether the claim is accepted and, if it is not accepted, the reasons why, together with an explanation as to which facts and parts of the claim are disputed and whether the defendant is making a counterclaim, as well as providing details of any counterclaim.
- The parties should disclose key documents relevant to the issues in dispute.

Both pre-action protocols and the PDPACP will be dealt with in turn below.

Pre-action protocols

Pre-action protocols contain specific guidance on the steps that should be taken by parties who have a dispute arising from one of 13 different legal causes of action. They are as follows:
- personal injury;
- resolution of clinical disputes;
- construction and engineering;
- defamation;
- professional negligence;
- judicial review;

- disease and illness;
- housing disrepair;
- possession claims by social landlords;
- possession claims for mortgage arrears;
- dilapidation of commercial property;
- low-value personal injury road traffic accident claims;
- low-value personal injury employers' liability and public liability claims.

If a particular pre-action protocol applies, this should be used instead of the PDPACP. Some protocols have template letters of claim annexed to them to ensure that compliance with the protocol can be achieved.

> **Revision tip**
>
> You will not be expected to learn the contents of each pre-action protocol for SQE1. However, you will be expected to know which types of claims have pre-action protocols associated with them, and the common series of steps that should be taken by parties prior to issuing proceedings (as set out on **page 26**).

Practice Direction on Pre-Action Conduct and Protocols (PDPACP)

In the event that a dispute does not have a relevant pre-action protocol, the requirements laid out in the PDPACP ought to be followed. It is important to note that it is not mandatory for parties to follow the guidance laid out; however, the court will consider whether the parties have complied in substance with the PDPACP when deciding whether sanctions are appropriate.

The key requirements of the PDPACP are laid out in **Table 2.2**.

Table 2.2: The key requirements of the PDPACP

Requirement	Explanation
Exchange of key information	Parties should look to disclose any evidence that allows them to achieve the objectives of pre-action conduct (set out on **page 26**).
Consideration of ADR	Parties are expected to explore and provide evidence that consideration has been given to resolving the dispute using a form of ADR.
Instruction of experts (where appropriate)	Parties should look to instruct a single joint expert instead of an expert for each side to save time and costs.
Proportionality	Only reasonable and proportionate steps should be taken by the parties to try to resolve the matter, and costs incurred in taking those steps should also be proportionate to the matter in dispute.

Although it is the court's expectation that pre-action conduct will take place in almost every claim, there are certain instances where this will not be appropriate, for example:
- where the application is 'without notice', meaning that it is made with the intention of giving the defendant no warning, such as a freezing order on assets to avoid them being disposed of;
- where the statutory or contractual limitation period is about to expire and compliance with the pre-action conduct requirements would mean that the defendant would have an absolute limitation defence against the action.

Consequences for failing to follow a pre-action protocol or PDPACP without good reason

Parties who fail to comply with the substance of the relevant protocol or PDPACP without good reason could be liable to penalties, or sanctions, being imposed upon them by the court. Examples of such sanctions include:
- an order that the party at fault pays the costs of the proceedings, or part of the costs of the other party or parties;
- an order that the party at fault pay those costs on an **indemnity basis**;
- if the party at fault is a claimant who has been awarded a sum of money, an order depriving that party of interest on that sum for a specified period, and/or awarding interest at a lower rate than would otherwise have been awarded;
- if the party at fault is a defendant, and the claimant has been awarded a sum of money, an order awarding interest on that sum for a specified period at a higher rate (not exceeding 10% above base rate) than the rate which would otherwise have been awarded.

Key term: indemnity basis
A term used in the context of costs recovery in civil litigation. If costs are awarded by the court on the indemnity basis, any dispute between the parties as to the value of those costs will be resolved in favour of the receiving party, and there is no requirement for the costs sought to be proportionate. This means that a party paying their opponent's costs on an indemnity basis are much more likely to have a higher costs liability than if they were awarded on the standard basis.

■ KEY POINT CHECKLIST

This chapter has covered the following key knowledge points. You can use these to structure your revision, ensuring you recall the key details for each point, as covered in this chapter.
- If there is an express declaration in a contract that the law of England and Wales applies to its terms, this will be the position.
- The limitation date is the last date on which a claimant can issue proceedings against a defendant.

- Pre-action protocols contain specific guidance on the steps that should be taken by parties who have a dispute arising from one of 13 different legal causes of action.
- In the event that a dispute does not have a specific relevant pre-action protocol, the requirements laid out in the Practice Direction on Pre-Action Conduct and Protocols (PDPACP) ought to be followed.
- Parties who fail to comply with the substance of the relevant protocol or PDPACP without good reason could be liable to penalties being imposed upon them by the court.

■ KEY TERMS AND CONCEPTS

- pre-action protocol (**page 21**)
- Practice Direction on Pre-Action Conduct and Protocols (PDPACP) (**page 24**)
- statute barred (**page 23**)
- latent damage (**page 24**)
- litigation friend (**page 26**)
- indemnity basis (**page 29**)

■ SQE1-STYLE QUESTIONS

QUESTION 1

Three years ago last week, a man ordered 15 mahogany desks from a company over the internet for use in his office. He paid for the items upfront. When they were delivered, he had no real use for them so stored them immediately. He did not use them until last week, when a scheduled refurbishment of the office was completed. Having been put into use for a week, it became clear that the desks are unfit for purpose and are a hazard to their users as they are creaking and wobbling.

Which of the following best summarises the man's position regarding limitation?

A. The man has another three years to bring a claim. The time limit for a breach of contract claim such as this is six years overall, and the limitation period began from the date on which the cause of action arose.

B. The man has six years from last week to bring a claim. The time limit for a breach of contract claim such as this is six years overall, and the limitation period began from the date on which the goods first appeared defective.

C. The man has another 12 years to bring a claim. The time limit for a breach of contract claim such as this is 15 years overall, and the limitation period began from the date of the breach and three years have passed already.

D. The limitation period has expired. The man had three years to bring the claim and failed to do so in the relevant time.
E. Limitation will not apply as the goods were purchased over the internet. Different rules therefore govern the limitation on making a claim.

QUESTION 2

A client instructs a solicitor in connection with a personal injury claim. The limitation period is due to expire the day after the client is expected to have a meeting with the solicitor.

Which of the following best represents the steps the solicitor should take?

A. The solicitor should gather evidence from the client and send a letter before action to the defendant in compliance with the pre-action protocol. Once the time period for responding has expired, the solicitor can issue proceedings.
B. The solicitor should send a letter before action to the defendant in compliance with the pre-action protocol. If the defendant fails to respond, the solicitor should make further repeated attempts to settle the matter using alternative dispute resolution as per the pre-action protocol.
C. The solicitor should issue proceedings immediately without complying with the pre-action protocol. Failing to issue proceedings within the relevant limitation period would be fatal to the claim.
D. The solicitor should send a letter before action to the defendant in compliance with the pre-action protocol. The solicitor should follow this with an application to the court to extend the limitation period so that the client's claim is preserved while still allowing the parties to engage in appropriate pre-action conduct.
E. The solicitor should issue proceedings immediately but also send a letter before action in compliance with the pre-action protocol.

QUESTION 3

A client instructs a solicitor in connection with a dispute over the supply of 50 boxes of fruit to their café. When the fruit arrived, much of it was rotten. The client paid upfront for the goods and now would like to recover the sums paid from the supplier. The client is furious and would like to issue proceedings immediately.

Which of the following best describes how the client should proceed?

A. The client should issue proceedings immediately. It is clear that there has been a serious breach of contract, and the court should therefore be involved without delay to resolve matters.

B. The client should send a letter before action to the supplier setting out details of their claim and enclosing key documents by way of evidence.

C. The client should issue proceedings immediately. Litigants are only required to engage with the Practice Direction on Pre-Action Conduct and Protocols (PDPACP) if to do so would be proportionate to the dispute, and that is not the case here.

D. The client should issue proceedings immediately but inform the supplier in writing that they are doing so, as well as offering to engage in alternative dispute resolution (ADR).

E. The client should send a letter to the supplier informing them that they are very disappointed with the service received. They should then issue proceedings.

QUESTION 4

A client company enters into a trade agreement with a Spanish company for the supply of coat hangers. The client company purchased the goods two weeks ago and paid for them upfront. The goods arrived yesterday; however, many of the coat hangers were damaged and cannot be used. The client now wishes to reject the goods, claim back the money paid and claim for compensation.

Which of the following best reflects the legal position of the parties?

A. The client company must issue proceedings in Spain as this is the local court to the Spanish company.

B. The client company must issue proceedings in England as this is where the goods were delivered.

C. The client company must investigate to see if the Spanish company has a registered office in England. If so, proceedings can be issued against the Spanish company through the English courts as they have accepted the English courts' jurisdiction.

D. The company must review the contract first to see if there is any express term indicating what the governing law is and which courts have jurisdiction in the event of a dispute arising.

E. The company must check the contract first; but even if there is an express term indicating that Spanish courts have jurisdiction, that can be overridden because Spain is an EU country.

QUESTION 5

A client has recently been in a car accident. The client was unharmed, but their 8-year-old child was seriously injured. The client wishes to make a claim against the driver at fault for the accident.

Which of the following best reflects the legal position?

A. The child is too young to conduct proceedings on their own behalf, so the client should apply to be the child's litigation friend. This means that they will be able to conduct proceedings for them.
B. The child is too young to conduct proceedings on their own behalf, so they should wait until they are 18 years old to make a claim. This will be within the 15-year time limit after the date of the negligent act, so they will not be statute barred from making a claim.
C. The client should issue proceedings in their own name on the child's behalf.
D. The child is too young to conduct proceedings on their own behalf, but the client would not be a suitable litigation friend as they are too close to the child. The court would therefore be unlikely to accept their application.
E. The child is too young to conduct proceedings on their own behalf and the limitation period is only three years from the date of the accident, so they will have to abandon the claim.

ANSWERS TO QUESTIONS

Answers to 'What do you know already?' questions at the start of the chapter

1) False. In very limited and exceptional circumstances, the court does have discretion to extend the limitation period, but only following an application by the prospective claimant.
2) If the claimant issues proceedings outside the relevant limitation period, the defendant has an absolute defence to an action against them.
3) Provided the contract was due to be carried out in England and Wales. If the work in connection with the contract was due to be carried out in the EU, then the claimant must issue proceedings in the defendant's home court.
4) False. The PDPACP is guidance only, but the court will impose sanctions on parties who fail to follow its substance.
5) If a party fails to follow a relevant pre-action protocol, the court is able to punish them by imposing sanctions or penalties.

Answers to end-of-chapter SQE1-style questions

Question 1:
The correct answer was A. Breach of contract claims run from the date on which the cause of action arose (when the goods were delivered) and the relevant limitation period is six years. This makes option B incorrect, and option C is wrong as the 15-year time period is only relevant to latent damage claims in tort. Option D is incorrect as the limitation period is

34   Resolving a dispute through a civil claim

six years, and therefore has not expired, and the medium over which the contract is formed is immaterial, making option E wrong.

Question 2:
The correct answer was C. Limitation will always trump the need to comply with the pre-action protocol. If the solicitor issues proceedings after limitation, then the defendant will have an absolute defence to the claim, which makes option B incorrect. Although the solicitor should write to the defendant explaining that the proceedings have been issued and inviting them to engage in ADR, the claim would still need to have been made by the limitation date, which makes options A and E incorrect. Finally, option D is incorrect as it is only in exceptional circumstances that the court will allow an application to extend limitation.

Question 3:
The correct answer was B. The PDPACP indicates that a letter before action, setting out concise details of the claim with accompanying evidence, should be sent to a prospective defendant before proceedings are issued. This assists with the 'cards on the table approach' and also means that option E is incorrect. Issuing proceedings immediately would only be justified where limitation is an issue, which means that options A, C and D are incorrect.

Question 4:
The correct answer was D. The first place to check is the contract to see if there has been an express agreement made regarding jurisdiction. If so, the parties are bound to follow that agreement. Default provisions for EU countries are only applicable where there is no express agreement, so option E is incorrect. Options A, B and C are incorrect as any default arrangements would only come into force where there was no contractual agreement in existence.

Question 5:
The correct answer was A. A minor is not capable of conducting proceedings on their own behalf, but the client would be able to apply to the court to be appointed as their litigation friend. Option B is incorrect as the 15-year time limit only relates to latent damage claims in tort (which this is not), and option C is incorrect as the client is not the injured party and therefore the true claimant, so cannot simply issue proceedings in their own name. Option D is incorrect as the client is the child's parent, and therefore is a suitable litigation friend. Finally, option E is not correct as the option is there for a litigation friend to conduct proceedings on the child's behalf rather than the claim being simply abandoned.

■ KEY CASES, RULES, STATUTES AND INSTRUMENTS

The SQE1 Assessment Specification does not require you to know any case names or statutory materials for the topic of resolving a dispute through a civil claim.

3

Commencing proceedings

■ MAKE SURE YOU KNOW

This chapter will cover commencement of a claim. It will cover the correct court in which to commence proceedings and how to issue and serve the claim form and associated documentation, including where you may need to serve proceedings outside of England and Wales. You are required to be able to apply these principles appropriately and effectively to realistic client-based and ethical problems and situations for your SQE1 assessment.

■ SQE ASSESSMENT ADVICE

As you work through this chapter, remember to pay particular attention in your revision to:
- where to start proceedings, including how business is allocated between the High Court and the County Court and jurisdiction of the specialist courts;
- issuing and serving proceedings, including issuing a claim form, joinder of parties and of causes of action;
- service of a claim form within and outside of the jurisdiction, and when the court's permission is required;
- when the deemed dates of service fall and the applicable time limits for serving proceedings;
- how to serve proceedings by an alternative method.

■ WHAT DO YOU KNOW ALREADY?

Have a go at these questions before reading this chapter. If you find some difficult or cannot remember the answers, make a note to look more closely at that subtopic during your revision.
1) A client has a claim worth £45,000. Which court should it be commenced in?
   [Which court should a claim be commenced in?, page 36]
2) How long after a claim form has been issued by the court does it need to be served on a defendant?
   [When to serve the claim form, page 42]

36   Commencing proceedings

3) Can a party be added to proceedings as claimant once a claim has been issued?
   [Adding, removing or substituting a party, page 45]
4) Which of the following methods cannot be used to serve proceedings on an opponent?
   a) Post
   b) Text message
   c) Phone call
   [How to serve the claim form, page 40]
5) What are the grounds that need to be proved to add a party to proceedings prior to the expiration of the limitation period?
   [Adding, removing or substituting a party, page 45]

INTRODUCTION TO COMMENCING PROCEEDINGS

This chapter sets out how to commence proceedings in the civil courts of England and Wales. The SQE requires you to know and understand the following:
- which court a claim should be commenced in;
- how a claim is issued at court;
- how to serve the **claim form** and **particulars of claim** on the defendant
- how the Civil Procedure Rules 1998 (CPR; see **Chapter 1**) treat time in relation to dates of service and time limits for serving proceedings;
- how to join other parties to proceedings or how to apply to substitute a party to proceedings;
- service of a claim outside the jurisdiction of England and Wales.

Key term: claim form
This is the form that is used to start proceedings in England and Wales.

Key term: particulars of claim
This is generally a separate document that is served either together with or after the claim form. The claim form generally includes a brief summary of the claim, whereas the particulars of claim sets out the material facts and the legal cause of action being brought by the claimant.

WHICH COURT SHOULD A CLAIM BE COMMENCED IN?

In England and Wales, civil claims must be issued in either the County Court or the High Court. Although other factors are taken into consideration, the following is a good rule of thumb:
- Claims worth £100,000 or less should be commenced in the County Court.

Which court should a claim be commenced in? 37

- Personal injury claims worth £50,000 or less should be commenced in the County Court.
- Claims worth £100,000 or more may be commenced in either the County Court or the High Court.

If the value of the claim is more than £100,000 (or £50,000 for personal injury claims), the High Court will be the most appropriate court where:
- the case has complex facts;
- the outcome of the case has an element of public interest.

Exam warning

The primary driving factor behind the most appropriate court in which to issue proceedings is the value of the claim. It is important that you know how the CPR regard how the value of a claim is calculated. CPR 16.3(6) sets out that the value of a claim is its financial worth *disregarding* the following:
- interest accumulated;
- the legal costs in pursuing the claim;
- the costs involved in pursuing any **counterclaim**;
- any amount that may be claimed for contributory negligence (eg where the claimant has contributed to their injuries by their own negligence).

Key term: counterclaim

A claim that is made by a defendant to offset the claimant's claim. For example, a claimant makes a claim for breach of contract to the value of £25,000. The defendant admits breaching the contract but argues that the claimant also breached the contract, costing him £15,000. The defendant would therefore make a counterclaim against the claimant, which would be considered by the court as part of the same action.

In the event that the claim is complex and valued at over £100,000 (or £50,000 for personal injury claims), it is likely that it will need to be issued in the High Court. We must therefore consider the structure of the High Court and what types of dispute it deals with.

The High Court is comprised of three distinct divisions. These are:
- the Queen's Bench Division;
- the Chancery Division;
- the Family Division.

For the purposes of this book, we will not be considering the Family Division as it does not hear civil claims in the areas of contract or tort.

The Queen's Bench Division
The Queen's Bench Division hears contract and tort disputes that are complex and/or involve substantial sums of money. It also contains several specialist courts, including:
- the Administrative Court;
- the Admiralty Court;
- the Commercial Court;
- the Mercantile Court;
- the Technology and Construction Court.

The Chancery Division
The Chancery Division also hears a wide range of civil cases. It typically hears business or property disputes that are complex and/or involve substantial sums of money. The Chancery Division also incorporates specialist courts. These include:
- the Insolvency and Companies Court;
- the Intellectual Property Enterprise Court;
- the Patents Court.

The Chancery Division can hear the following types of cases:
- land and property disputes;
- mortgages;
- trusts, administration of estates and probate matters;
- bankruptcy;
- partnerships and company matters;
- intellectual property.

For claims that are complex or high-value, and are therefore appropriate to be issued in the High Court, you must be able to identify which Division or Specialist Court the matter is likely to be allocated to for your SQE assessment. Test whether you are able to identify the correct court to consider a claim in **Practice example 3.1**.

> **Practice example 3.1**
>
> Grantham Construction Limited were contractually engaged as structural engineers two years ago by Bright Houses Limited to design, assess and inspect the building of a block of flats in Manchester city centre. Midway through the project, it became apparent that the building was at risk of structural failure. Engineering experts were brought in to provide reports, some of which support the argument that structural failure is imminent and others which do not support it. The parties have been locked in dispute ever since. Bright Houses Limited now wishes to commence proceedings against Grantham Construction Limited for breach of contract, with a claim value of approximately £450,000. Which would be the correct court to consider this claim?

The correct court to issue proceedings would be the High Court. The matter would be heard by the Technology and Construction Court within the Queen's Bench Division. This is due to the fact that it is valued at over £100,000 and is quite clearly complex factually, given the disagreements in expert evidence.

HOW TO ISSUE A CLAIM AT COURT

It is a common misconception that the term 'issuing proceedings' refers to an act done by the claimant. This is not the case. Proceedings are actually issued by the court, once the claimant has filed the claim form, the particulars of claim and any supporting evidence (see **Chapter 1, Table 1.5**). The court issues the claim by sealing the claim form (which stops the limitation time running, see **Chapter 2**) and allocating a claim number to the case. Once these steps have been taken, the claim is regarded as being formally issued.

Once issued, the claim form is valid for four months. Either the court or the claimant must then take a relevant step to serve the claim on the defendant within that four-month period (see **Chapter 1, Table 1.5**).

The claim form and particulars of claim

The claim form is the document that is used by a claimant to commence proceedings against a defendant. In the majority of civil cases, the claim form to be used is form N1. This asks for the following information:
- claimant name and address;
- defendant name and address;
- brief details of claim;
- claim value;
- preferred County Court hearing centre for the hearing(s);
- defendant's address for service;
- particulars of claim;
- statement of truth;
- claimant's or their legal representative's address for correspondence.

The particulars of claim can either be included on the form N1 or attached to the form N1 in a separate document. The particulars of claim set out a detailed chronology of the facts of the case, as well as specifying the legal elements of the claim that is being brought. Evidence will accompany the particulars of claim, where appropriate, directed by the CPR.

SERVICE OF THE CLAIM FORM AND PARTICULARS OF CLAIM

We now know how proceedings are issued by the court. The claim form must be served on all parties to the action within four months of the date of issue.

For SQE1, you may have to establish whether a claim form has been validly served. You therefore need to know the following:
- how to serve the claim form;
- where to serve the claim form;
- when to serve the claim form.

How to serve the claim form

There are two elements of how to validly serve the claim form. First, the claimant must identify the appropriate method of service. Then the claimant must complete the relevant step (ie what needs to be done by the claimant to validly serve the claim form for that particular method of service). For the SQE, you may be asked to identify whether a claim form has been validly served by a claimant.

The permitted methods of service are set out in CPR 6.3. Once you have established which method of service the claimant has chosen, you can then check whether they have completed the relevant step correctly to validly serve the claim form. The permitted methods of service and relevant steps are set out in **Table 3.1**.

Table 3.1: Permitted methods of service and relevant step required for valid service

Method of service	Explanation	Step required for valid service
Personal service	Effective personal service of the claim form depends on leaving it with the right person.	(a) If the defendant is an individual, the claim form should be left with that individual. (b) If the defendant is a company or other corporation, the claim form should be left with a person holding a senior position within the company or corporation. (c) If the defendant is a partnership, the claim form should be left with a partner or a person who, at the time of service, has the control or management of the partnership business at its principal place of business.

Table 3.1: (continued)

Method of service	Explanation	Step required for valid service
First-class post or Document Exchange	If sending by post, the claim form will only be considered validly served if sent by first-class post or by Document Exchange (which is a private postal service used by solicitors that guarantees next-day delivery).	Posting, leaving with, delivering to or collection by the relevant service provider.
Leaving the claim form at a specified place	Directly delivering the document to the location at which it is to be served (discussed in greater detail in **Table 3.2**).	Delivering to or leaving the document at the relevant place.
Fax or other means of electronic communication	Provided the recipient has expressly confirmed that they are happy to accept service by fax or email, the claim form can be sent via either of those means.	(a) Completing the transmission of the fax. (b) Sending the email or other electronic transmission.
Any other method authorised by the court	In certain exceptional circumstances, the court can authorise service of the claim form by a different method, such as posting or delivering it to someone who knows the defendant or authorising service by text message.	

Once you have established how the claimant has served the claim form, you then need to move on to consider where the claim form has been served.

Where to serve the claim form
The correct address for service, depending on the nature of the defendant who is to be served, is set out in CPR 6.9 and **Table 3.2**.

Table 3.2: Appropriate place of service

Nature of defendant to be served	Appropriate place of service
Individual	Usual or last known residence.
Individual being sued in the name of a business (eg a sole trader)	Usual or last known residence of the individual, or principal or last known place of business.

Table 3.2: (continued)

Nature of defendant to be served	Appropriate place of service
Individual being sued in the name of a business name of a partnership	Usual or last known residence of the individual, or principal or last known place of business of the partnership.
Limited liability partnership	Principal office of the partnership, or any place of business of the partnership within the jurisdiction that has a real connection with the claim.
Corporation incorporated in England and Wales	Principal office of the corporation, or any place within the jurisdiction where the corporation carries on its activities and which has a real connection with the claim.
Company registered in England and Wales (with 'Ltd.' or 'Limited' after the company name)	Principal office of the company, or any place of business of the company within the jurisdiction that has a real connection with the claim.

Exam warning

An SQE question could specify that the defendant has instructed solicitors to accept service on their behalf. If this is the case, then the claim form and associated documentation should be served on the defendant's solicitors at their principal or last known place of business, if a partnership, or registered office, if a company. If the question does not specify that the defendant's solicitors are instructed to accept service, the claim form and associated documentation must be served on the defendant.

Once you have established where the correct place for service is, the final step is to find out if the claim form has been served within the correct time limitations.

When to serve the claim form

Before considering the rules regarding time limits for service of the claim form, it is important that you are clear on how the CPR count days so you can calculate your time limits accurately. The rules set out in the CPR are as follows:
- 'Days' always means clear days. This means that the day on which the period begins is *not* included.
- If the day on which the period ends is a specific date (ie 15 July), then the final day is counted as a clear day.

Service of the claim form and particulars of claim   43

- If the day on which the period ends is by reference to an event (ie 14 days before the hearing), then the date of the event is not regarded as a clear day.
- Where a period specified is five days or less, Saturdays, Sundays and bank holidays are not counted.

Once a claim has been issued, the claimant has four months within which to serve it on the defendant. This means four straight months; so if a claim was issued on 14 May, then it would need to be served by midnight on 14 September.

Bear in mind that there is an exception with the particulars of claim if it is drafted as a separate document to the claim form. The CPR allow for the particulars of claim to be served up to 14 days after the claim form, provided this does not fall outside the four-month time period from the date on which the claim form was issued. Therefore, using the example above, if the claim was issued on 14 May and the claimant wished to serve the claim form and particulars of claim separately, they would have to make sure that both documents were served by midnight on 14 September.

On occasion, the defendant may argue that they have not actually received the claim form from the claimant. It is for this reason that the CPR use the concept of **deemed service** to determine the date on which the claim form was served.

Key term: deemed service
When a document or application is legally treated by the CPR as having been served on a person, irrespective of whether it actually arrived.

A claim form is deemed served on the second business day after the relevant step has taken place (see **Table 3.1**). A business day is defined by the CPR as any day except Saturday, Sunday, a bank holiday, Good Friday or Christmas Day.

It is important to note that the rules on deemed service differ depending on the nature of the document to be served. Above is the rule concerning deemed service of the claim form. **Table 3.3** sets out the rules governing when *all* other types of documents will be deemed served. This is to include the particulars of claim, if served separately, and the defence.

Exam warning
An SQE question may try to catch you out by asking you a question about when a document other than a claim form is deemed served. Make sure that you pay close attention to the nature of the document before answering the question. The right answer will depend on the method of service that has been adopted, as laid out in **Table 3.3**.

44 Commencing proceedings

Table 3.3: Rules governing methods of service other than claim forms

Method of service	Deemed date of service
If the document is served by personal service, fax, email or by delivering the document to an address	If served before 4.30 p.m. on a business day, the deemed date of service is the same day. If served after 4.30 p.m. on a business day or not on a business day, the deemed date of service is the next business day.
If the document is served by first-class post or Document Exchange	The second day after it is posted, if it is a business day. So, if a defence is sent by first-class post on a Wednesday, it will be deemed served on Friday. If the second day after the document is posted is not a business day, the document will be deemed served the next business day. So, if a defence is sent by first-class post on a Friday, the second day after posting will be Sunday, which is not a business day. It will therefore be deemed served on Monday.

Where the claimant serves the claim form, they must file a certificate of service with the court within 21 days of the date of service of the particulars of claim. Now test your ability to apply your knowledge to a scenario in **Practice example 3.2**.

Practice example 3.2

Samantha sends a claim form and particulars of claim to the court for issue. She indicates that she wishes to serve the claim on the defendant, Borthwaite Homes Limited, personally. She decides that she will serve the claim by first-class post, and she sends the claim form and particulars of claim to the registered address of Borthwaite Homes Limited on the afternoon of Friday 12 May. Has Samantha validly served the claim form and particulars of claim; and if so, when will the court regard the documents as deemed served?

First, Samantha has picked a valid method of service in sending the documents by first-class post. The relevant step for that method of service is posting the document, which she has done. The address to which she has sent the documentation is compliant with CPR 6.9, being the registered address of the company. She has therefore effected valid service of the claim form and particulars of claim. In terms of deemed service, we are dealing with a claim form, and therefore the date of deemed service is the second business day after the relevant step is taken, in this case the posting of the documents on Friday 12 May. The

> second day after the document is posted is Sunday 14 May, which is not a business day. The claim form and particulars of claim will therefore be deemed served on Monday 15 May.

HOW TO JOIN OTHER PARTIES OR CAUSES OF ACTION TO PROCEEDINGS OR HOW TO APPLY TO SUBSTITUTE A PARTY TO PROCEEDINGS

Sometimes the need arises to add (joinder), remove or substitute a party to proceedings. This can be because a party has died, the incorrect defendant has been identified, or it transpires that an additional party is potentially liable in the action and therefore needs to be added. It can also be the case that a party re-evaluates their claim and needs to add to or amend their cause of action. This can sometimes be as a result of commencing proceedings without legal advice and subsequently receiving advice that they have pleaded an incorrect cause of action.

Each of these will be considered in turn below.

Adding, removing or substituting a party

This section is divided into three: Who can make an application? What are the grounds of the application? And what needs to happen if the court grants the application.

Who can make an application?

An application can be made by either an existing party or by a person who wishes to become a party. The court is also entitled to add a party on its own initiative. The following documents need to be filed with the court:
- the application notice;
- an amended copy of the claim form and particulars of claim;
- in the case where a claimant is being added, the signed written consent of that new claimant must be filed with the court or they will not grant the application.

What are the grounds of the application?

The grounds of the application depend on whether the application is made inside or outside the limitation period.

If the application is made inside the limitation period, the criteria that the applicant needs to meet are:
- it is desirable to add the new party so that the court can resolve all the matters in dispute in the proceedings, or;
- there is an issue involving the new party and an existing party which is connected to the matters in dispute in the proceedings, and it is desirable to add the new party so that the court can resolve that issue.

> **Exam warning**
> Note the use of the word 'desirable' in the test. If an SQE question asks you about substituting a party within the limitation period, make sure you select the option that makes specific reference to the amendment being 'desirable'.

If the application is made outside the limitation period (but the original claim was made inside the limitation period), the criteria that the applicant needs to meet are:
- the new party is to be substituted for a party who was named in the claim form in mistake for the new party, or;
- the claim cannot properly be carried on by or against the original party unless the new party is added or substituted as claimant or defendant, or;
- the original party has died or had a bankruptcy order made against them, and their interest or liability has passed to the new party.

What needs to happen if the court grants the application?
A copy of the order must be served on every party to the proceedings and on any other person affected by the order.

Adding or amending a cause of action
If you are asked about amending a statement of case (particulars of claim or defence) to reflect a change of cause of action, remember the following rules:
- If the document *has not* been served on any other party to the proceedings, then permission of the court is *not* required.
- If the document *has* been served, the party making the application to amend will either need:
  - the written consent of all other parties to the action to amend the document;
  - permission of the court.

SERVICE OUTSIDE THE JURISDICTION
Where the claim form is to be served outside the jurisdiction, (ie outside England and Wales), it must be served within six months of the date of issue, not four months.

Different rules exist for where service of the claim form needs to take place in a country within the EU or outside the EU.

Within the EU
Provided the English courts have jurisdiction over the claim and the claim was issued after 1 January 2021 (post EU withdrawal), permission from the court to serve a claim form and documents in an EU country will need to be sought prior to service taking place. If the claim was issued before 1 January 2021, no permission of the court to serve the document in the EU state will be needed.

Outside the EU
Permission from the court will have to be sought to serve the claim form and associated documentation in a country outside the EU. When the court grants permission, they will automatically extend the time period for service to six months after the claim form was issued.

Methods of service outside the jurisdiction
Once permission to serve outside the jurisdiction has been obtained from the court, service itself needs to be carried out in accordance with the procedures under the law of the country concerned. The claimant should provide the claim form, and other documentation is provided to the authorities in England and Wales, who then submit that to the authorities in the country in which the defendant is to be served. The foreign authorities will then serve the document and provide a certificate of service.

■ KEY POINT CHECKLIST
This chapter has covered the following key knowledge points. You can use these to structure your revision, ensuring you recall the key details for each point, as covered in this chapter.
- Civil proceedings should either be commenced in the County Court or the High Court, generally depending on the value of the claim.
- Proceedings are commenced using a claim form, particulars of claim and any supporting evidence.
- The court issues the claim by sealing the claim form and allocating a claim number to the case.
- Proceedings must be validly served within four months of the date of issue.
- The methods of validly serving proceedings are first-class post or Document Exchange, personal service, delivery of the document or leaving it at a relevant place, and fax or other electronic method.
- Once a claim has been issued, the claimant has four months within which to serve it on the defendant.
- A party can apply to add, substitute or remove a party from a claim in appropriate circumstances.
- When a claim form is to be served outside England and Wales, it must be served within six months of the date of issue.

■ KEY TERMS AND CONCEPTS
- claim form (**page 36**)
- particulars of claim (**page 36**)
- counterclaim (**page 37**)
- deemed service (**page 43**)

48 Commencing proceedings

■ SQE1-STYLE QUESTIONS

QUESTION 1

A claimant wishes to commence proceedings against a company for breach of contract that led the claimant to suffer losses of £95,000. Interest calculated on the damages is £7,496, meaning the total claim is worth £102,496. Evidence is required from multiple experts to determine whether the defendant breached the contract and to quantify the losses that the claimant is arguing they suffered.

Which of the following best represents the court in which the claim should be commenced, and why?

A. The claim must be commenced in the High Court. The value of the claim is above £100,000 and the matter is complex.

B. The claim may be commenced in the High Court. The value of the claim is above £100,000 and the matter is complex.

C. The claim must be commenced in the County Court. The value of the claim is over £100,000, but a breach of contract matter is not complex enough to warrant being commenced in the High Court.

D. The claim must be commenced in the County Court. The matter is complex, requiring multiple experts, but the value of the base claim is under £100,000.

E. The claim may be commenced in the High Court. Even though the value of the base claim is under £100,000, the matter is sufficiently complex to warrant being commenced in the High Court.

QUESTION 2

A claimant commences proceedings against their former solicitors (a partnership with three partners) for negligence. The claimant indicates to the court that they intend to serve the claim form and associated documentation themselves personally. The partnership has instructed solicitors through their insurance company to deal with the matter.

Which of the following best reflects the way in which the claimant can achieve valid service of documentation?

A. The claimant should serve the claim form and associated documentation on somebody who has a controlling interest in the partnership's solicitors.

B. The claimant should investigate the registered address or last known place of business of the partnership's solicitors and serve the claim form and associated documentation on an employee of that firm at the relevant address.

C. The claimant should serve the claim form and associated documentation on a member of the partnership at their principal or last known place of business.

D. The claimant should serve the claim form and associated documentation on any employee of the partnership at their principal or last known place of business.

E. The claimant should serve the claim form and associated documentation on all members of the partnership together at their principal or last known place of business.

QUESTION 3

A claim form is issued by the court on Monday 23 August and sent to the claimant to effect service personally. The claimant posts the claim form through the letterbox of the correct address of the defendant at 5.15 p.m. on Friday 27 August. Monday 30 August is a bank holiday.

Which of the following best reflects the correct date of deemed service?

A. The claim form is deemed served on Sunday 29 August.
B. The claim form is deemed served on Monday 30 August.
C. The claim form is deemed served on Tuesday 31 August.
D. The claim form is deemed served on Wednesday 1 September.
E. The claim form is deemed served on Thursday 2 September.

QUESTION 4

A claimant commences proceedings and indicates to the court that they will deal with the service of those proceedings. Prior to serving the claim form and associated documentation on the defendant, the claimant takes legal advice on the matter from a solicitor. The solicitor informs the claimant that their claim form and particulars of claim do not plead a proper cause of action, although the limitation period has four years left to run. The claimant therefore needs to amend the proceedings.

Which of the following best reflects the claimant's position?

A. The claimant will need to apply for permission from the court to amend the proceedings. If permission is granted, the claimant will have four months from the date of the order granting permission to serve the amended claim form on the defendant.

B. The claimant will need to apply for permission from the court to amend the proceedings. If permission is granted, the claimant will have four months from the date that the proceedings were originally issued to serve the amended claim form on the defendant.

50 Commencing proceedings

C. The claimant does not need the permission of the court to amend the proceedings but must serve the amended claim form on the defendant within four months of the date on which the proceedings were originally issued.

D. The claimant does not need the permission of the court to amend the proceedings but must serve the amended claim form on the defendant within four months of the date of amendment.

E. The claimant does not need the permission of the court to amend the proceedings but must serve the amended claim form on the defendant immediately.

QUESTION 5

A claimant commenced proceedings last week against the defendant, a French company, over breach of a contract with an express provision that the terms will be governed by the law of England and Wales. The claim form is issued by the court and returned to the claimant for service.

Which of the following responses best explains the timescales and steps that the claimant now needs to take to validly serve the proceedings?

A. The claimant is required to serve the claim form and associated documentation within six months of the date of issue. They will first need to seek the permission of the court to serve the proceedings outside the jurisdiction, and then send the documentation to the French authorities to serve on the defendant in accordance with French procedural requirements.

B. The claimant is required to serve the claim form and associated documentation within six months of the date of issue. They do not need to seek the permission of the court to serve the proceedings outside the jurisdiction, so they can proceed to sending the documentation to the French authorities to serve on the defendant in accordance with French procedural requirements.

C. The claimant is required to serve the claim form and associated documentation within six months of the date of issue. They will first need to seek the permission of the court to serve the proceedings outside the jurisdiction, and then post the proceedings to the registered office of the company in France in accordance with the requirements of the CPR.

D. The claimant is required to serve the claim form and associated documentation within four months of the date of issue. They will first need to seek the permission of the court to serve the proceedings outside the jurisdiction, and then send the documentation to the French authorities to serve on the defendant in accordance with French procedural requirements.

E. The claimant is required to serve the claim form and associated documentation within four months of the date of issue. They will first need to seek the permission of the court to serve the proceedings outside the jurisdiction, and then post the proceedings to the registered office of the company in France in accordance with the requirements of the CPR.

■ ANSWERS TO QUESTIONS

Answers to 'What do you know already?' questions at the start of the chapter

1) The County Court. Any claim with a financial value of less than £100,000 must be commenced in the County Court.
2) The claimant has up to four months after the date the claim form was issued to serve it on the defendant.
3) Yes. Provided the court has received the relevant application, an amended copy of the claim form and particulars of claim showing the name of the new party and the written and signed consent of the party to be added, that party can be added as claimant after the claim has been issued.
4) The correct answer was (c). A phone call is the only method that is not appropriate. Service by text message can only happen with the prior permission of the court and only in exceptional circumstances, and service by post is most common.
5) The applicant must prove to the court that either it is desirable to add the new party so that the court can resolve all the matters in dispute in the proceedings, or there is an issue involving the new party and an existing party which is connected to the matters in dispute in the proceedings, and it is desirable to add the new party so that the court can resolve that issue.

Answers to end-of-chapter SQE1-style questions

Question 1:
   The correct answer was D. The County Court is the correct court to commence proceedings (this discards options A, B and E). For the purposes of valuing the claim, the CPR disregard any interest or legal costs; therefore, the base figure of £95,000 is the true value. Any claim worth under £100,000 must be commenced in the County Court, which also discards option C.

Question 2:
   The correct answer was C. As the claimant has elected to serve the claim form and associated documentation personally, they need to identify the correct person at the correct place to effect valid service. In this case, that is a member of the partnership or somebody who at the time of service had control or management of the partnership business at their principal or last known place of business. An employee will not have

control or management of partnership business, which means that option D is not correct. Although we are told that the partnership instructed solicitors through their insurance company, we are not expressly told that they are instructed to accept service of proceedings, making options A and B incorrect. Finally, there is no requirement to serve proceedings on the partners together, making option E incorrect.

Question 3:
The correct answer was D. The document in question is a claim form, and therefore this is deemed served two business days after the relevant step is taken (in this case, posting it through the letterbox). The relevant step is taken on Friday, which is a business day; Saturday and Sunday are not business days (meaning that option A is incorrect), Monday is a bank holiday (making option B incorrect), and Tuesday is the first business day after the relevant step is taken (making option C incorrect – although this would be correct if the document were not a claim form, as the document was posted after 4.30 p.m. on Friday, meaning it would be deemed served the next business day, which in this case would be Tuesday). Therefore, the second business day after posting (which is applicable to claim forms) is Wednesday 1 September. Option E is incorrect as it is too late.

Question 4:
The correct answer was C. As the claimant has not already served proceedings on the defendant, they can amend the cause of action without having to apply for the permission of the court. This discards options A and B. Despite the amendment, the claim form still needs to be served on the defendant within four months of the original date of issue, making option C the correct answer and rendering options D and E incorrect.

Question 5:
The correct answer was A. The court automatically extends the time limit for service to six months from four months on issue. This makes options D and E incorrect. France is an EU country, but the claimant will need to seek the court's permission as proceedings were issued after 1 January 2021. This makes option B incorrect. Finally, service needs to be in accordance with the procedural rules of the country in which the proceedings are being served, which renders option C incorrect.

■ KEY CASES, RULES, STATUTES AND INSTRUMENTS

The SQE1 Assessment Specification does not require you to know any case names or statutory materials for the topic of commencing proceedings.

Responding to a claim

■ MAKE SURE YOU KNOW
This chapter will cover the ways in which a defendant can respond to a claim made against them. It will cover the range of possible initial responses from a defendant when they are served with proceedings, as well as the time limits for them to act, what a claimant can do if the defendant fails to act, and the way in which a claim can be discontinued or settled at this early stage. You are required to be able to apply these principles and rules appropriately and effectively to realistic client-based and ethical problems and situations for your SQE1 assessment.

■ SQE ASSESSMENT ADVICE
As you work through this chapter, remember to pay particular attention in your revision to:
- the method and consequences of admitting the claim;
- the method and consequences of acknowledging service and filing a defence against the claim;
- the relevant timescales for responding to a claim;
- the way in which a party could dispute the court's jurisdiction;
- the way in which a claim can be discontinued or settled;
- how and when a claimant can apply for judgment in default and in what circumstances a defendant can apply to set it aside.

■ WHAT DO YOU KNOW ALREADY?
Have a go at these questions before reading this chapter. If you find some difficult or cannot remember the answers, make a note to look more closely at that subtopic during your revision.
1) What is the difference between a specified claim and an unspecified claim?
   [Admitting the claim in whole or in part, page 55]
2) What four options does a defendant have when they are served with a claim form and a particulars of claim?
   [Introduction to responding to a claim, page 54]

3) True or false? If a defendant applies to set aside a judgment in default, the court must grant the defendant's application.
[Judgment in default, page 58]
4) Why is a Tomlin order a beneficial type of consent order for a claimant to use following settlement of a claim with the defendant?
[Settlement, page 62]
5) What procedural steps does the claimant need to take if they want to discontinue proceedings?
[Discontinuance, page 61]

INTRODUCTION TO RESPONDING TO A CLAIM

When a defendant is served with claim documentation, the first step they must take is to ascertain exactly what that documentation is. This will dictate how they should respond to it. **Table 4.1** sets out how a defendant should act in response to particular types of documentation being served on them.

Table 4.1: Responses to claim documentation

Type of document served	Response
Claim form alone where the particulars of claim are to follow as a separate document.	There is no need for the defendant to do anything if they have only been served with a claim form without the particulars of claim.
Claim form with the particulars of claim attached, or particulars of claim when the claim form has already been served.	The defendant needs to act at this point. They have several options of how to deal with a claim once the particulars of claim have been served on them. They can: • admit the claim in whole or in part; • file an **acknowledgment of service**; • file a defence; • ignore the claim and allow the claimant to apply for **judgment in default**.

Key term: acknowledgment of service
This is a formal document which is filed with the court by the defendant to acknowledge that they have been served with the claim form and particulars of claim.

Key term: judgment in default
This is the term for judgment being awarded in the claimant's favour on the basis that the defendant has failed to respond to the claim form and particulars of claim being served on them within the relevant time.

When a defendant is served with a claim, they are also provided with a 'response pack'. This contains the following forms, which give the defendant options in terms of how they wish to respond:
- an admission form;
- an acknowledgment of service form;
- a defence and counterclaim form.

Each of the possible ways in which a defendant can respond will now be considered in turn.

ADMITTING THE CLAIM IN WHOLE OR IN PART

If the defendant acknowledges that they are liable for the whole or part of the claim, it makes good sense for them to admit that at as early a stage as possible to enable matters with the court to be concluded. The process for this differs depending on whether they admit the whole of the claim or just part of it, and whether the claim is **specified** or **unspecified**.

Key term: specified claim
A type of claim that is issued for a fixed amount of money allegedly owed by the defendant to the claimant.

Key term: unspecified claim
A particular type of claim in tort where the amount of money to be awarded is left to the court to determine.

Specified claims

Table 4.2 sets out how the defendant and claimant should deal with admissions of specified claims.

Table 4.2: Dealing with admissions of specified claims

Whole or part of claim admitted?	Steps for defendant and claimant
Whole of claim admitted	• Defendant to complete the admission form offering to pay the claim in full within a specified time period. • Defendant to provide details on the admission form (N9A) of assets, income, expenditure and a proposal for instalment payments. This will be sent to the claimant by the court. • Claimant will either accept the terms or raise objection to them. If the claimant raises objection, the court will either set the instalment figures and time period or set the matter down for a hearing to hear each side's point of view. This is called a disposal hearing.

Table 4.2: (continued)

Whole or part of claim admitted?	Steps for defendant and claimant
	• Following receipt of the admission from the defendant, the claimant will also be entitled to apply for judgment in their favour based on the defendant's admission.
Part of claim admitted	• Defendant to complete the admission form admitting part of the claim and often making an offer to the claimant to settle the whole matter. • Claimant will have 14 days to make a decision on the offer. • If the claimant accepts the offer, the court will proceed to make a judgment for the sum agreed if the claimant requests it to do so. • If the claimant accepts the offer amount but rejects the proposals for payment, then the court will list the matter for a disposal hearing. • If the claimant rejects the offer, the matter will proceed as a disputed case and the defendant will be required to file a defence.

Unspecified claims

If the defendant files an admission of liability in an unspecified claim, the court will stay, or put on hold, proceedings and arrange to list the matter for a disposal hearing. At this hearing, the court will determine the sum that is payable by the defendant to the claimant in respect of the claim.

Revision tip
In unspecified claims, the defendant can make an offer to settle that accompanies their admission of liability. The court will serve a notice on the claimant asking if they accept the offer. If the claimant accepts, the court will enter judgment in that amount. If the claimant accepts the amount offered but not the defendant's proposals for payment, the court will make an order based on the assets, income and expenditure of the defendant.

FILING AN ACKNOWLEDGMENT OF SERVICE

If the defendant does not wish to admit the claim but is not immediately in the position where they feel able to submit a full defence to it, they can file an acknowledgment of service with the court. This essentially extends the amount of time they have to file a full defence from 14 days after the particulars of claim is served on them to 28 days. Timescales are dealt with in more detail on **page 57**.

FILING A DEFENCE

The third option for a defendant when they are served with the particulars of claim is to file a full defence to the claim. This will involve completing the defence form found in the response pack sent to the defendant alongside the particulars of claim. What to include in the defence is set out in more detail in **Chapter 5**.

It is also open to the defendant to submit a counterclaim, if relevant, at the same time as the defence (also discussed in **Chapter 5**).

IGNORING THE CLAIM

If the defendant simply ignores the claim, the claimant will apply for judgment in default once the maximum period for filing an acknowledgment of service or defence has passed. The court, in the absence of any defence from the defendant and on application from the claimant, will grant judgment on the amount claimed. This is called judgment in default and is dealt with in more detail on **page 58**. The defendant will then be required to pay the full amount of the judgment to the claimant.

THE RELEVANT TIMESCALES FOR RESPONDING TO A CLAIM

After service of proceedings, the defendant has the following timescales to respond:
- a maximum of 14 days from the date of service of the particulars of claim to file an acknowledgment of service;
- if an acknowledgment of service is filed, a maximum of 28 days from the date of service of the particulars of claim to file a defence and counterclaim (if applicable).

> **Exam warning**
>
> The Civil Procedure Rules 1998 (CPR; see **Chapter 1**) do allow parties to agree to extend the deadline for filing a defence and, if applicable, a counterclaim between themselves without any court involvement. Such an extension is limited to a further 28 days, which would mean that the defendant would have a total of 56 days to file their defence and counterclaim (if appropriate).

Once a defence and counterclaim have been filed with the court, they will serve the relevant documents on the claimant unless the defendant has indicated in their response that they wish to serve the document on the claimant directly.

DISPUTING THE COURT'S JURISDICTION

If the defendant does not believe that the court of England and Wales has jurisdiction to hear the claim, they *must* indicate this on the acknowledgment of service form. The defendant then has 14 days from the date of filing the acknowledgment of service to make an application to the court disputing jurisdiction. The defendant would need to submit supporting evidence to show the court why they do not have jurisdiction.

If the court grants the defendant's application, the claim form will be set aside and the proceedings closed. If the court rejects the defendant's application, the defendant will be required to file a further acknowledgment of service within 14 days of the date of the order dismissing the application, and the proceedings can continue.

If the defendant fails to make an application within the 14-day time window of filing their acknowledgment of service, the court will assume that the defendant accepts the court's jurisdiction and a defence must then be filed.

JUDGMENT IN DEFAULT

As discussed above, one of the options available to the defendant after they have been served with the particulars of claim is to simply ignore it. If they fail to file either an acknowledgment of service or a defence within 14 days, or file an acknowledgement of service and fail to file a defence within 28 days, the claimant is entitled to apply for judgment in default. This is essentially a judgment in favour of the claimant that is based on the defendant's failure to plead their defence.

SQE1 may ask you about the procedure the claimant must follow to apply for judgment in default, or the way in which an application can be made and the grounds that must be proven by the defendant to **set aside** the judgment in default. Each of these will be discussed in turn below.

> **Key term: set aside**
>
> When the court declares a previous decision invalid (eg when a judgment in default is set aside, the court action will proceed as if that judgment was never granted).

Applying for judgment in default

The court will not grant judgment in default on its own; the claimant needs to specifically apply for and ask the court to grant them the judgment. The CPR set out the criteria that the claimant must satisfy. They are:
- the particulars of claim have been validly served on the defendant, and;
- the defendant has not filed an acknowledgment of service or defence within the relevant time period.

Given the fact that the court's record is likely to prove both of these criteria (unless the claimant has requested to serve the claim form and particulars of claim themselves), it is factually easy for a claimant to meet them and therefore be awarded judgment in default. The only circumstances in which the claimant will fail is if the defendant has already made an application for either **summary judgment** or to have the claimant's claim form and particulars of claim **struck out**.

> **Key term: summary judgment**
> A special type of application that is made by either the claimant or defendant on the basis that the claim or defence has no reasonable prospect of success at trial.

> **Key term: struck out**
> When the court orders written material to be deleted so that a party can no longer rely on it.

If the claim is for a specified sum, to allow the court to make judgment in default, the claimant will have to provide the court with confirmation of the date that payment was due, as well as an up-to-date interest figure and daily rate of interest. This enables the court to enter judgment for a specific and up-to-date amount, as well as ordering that additional daily interest is payable by the defendant until the point at which they settle the debt.

If the claim is for an unspecified sum, the court will enter judgment in the claimant's favour but then schedule a hearing so that they can determine the amount which the defendant should pay.

Applying to set aside judgment in default

If the defendant receives the judgment in default and wishes to contest the proceedings, they can apply to set aside the judgment in default. If successful, this would have the effect of the judgment being declared invalid and the proceedings continuing as if judgment were never entered.

The CPR set out two grounds on which a defendant can make an application to set aside judgment in default. The first is a mandatory ground, which means the court *must* set the judgment aside if the defendant can prove that they meet the relevant criteria. The second is a discretionary ground, which means the court *may* set judgment aside depending on the circumstances pleaded by the defendant. **Table 4.3** sets out what the defendant must prove for each ground.

Table 4.3: Grounds for setting aside judgment in default

Ground	What the defendant must show
Mandatory	In cases where the claimant has obtained judgment because the defendant has not filed their acknowledgment of service or defence within the relevant time, the defendant must show that they did file the document before the relevant deadline, or that the defendant settled and paid the claim prior to judgment in default being entered.

Table 4.3: (continued)

Ground	What the defendant must show
Discretionary	The defendant must show either that they have a real (and not fanciful) prospect of defending the claim, or that there is some other good reason why they should be allowed to defend the claim (such as the defendant being in hospital or abroad when the proceedings were served). The court must also take into consideration whether the defendant applied promptly upon receipt of the judgment in default. If the application has not been made promptly with no real explanation as to why from the defendant, the court has the discretion to reject the application. This means that the judgment will stand and the defendant will be required to pay the judgment sum.

Once the court has considered the application, they can make one of the following orders:
- The application is successful, meaning that the judgment against the defendant is set aside and they are allowed to defend the court proceedings.
- The application is unsuccessful, meaning that the judgment against the defendant stands and the claimant can enforce that judgment.
- The application is successful, but the court attaches a condition that judgment will not be set aside unless the defendant pays a certain amount of money into court as security by a specific deadline. If the defendant fails to pay the amount into court, the judgment in default will stand.

Now test your understanding of this subject in **Practice example 4.1**.

Practice example 4.1

Climpton Finance Limited are served with proceedings on 4 January. Due to an administrative mix-up, they fail to open the letter in which the claim form and particulars are enclosed. They receive a further letter from the court enclosing an order awarding judgment in default to the claimant on the basis of Climpton Finance Limited's failure to file an acknowledgment of service or a defence by the relevant date. Climpton Finance Limited wish to defend the proceedings. What can they do?

Climpton Finance Limited can apply to set aside the judgment in default. They would have to do so on a discretionary ground, and they would therefore need to provide the court with supporting evidence that they had a real prospect of successfully defending the claim or that there exists some other good reason why they should be allowed to defend the claim. They would also need to apply promptly after having

received the judgment in default, as the court are obligated to take this into consideration before exercising their discretion on whether to set judgment aside.

DISCONTINUATION OR SETTLEMENT OF A CLAIM

There are two ways in which a claimant can voluntarily bring an end to proceedings without progressing to a judgment. These are through **discontinuance** or by settlement.

> **Key term: discontinuance**
> The termination of a legal action by a claimant.

Discontinuance

A claimant is entitled to discontinue all or part of their proceedings at any point of a court action. They may decide to discontinue a claim for a variety of reasons, but mainly this is because:
- the court action is taking too long and is too expensive for the claimant to continue;
- the claimant has discovered that the defendant does not have, and is unlikely to have in the future, the means to pay any judgment awarded in favour of the claimant;
- the claimant has re-evaluated the strength of their claim and decided that it is unlikely they will be successful.

SQE1 may ask you about the procedure that a claimant would need to follow to discontinue proceedings and the potential consequences of them doing so.

Table 4.4 sets out how a claimant should proceed if they wish to discontinue proceedings.

Table 4.4: Steps that a claimant needs to take to discontinue proceedings

What steps does the claimant need to take?	• The claimant must first file and serve a notice of discontinuance on all of the parties to proceedings. • If there is more than one claimant, the other claimants must provide their written consent to the proceedings being discontinued, which should be attached to the notice of discontinuance. • If there are multiple claimants and they refuse to provide their consent, the claimant who wishes to discontinue must apply for the permission of the court to do so.

Table 4.4: (continued)

When will proceedings be deemed discontinued?	• As soon as the notice of discontinuance is served on all other parties to the action, the claim will be discontinued.
What penalties does the claimant face for discontinuing proceedings?	• The claimant will be liable to pay the defendant's costs on the **standard basis** in relation to either the whole of the action or, alternatively, the part of the action that has been discontinued.

> **Key term: standard basis**
>
> One of the two methods by which the court calculates the level of legal costs, fees and expenses payable by one party to another. Using this method, costs, fees and expenses associated with the legal action and claimed from the opposition must have been reasonably incurred and must be proportionate to the issues that the court has been asked to resolve.

Settlement

The second way for a claimant to voluntarily bring proceedings to an end is through reaching a settlement with the defendant while the litigation is ongoing. If an agreement is reached, the parties will need to draw up and agree the terms of a **consent order**.

> **Key term: consent order**
>
> An umbrella term for all orders that record settlements which are reached between parties to litigation.

A consent order is essentially a contract by which the claimant agrees to terminate the proceedings in exchange for a settlement sum. If the defendant breaches any of the terms of a consent order, the claimant will need to issue a new set of proceedings (based on breach of contract, the contract being the consent order) to enforce the terms of that order. In many cases, this is far from ideal from the claimant's perspective. The claimant will already have issued proceedings once and will not wish to issue proceedings again to simply get what they should have been entitled to had they continued with the original court action. A special type of consent order, known as a **Tomlin order**, can therefore be drafted and agreed to avoid this eventuality.

> **Key term: Tomlin order**
>
> A court order under which a claim is stayed or paused on terms that have been agreed between the parties and are then attached to the order in the form of a confidential schedule. This avoids the need for having to issue fresh proceedings if a term of the order is breached by one of the parties.

A Tomlin order does not set out the terms of agreement between the parties (those are set out in the confidential schedule, which is attached to the order). The order itself simply includes:
- a statement that the parties have agreed terms of settlement;
- a statement that all further proceedings are stayed;
- confirmation that the stay is based on the terms set out in the attached schedule being complied with;
- a statement that if the terms of the schedule are breached, the innocent party can make an application to the court and request that they lift the stay, thereby allowing the innocent party to ask the court to enforce the settlement (methods of enforcement are dealt with in more detail in **Chapter 11**);
- a direction as to which party is paying the other's costs and whether those costs are to be assessed (this is dealt with in more detail in **Chapter 10**).

Whichever type of consent order is used, the immediate proceedings are either brought to an end completely or paused subject to the terms of the order being complied with. This therefore prevents further costs being incurred by either party in connection with the action.

■ KEY POINT CHECKLIST

This chapter has covered the following key knowledge points. You can use these to structure your revision, ensuring you recall the key details for each point, as covered in this chapter.
- Upon receiving a claim form and a particulars of claim, a defendant may admit the claim in whole or in part, file an acknowledgment of service, file a defence, or ignore the claim.
- The defendant may admit liability in respect of the whole claim or part of the claim.
- In a specified claim, the defendant may admit liability and offer to pay the claim in full within a specified time. If the defendant admits part of the claim, they may offer to settle the whole matter, and the claimant will have 14 days to decide whether to accept the offer.
- If the defendant files an admission of liability in an unspecified claim, the court will stay proceedings and arrange to list the matter for a disposal hearing. At this hearing, the court will determine the sum that is payable by the defendant to the claimant in respect of the claim.
- If the defendant does not wish to admit the claim but is not immediately in the position where they feel able to submit a full defence to it, they can file an acknowledgment of service with the court. This essentially extends the amount of time they have to file a full defence from 14 days after the particulars of claim is served on them to 28 days.
- Alternatively, the defendant may file a full defence to the claim. If relevant, the defendant can also submit a counterclaim at the same time as their defence.

64 Responding to a claim

- If the defendant simply ignores the claim, the claimant can apply for judgment in default. A claimant can apply for judgment in default on the basis that the particulars of claim have been validly served on the defendant and the defendant has not filed an acknowledgment of service or defence within the relevant time period. If the court grants an order in default, the defendant will be required to pay the full amount of the judgment to the claimant.
- A defendant may make an application to set aside the judgment in default if they meet the relevant criteria laid out in the CPR.

■ KEY TERMS AND CONCEPTS

- acknowledgment of service (**page 54**)
- judgment in default (**page 54**)
- specified claim (**page 55**)
- unspecified claim (**page 55**)
- set aside (**page 58**)
- summary judgment (**page 58**)
- struck out (**page 59**)
- discontinuance (**page 61**)
- standard basis (**page 62**)
- consent order (**page 62**)
- Tomlin order (**page 62**)

■ SQE1-STYLE QUESTIONS

QUESTION 1

A defendant has been served with a claim form. On the form, it states that the particulars of claim are to follow.

Which of the following responses best explains what the defendant should do?

- A. The defendant does not need to respond after being served with the claim form.
- B. The defendant needs to file an acknowledgment of service within 14 days of the date on which the claim form was deemed served.
- C. The defendant needs to file a defence within 14 days of the date on which the claim form was deemed served.
- D. The defendant needs to file an acknowledgment of service within 14 days of the date on which the claim form was deemed served and a defence within 28 days.
- E. The defendant needs to file a defence within 28 days of the date on which the claim form was deemed served.

QUESTION 2

A defendant is served with a claim form and particulars of claim for an unspecified amount. The defendant wishes to admit liability and so completes the relevant admission form. They also wish to make an offer of settlement to the claimant to save matters going any further.

Which of the following best represents how the court will deal with the situation?

A. Due to the claim being unspecified, the court will note the defendant's admission of liability and set the matter down for a disposal hearing within 14 days of the admission and offer being received.
B. Due to the claim being unspecified, the court will note the defendant's admission of liability and make a decision on whether they think the offer is reasonable. If the court believes the offer is unreasonable, they will set the matter down for a disposal hearing.
C. Due to the claim being unspecified, the court will stay the proceedings and send a notice to the claimant including the offer. If the claimant indicates that the offer is acceptable, the court will make a judgment in that amount.
D. Due to the claim being unspecified, the court will send a notice to the claimant including the offer, but the proceedings will remain ongoing until the claimant has either accepted or rejected the offer.
E. Due to the claim being unspecified, the court will stay the proceedings and make a decision on whether they think the settlement offer is reasonable.

QUESTION 3

A defendant is served with a claim form and particulars of claim and visits their solicitor the day afterwards. The solicitor explains that provided an acknowledgment of service is filed, the defence will need to be filed within 28 days of the date of deemed service of the particulars of claim. The defendant will be abroad for 40 days from the day afterwards and does not have time to gather the relevant information to enable the solicitor to draft a full defence.

Which of the following best describes how the defendant can proceed?

A. The defendant should gather as much information as possible before they go abroad and instruct their solicitor to file a defence within 28 days of the particulars of claim being deemed served. Failure to file a defence will leave the defendant open to a judgment in default being made against them.

Responding to a claim

B. The CPR allow parties to agree an extension of up to 28 days for filing their defence. The defendant should therefore instruct their solicitor to negotiate an extension with the claimant's solicitor.

C. The defendant will need the court's permission for an extension. They will therefore need to instruct their solicitor to prepare an application immediately so that it can be sent to the court before they go abroad.

D. The defendant should instruct their solicitor to file an acknowledgment of service and indicate that they intend to defend all of the claim. This prevents the claimant's solicitor from applying for judgment in default. The defence can then be filed when the client returns from abroad.

E. The CPR allow a party in extreme circumstances to have an extension of 28 days to file a defence without the agreement of the claimant. The defendant is therefore entitled to file a defence once they return from abroad.

QUESTION 4

Two defendants are served with a claim form and particulars of claim. However, at the time, they are abroad and do not return for a further six weeks. In that time, the claimant applies for judgment in default against them. As soon as they return home and discover the proceedings and the order, they contact their solicitor and visit them that day. The defendants deny the claim.

Which of the following best reflects the defendants' legal position?

A. The defendants should simply pay the amount in the judgment. The defendants have failed to file an acknowledgment of service within 14 days of the particulars of claim being served on them, and therefore they can do nothing.

B. The defendants should contact the claimant and try to negotiate. The CPR require parties to attempt alternative methods of dispute resolution before engaging the court, and therefore the defendants should try to agree to mediate the dispute before going back to the court.

C. The defendants should apply to the court to set aside the judgment in default on the mandatory ground that the claimant has failed to serve the claim documentation on them properly. They were out of the country and therefore valid service has not taken place.

D. The defendants should file an acknowledgment of service within 14 days of returning home and their defence within 28 days of returning home. Valid service has not taken place until they returned from abroad, leaving them unable to defend the proceedings.

E. The defendants should apply to the court to set aside the judgment in default on the discretionary ground that they had some other good reason for not dealing with the claim immediately, the good reason being that they were out of the country. Provided they make the application promptly, it is likely that the court will set aside the judgment and allow them to defend the claim.

QUESTION 5

A claimant has commenced proceedings against a defendant. In the initial stages, neither party was prepared to negotiate, but after eight months both sides engage in negotiations and agree a settlement. The settlement involves the defendant paying the claimant the full judgment sum in instalments over 24 months.

Which of the following best represents how the parties should proceed?

A. The parties should draft the terms of settlement into the schedule of a Tomlin order, sign it and send it to the court.
B. The parties should draft the terms of settlement into a consent order, sign it and send it to the court.
C. The parties should draft the terms of settlement into open correspondence between them and ask the court to vacate the listed trial date.
D. The parties should draft the terms of settlement into a contract that both parties sign and the claimant should discontinue proceedings against the defendant.
E. The parties should proceed to the trial date and inform the court at that stage that the matter has been settled.

■ ANSWERS TO QUESTIONS

Answers to 'What do you know already?' questions at the start of the chapter

1) A specified claim is a type of claim that is issued for a fixed amount of money allegedly owed by the defendant to the claimant. An unspecified claim is a particular type of claim in tort where the amount of money to be awarded is left to the court to determine.
2) The defendant can either admit the claim, file an acknowledgment of service, file a defence or ignore the claim.
3) False. If the defendant applies on a mandatory ground and is able to provide evidence to prove their application, the court must set judgment aside. Alternatively, the court has discretion over whether to grant the application.
4) A Tomlin order is appropriate where the parties have agreed a settlement and payment terms but there is a risk that the defendant will default on those terms in the future. A Tomlin order stays proceedings

rather than terminating them, meaning it is much easier for the claimant to return to court to enforce the terms of the judgment.
5) The claimant must first file and serve a notice of discontinuance on all of the parties to proceedings. If there is more than one claimant, the other claimants must provide their written consent to the proceedings being discontinued, which should be attached to the notice of discontinuance. If there are multiple claimants and they refuse to provide their consent, the claimant who wishes to discontinue must apply for the permission of the court to do so.

Answers to end-of-chapter SQE1-style questions

Question 1:
The correct answer was A. We are told that only the claim form has been served, with particulars of claim to follow. The defendant is not required to do anything until the particulars of claim has been served on them. This therefore makes options B, C, D and E incorrect, as the claimant does not need to take any action.

Question 2:
The correct answer was C. On receipt of an admission to an unspecified claim, the court will stay, or pause, the claim immediately (making option D incorrect) and send the offer to the claimant in the form of a notice for their consideration. If the claimant accepts the offer, then the court will make a judgment in that amount. The court will not take a decision on their own on the settlement amount unless the claimant rejects the offer and asks the court to make a judgment on the amount, making options B and E incorrect. Finally, option A is incorrect as the court will not set the matter down for a disposal hearing upon receipt of a settlement offer in an unspecified claim.

Question 3:
The correct answer was B. The CPR include a provision that enables parties to agree a 28-day extension for the defendant to file a defence without needing the permission of the court (making option C incorrect). Filing an acknowledgment of service does not prevent the claimant from applying for judgment in default, making option D incorrect, and the CPR do not allow a party to unilaterally extend its own deadline, rendering option E wrong. Finally, option A is not the best option as the defendant needs their defence to be as strong as possible to ensure they can defend the claim effectively. An extension allowing them time to prepare it properly is therefore the best option.

Question 4:
The correct answer was E. Being absent at the time the particulars of claim was served is a good reason for not responding to it, and that is a discretionary ground to set aside default judgment under the CPR. The defendants have not filed an acknowledgment of service or their defence

on time, nor was there an ongoing application for summary judgment or to strike out the claimant's claim, which removes any mandatory ground from their options (and makes option C incorrect). The particulars of claim is deemed served on the second business day after posting, so they do seem to have been validly served, making option D incorrect. Although the CPR do require the parties to try to pursue alternative dispute resolution, promptness of the application to set aside default judgment will take precedence, making option B incorrect. Option A is not correct as the defendants can apply to set aside default judgment. They therefore do not need to just pay the judgment debt immediately.

Question 5:
The correct answer was A. A Tomlin order allows the proceedings to be stayed, or paused, subject to the defendant complying with the terms of settlement. It is most suitable here as the defendant is paying the settlement amount in 24 monthly instalments – plenty of opportunity for things to go wrong. All that the claimant would need to do in the event of non-payment is ask for proceedings to be reinstated and apply for the court to deal with enforcement of the terms of the Tomlin order. A consent order would bring proceedings to an end, which means the claimant would have to commence proceedings again for breach of contract if the defendant defaulted, meaning option B is incorrect. Discontinuing proceedings would only be applicable where the claimant felt they did not have a good prospect of success and therefore wished to withdraw, meaning option D is incorrect. Option E is wrong, as to allow the matter to continue to trial when it is settled would be a waste of money and the court's time. Finally, option C would leave the proceedings open (the trial date being vacated would mean it would have to be relisted) and so is not correct.

■ KEY CASES, RULES, STATUTES AND INSTRUMENTS

The SQE1 Assessment Specification does not require you to know any case names or statutory materials for the topic of responding to a claim.

5

Statements of case

■ MAKE SURE YOU KNOW

This chapter will cover the purpose, structure and contents of a claim form, particulars of claim, or defence in relation to claims in contract and tort. It will also consider Part 20 claims, defence to Part 20 claims and requests for further information. You are required to be able to apply these principles and rules appropriately and effectively to realistic client-based and ethical problems and situations for your SQE1 assessment.

■ SQE ASSESSMENT ADVICE

As you work through this chapter, remember to pay particular attention in your revision to:
- the purpose, content and structure of a claim form, particulars of claim or defence relating to a claim in either contract or tort;
- the purpose, content and structure of a reply to defence, a Part 20 claim, or defence to a Part 20 claim;
- how to deal with requests for further information about a party's statement of case.

■ WHAT DO YOU KNOW ALREADY?

Have a go at these questions before reading this chapter. If you find some difficult or cannot remember the answers, make a note to look more closely at that subtopic during your revision.

1) What document(s) are needed to commence a claim against a defendant?
   [Claim form, page 71; Particulars of claim, page 73]
2) True or false? When a defendant receives a claim, they are limited to two responses only: they can either admit it or defend it completely.
   [Purpose of the defence, page 76]
3) Can a defendant party also make a separate claim against the claimant?
   [Part 20 CPR claims, page 77]
4) What steps can a defendant take if the claimant's particulars of claim need to be clarified?
   [Requests for further information about a statement of case, page 79]

5) What is the purpose of a defence?
   [Purpose of the defence, page 76]

INTRODUCTION TO STATEMENTS OF CASE

A statement of case is a document that is used to set out a party's case in civil litigation. Statements of case can take various forms depending on the circumstances and whether the party is a claimant or a defendant. Examples of statements of case are:
- claim form;
- particulars of claim;
- defence;
- reply to defence;
- Part 20 claim;
- defence to Part 20 claim.

The SQE1 Assessment Specification requires you to know the purpose of the documents listed above, as well as their structure and content. This chapter therefore covers each of the documents in turn, as well as requests for further information about a statement of case.

CLAIM FORM

The claim form is one of two primary documents that is used to commence a civil claim. Once the claim form is issued, this commences the claim against the defendant. The second document is the particulars of claim. You will hopefully remember from **Chapter 2** that the claim form (form N1) does include a space for the particulars of claim to be included; however, commonly it is drafted as a separate document and attached to the claim form.

Purpose of the claim form

The claim form is the document used to start proceedings and contains information relevant to the proceedings.

Structure and content of the claim form

The claim form requests that the claimant completes the information set out in **Table 5.1**.

Table 5.1: Information required on the claim form

Information requested	Explanation
Claimant name and address	Make sure you insert the details of the correct claimant. If the claimant is a company or a partnership, you must ensure that they are identified as the claimant party.

Table 5.1: (continued)

Information requested	Explanation
Defendant name and address	Ensure that this is accurate. Inserting the incorrect identity of the defendant will potentially lead to the claim being struck out or, at best, you having to make an application to amend the statement of case (see **Chapter 3, page 46**).
Brief details of claim	This box must contain: • a concise (preferably single) statement of the nature of the claim; • the remedy that the claimant is seeking.
Claim value	In specified claims, this is the amount that is being claimed without including interest. In unspecified claims, the claimant must enter '*I expect to recover ...*' followed by one of the following value brackets: • not more than £10,000; • more than £10,000 but not more than £25,000; • more than £25,000. There will be circumstances where the claimant cannot estimate how much they are expecting to recover. In this case, they must write, '*I cannot say how much I expect to recover.*'
Preferred County Court hearing centre for the hearing(s)	The most convenient County Court for a face-to-face hearing must be inserted here so that the court can transfer the claim after it has been issued, if it thinks appropriate.
Defendant's address for service	If the court is serving the claim form, the title, full name, address and postcode of the defendant's address for service must be inserted here.
Particulars of claim	This is dealt with separately on **page 73**.
Statement of truth	The statement of truth confirms that the party signing the document believes that the facts stated in it are true. In the case of the N1 claim form, it is signed by either the claimant, their legal representative or their litigation friend (if applicable).
Claimant or their legal representative's address for correspondence.	This is the address that the claimant would like the court to use to write to them.

Particulars of claim 73

> **Exam warning**
>
> If you are asked about the defendant's appropriate address for service, remember that the Civil Procedure Rules 1998 (CPR) prescribe the location of this depending on the status of the defendant. This was discussed in **Chapter 3** on **page 35**.

PARTICULARS OF CLAIM

The particulars of claim is a document setting out the case of the claimant and specifying the facts relied upon.

Purpose of the particulars of claim

The purpose of the particulars of claim is set out in CPR 16.4(1), which states that it should provide the following:

- a concise statement of the facts on which the claimant is relying;
- details of any interest that the claimant is claiming;
- a statement and accompanying grounds if the claimant is seeking either **exemplary damages** or **aggravated damages**;
- any other matters required for the type of claim as set out in the relevant Practice Direction (see **Chapter 1**).

> **Key term: exemplary damages**
>
> Also known as punitive damages. They are designed to punish the defendant if the allegations regarding their poor conduct contained in the particulars of claim are proven. The aim of exemplary damages being awarded is to deter the defendant and others from behaving in the same way in the future.

> **Key term: aggravated damages**
>
> These are additional damages claimed because the defendant's behaviour has caused the claimant mental distress, injury to feelings or anguish.

Structure and contents of the particulars of claim

The SQE requires you to know the structure and contents of a particulars of claim document depending on whether the legal claim is in the area of contract or tort.

Table 5.2 sets out the structure and contents of a particulars of claim for breach of contract.

Table 5.3 sets out the structure and contents of a particulars of claim in tort.

Table 5.2: *The structure and contents of a particulars of claim in contract*

Structure and contents	Explanation
Parties to the claim and their status	The opening paragraph of the particulars of claim sets out who the parties are and what their status is for the purposes of the claim. For example, *'At all material times, the Claimant was a company specialising in the design, manufacture and supply of bolts. At all material times, the Defendant was a customer of the Claimant.'*
Factual chronology	The court expects a concise chronology that covers all of the material facts which relate to the legal basis of the claim.
The contract and its terms	The court will expect to see details of how the contract was made, what discussions took place beforehand, what terms were agreed and what evidence exists. If the contract is written, the CPR require a copy of the contract to be attached to the particulars of claim. If the contract is oral, the particulars should set out the contractual words used and state by whom, to whom, when and where they were spoken.
How the contract was allegedly breached	The next step is to outline the term(s) of the contract that have allegedly been breached and how the defendant has breached them.
Consequences of breach	This section sets out what happened as a result of the defendant's alleged breach, specifically how it impacted the claimant.
Damages claimed	This sets out the nature and amount of the losses the claimant suffered as a result of the defendant's alleged breach.
Interest claimed	It is very important to include this, as the court will not award interest unless it is specifically claimed. The rate of interest claimed on a specified amount is determined by one of the following: • if there is a rate of interest specified in the contract, the court will apply this; • an annual statutory rate of 8% if the rate is not specified in the contract; • a rate of interest decided by the court exercising its discretion. The interest sum claimed should be broken down into the daily rate of interest and how many days have elapsed since the date of breach to the date of commencement of proceedings. The paragraph should make a claim for ongoing interest on a daily basis until the date that a final judgment or order is made.
Statement of truth	The statement of truth confirms that the party signing the document believes that the facts stated in it are true. It is signed by either the claimant, their legal representative or their litigation friend (where applicable).

Table 5.3: The structure and contents of a particulars of claim in tort

Structure and contents	Explanation
Parties to the claim and their status	The opening paragraph of the particulars of claim sets out who the parties are and what their status is for the purposes of the claim. For example, 'At all material times, the Claimant was the driver of a grey Nissan motor vehicle, registration number AB65 XYZ. At all material times, the Defendant was the driver of a red Ford motor vehicle, registration number ZC70 HVA.'
Factual chronology	As with the particulars of claim for breach of contract, this covers all of the material facts that relate to the legal basis of the claim.
The relevant duty of care and why the defendant owed it to the claimant	This should set out the relevant duty of care and how the circumstances and facts of the case support the fact that: • the defendant had a duty of care; • the defendant owed a duty of care to the claimant.
How the duty of care was allegedly breached	This section should set out how, when and where the defendant allegedly breached the duty of care they owed to the claimant.
Causation	As you will know from your study of tort, the defendant is only liable if the claimant can establish that the defendant's breach has resulted in some harm. This is called causation and it must be set out in the particulars of claim. Only strict liability torts (eg trespass against the person claims) are exempt from this.
Damages claimed	For specified claims, this section sets out the nature and amount of the losses that the claimant suffered as a result of the defendant's alleged breach. This should be broken down where possible so that the court can see exactly how the claimant has calculated the overall damages claimed. For unspecified claims, the claimant should indicate the value bracket for the damages they are seeking (less than £10,000, more than £10,000 but not more than £25,000, or more than £25,000) or alternatively inform the court that they do not know the value of the claim they are making.
Interest claimed	It is very important to include this, as the court will not award interest unless it is specifically claimed. The statutory basis of the interest claimed is set out by the claimant in the particulars of claim, but the rate is decided by the court using their discretion under either section 35A Supreme Courts Act 1981 (for High Court claims) or section 69 County Courts Act 1984 (for County Court claims).
Statement of truth	The statement of truth confirms that the party signing the document believes that the facts stated in it are true. It is signed by either the claimant, their legal representative or their litigation friend (where applicable).

DEFENCE

The defence is the document that is prepared and submitted by the defendant in response to receiving a claim form and particulars of claim.

Purpose of the defence

The purpose of the defence is to allow the defendant to indicate to the court what their position is in relation to each of the allegations which have been made against them. This is with the intention of narrowing the issues between the parties and ensuring that only the matters that are actually in dispute are brought before the court. The defendant can respond to each allegation made against them in one of three ways:
- they admit the allegation;
- they do not admit the allegation (this is called a **non-admission**) and require proof from the claimant as to its truth;
- they deny the allegation.

The defendant will respond to each of the numbered paragraphs in the particulars of claim, setting out their position in relation to each of those numbered paragraphs (eg *'Paragraph 1 is admitted'*). If the defendant denies an allegation, they must explain their reasons for the denial, set out their own version of events and explain how that differs from that of the claimant.

Key term: non-admission
This is where the defendant neither admits nor denies an allegation. A defendant will make a non-admission where they have no knowledge about the facts or allegations that have been made against them in a particular paragraph of the particulars of claim.

The defendant will state their position in relation to each of the allegations made. If they admit the paragraph, the court will consider that paragraph an agreed point. If they make a non-admission or denial, the burden of proof rests with the claimant to prove the allegation on the balance of probabilities.

Structure and contents of the defence

The defence will follow the structure that is set out in the particulars of claim where possible. If the particulars of claim have been properly drafted, they will set out the claimant's factual case in chronological order in a series of numbered paragraphs. The defendant will simply follow this lead and respond to each of the allegations made with either a denial, a non-admission or an admission.

If the particulars of claim has not been drafted as concisely as it perhaps should have been, the defendant should ensure that their defence deals with each allegation made in chronological order where possible, setting out the reasons for denial and explaining their version of events. The defence should also include:

- the claim number (which was allocated to the claim when it was issued);
- the parties to the dispute;
- the location of the court to which the claim has been allocated;
- a statement of truth signed by the defendant, their legal advisor or, where applicable, their litigation friend.

REPLY TO DEFENCE

This is an option for the claimant if the defence raises issues that have not been covered in the particulars of claim. The reply to defence is a formal statement of case that responds to any such issues. The claimant is not required to file a reply to defence; it is entirely optional.

The structure and contents of a reply to defence is reasonably straightforward. The claimant simply needs to specify the areas of the defence that they wish to respond to and put to the court their version of events. For example, *'The Defendant claims in paragraph 3 of the defence that the meeting to negotiate the contract took place on 15 July at their factory in Manchester. This is denied. The Defendant was in London all day on 15 July and has evidence to support this.'*

PART 20 CPR CLAIMS

A **Part 20 claim** is an additional claim that is brought by the defendant to an action. It is drafted as part of the same document as the defence, but the defence and Part 20 claim perform entirely different functions for the purposes of the proceedings overall. In a defence and Part 20 claim, the defence is therefore drafted first, and this is followed by the Part 20 claim. The CPR separate Part 20 claims into two common categories: counterclaims and other additional claims.

> **Key term: Part 20 claim**
> This is an additional claim that is brought by the defendant to proceedings after they have been served with the claim form and particulars of claim. A Part 20 claim is most commonly a counterclaim, which is a claim made by a defendant against a claimant, but which is considered part of the same overall proceedings. It is essentially a new cause of action, and the burden of proof for the counterclaim is on the defendant as it would be had they issued the counterclaim as a separate standalone claim.

Purpose, content and structure of counterclaims

The purpose of a counterclaim is to allow the defendant to bring a cause of action against the claimant for losses that they have allegedly suffered. It is important to note that this needs to be a claim in its own right and so must be more than just a denial of the claim. It can be based around the same set of facts as the initial claim or it can be entirely different. A counterclaim is

78 Statements of case

generally raised to save the cost, time and inconvenience of the defendant issuing a separate claim against the claimant.

The rules relating to drafting a counterclaim are the same as those for drafting a particulars of claim, which can be found in **Tables 5.2** and **5.3**. You can test your understanding of counterclaims in **Practice example 5.1**.

Practice example 5.1
Robert commences proceedings against Shelby for recovery of a debt of £6,000 based on breach of contract. Four years ago, Shelby loaned Robert £3,000 to assist him with purchasing a vehicle. Despite the terms of the agreement being that he would pay the amount back in 30 monthly instalments, Robert has failed to make any repayments to Shelby. Can Shelby bring a counterclaim against Robert for the £3,000 despite it having nothing to do with Robert's initial claim?
Yes. Shelby would need to file a defence to Robert's claim and commence a Part 20 claim against Robert. The defence and counterclaim would form part of the same document; but as they perform different roles in the context of proceedings, Shelby would draft the defence first followed by the counterclaim. She would also have to pay a court fee in connection with the counterclaim.

Exam warning
A defendant is entitled to enter a counterclaim against the claimant without permission *provided* it is submitted at the same time as the defence. If the defendant wishes to issue a counterclaim against the claimant after the time period for filing the defence has elapsed, then they will require the permission of the court under CPR 20.4(2)(b).

Purpose, content and structure of other additional claims
It is important that you know and understand what is meant by 'other additional claims' for the SQE. Other additional claims can be:
- where the claimant has issued proceedings against two defendants in a building dispute and the first defendant wishes to seek a contribution or indemnity from the second defendant as they do not believe they were responsible for the loss;
- where the defendant wishes to add a party who is not named in the original proceedings in a breach of contract action, such as in a building dispute where the main builder wishes to add a subcontractor to proceedings, as the act that led to the loss was committed by the subcontractor.

In the same way as counterclaims, any other additional claim would follow from the defence and be filed with the court as one document.

DEFENCE TO COUNTERCLAIM

The claimant is entitled to file a defence to a Part 20 counterclaim that is made against them by the defendant within 14 days of it being served on them. The claimant and defendant can agree between themselves an extension of up to 28 days for the claimant to file a defence to counterclaim, if appropriate.

REQUESTS FOR FURTHER INFORMATION ABOUT A STATEMENT OF CASE

Part 18 of the CPR allows either the court or any party to proceedings to request further information about a statement of case. The party who requests the information must do as follows:
- Send a preliminary request in writing to the other party stating a reasonable date by which a response should be received.
- If a response is received but is insufficient, or the other party ignores the request, the party making the request can apply to the court for a Part 18 order requiring the other party to provide the information requested.

If a party receives such a request, they are obliged to:
- clarify any matter that is in dispute in the proceedings;
- give additional information in relation to any such matter.

This applies whether or not the matter is contained or referred to in a statement of case. However, the request must be proportionate to the proceedings; parties cannot simply submit requests that are entirely irrelevant to the matter in dispute.

Once a party has received a request for further information from either the opposition or the court, they must:
- file their response;
- serve it on the other parties.

This must be done within the time limit set out by the court and must be accompanied by a statement of truth.

■ KEY POINT CHECKLIST

This chapter has covered the following key knowledge points. You can use these to structure your revision, ensuring you recall the key details for each point, as covered in this chapter.
- The claim form is one of two primary documents that is used to commence a civil claim. The other is a particulars of claim. The structure of a particulars of claim includes introducing the parties to the claim and their status, a factual chronology, the relevant legal cause of action, the level of damages and interest claimed, and a statement of truth.
- The reply to defence is a formal statement of case that responds to any issues raised in the defence which have not been covered in the particulars of claim.

80 Statements of case

- A Part 20 claim is an additional claim, most commonly a counterclaim, that is brought by the defendant to proceedings after they have been served with the claim form and particulars of claim.
- Part 18 allows either the court or any party to proceedings to request further information about a statement of case.

■ KEY TERMS AND CONCEPTS

- exemplary damages (**page 73**)
- aggravated damages (**page 73**)
- non-admission (**page 76**)
- Part 20 claim (**page 77**)

■ SQE1-STYLE QUESTIONS

QUESTION 1

A claimant commences proceedings by filing a completed claim form and particulars of claim with the court. At trial, the claimant is successful and asks the court to use its discretion to add interest to the judgment sum.

Which of the following responses best reflects the claimant's legal position?

A. The court can exercise its discretion and add interest at an appropriate rate to the claimant's award.

B. If the claimant has included a claim for interest in their particulars of claim, the court can exercise its discretion and add interest at either the rate claimed or at an appropriate rate to the claimant's award.

C. If the claimant has included a claim for interest in their particulars of claim but failed to specify the rate, the court will refuse to order interest be added to the judgment sum.

D. If the claimant has failed to include a claim for interest in their particulars of claim, the court will order that interest be awarded at the standard rate of 8%.

E. If the claimant has included a claim for interest in their particulars of claim but failed to specify the rate, the defendant will be able to argue that the rate of interest should be 1% as a sanction for failing to specify the rate claimed.

QUESTION 2

A defendant is served with a claim form and particulars of claim. The defendant admits some of the allegations and denies others. The claimant has, however, also made several allegations against the defendant that are outside the scope of the defendant's knowledge.

Which of the following best represents how the defendant should proceed?

A. The defendant should deny all allegations that he does not admit. The burden of proof is on the claimant to prove the allegations stated.

B. The defendant should ignore any allegations that are outside his sphere of knowledge. The burden of proof is on the claimant to prove the allegations stated.

C. The defendant should deny all allegations made against him in the particulars of claim. The burden of proof is on the claimant to prove the allegations stated.

D. The defendant should admit or deny the allegations that are within his sphere of knowledge and submit non-admissions against the remainder. The defendant should state that the claimant is required to prove the allegations that are the subject of the non-admissions.

E. The defendant should submit non-admissions against all of the allegations made against him in the particulars of claim. The defendant should state that the claimant is required to prove the allegations that are the subject of the non-admissions.

QUESTION 3

A claimant contracts a building company to build an extension to their house. The building company subcontract the electrical work to an independent contractor. Once work is completed, there is a fault with the wiring that causes a small fire. The claimant suffers losses of £25,000 due to the fire. The claimant sues the building company as their contractual agreement exists only with them.

Which of the following best describes how the defendant can proceed?

A. The defendant should defend the claim and also issue an additional claim under Part 20 Civil Procedure Rules 1998 (CPR) against the electrical contractor so that it can be considered part of the overall proceedings.

B. The defendant should defend the claim on the basis that it was not their fault or responsibility. If the claimant is successful, the defendant can issue a separate claim against the electrical contractor.

C. The defendant should defend the claim on the basis that it was not their fault. The court will not find the defendant liable as they did not carry out the work on the claimant's property.

D. The defendant cannot defend the claim as they were contractually obligated to the claimant and it is clear that the breach has caused the damage. They should offer to settle with the claimant, file a consent order and conclude court proceedings. The defendant can then issue a separate claim against the electrical contractor.

E. The defendant should not file a defence; however, they can issue a Part 20 claim against the electrical contractor. This will mean that the defendant will no longer be party to proceedings.

QUESTION 4

A defendant is served with a claim form and particulars of claim. The defendant files a defence within the relevant time period and denies all of the allegations made. Eight weeks after the particulars of claim were served, the defendant seeks legal advice about some money that the claimant owes her in relation to a different matter and is told she would have a good claim.

Which of the following reflects the best way the defendant can proceed?

A. The defendant should file a counterclaim against the claimant immediately. It does not matter that the facts are unconnected to the original claim; the defendant is entitled to commence a counterclaim at any point.

B. The defendant should file a separate claim against the claimant immediately. As the facts are unconnected to the original claim, it cannot be dealt with by way of counterclaim; however, the defendant is entitled to issue proceedings against the claimant separately.

C. The defendant should seek the court's permission to bring a separate claim against the claimant immediately. As the facts are unconnected to the original claim, it cannot be dealt with by way of counterclaim; however, the defendant is entitled to issue proceedings against the claimant separately with permission of the court.

D. The defendant should wait until the current proceedings are concluded and then issue a claim against the claimant separately. As the facts are unconnected to the original claim, it cannot be dealt with by way of counterclaim; however, the defendant is entitled to issue proceedings against the claimant separately.

E. The defendant should apply for the permission of the court to file a counterclaim against the claimant immediately. It does not matter that the facts are unconnected to the original claim; the defendant is entitled to commence a counterclaim. However, as the time period for a defence being submitted has now expired, the defendant will need permission from the court to do so.

QUESTION 5

A claimant commences proceedings against a defendant. When the defence is received, the claimant does not feel able to respond as the defence is confusing.

Which of the following best describes how the claimant should proceed?

A. The claimant should file a reply to defence and indicate that the defence is not sufficiently clear to respond properly.
B. The claimant should write to the defendant asking them to clarify the parts of their defence that are confusing in a reasonable timescale.
C. The claimant should apply to the court and request that they order the defendant to clarify the parts of their defence that are confusing.
D. The claimant should write to the defendant asking them to clarify the parts of their defence that are confusing immediately, failing which the claimant will make an application for the defence to be struck out.
E. The claimant should apply to the court to have the defendant's statement of case struck out.

■ ANSWERS TO QUESTIONS

Answers to 'What do you know already?' questions at the start of the chapter

1) A claim form and, if being prepared separately, a particulars of claim are required to commence a claim.
2) False. The defendant responds to each allegation made in one of three ways: admit the allegation, defend the allegation or enter a non-admission against the allegation.
3) Yes. If the defendant has a separate claim against the claimant, they can enter a counterclaim at the same time as filing their defence to the principal claim.
4) A defendant is entitled to make a request for further information about the points in the particulars of claim that require clarification. They would submit that request in writing to the claimant, allowing them a reasonable time limit to respond.
5) The purpose of the defence is to allow the defendant to indicate to the court what their position is in relation to each of the allegations that have been made against them.

Answers to end-of-chapter SQE1-style questions

Question 1:
  The correct answer was B. Provided the claimant has included a claim for interest in their particulars of claim, then the court is able to exercise its discretion with regard to awarding interest. If the claimant has failed to make any claim for interest, the court will not award it, which makes option D incorrect. Option A is not the best answer as the question

does not specify whether or not the claimant has claimed for interest in the particulars of claim. If the claimant has included a claim for interest but not specified the rate, the court will use a default rate; they will not refuse to award interest or penalise the claimant for not having specified a rate. This makes options C and E incorrect.

Question 2:
The correct answer was D. Any allegations that are outside the defendant's knowledge should be dealt with as non-admissions and the claimant should be put to strict proof on them. Although the burden of proof is on the claimant, the defendant should not just blanket deny everything as this implies that he has knowledge of the facts (making options A and C incorrect), nor should he ignore any allegations made (making option B incorrect). Finally, option E is not right as we are told that the defendant admits some of the allegations and denies others; his response must therefore reflect this.

Question 3:
The correct answer was A. The defendant will need to file a defence to the claim and issue an additional Part 20 against the electrical contractor at the same time. This will bring the electrical contractor into proceedings. Option B is not the best answer as there is no need for the defendant to incur the cost, time and inconvenience by waiting for the conclusion of proceedings to commence a separate claim against the electrical contractor (thus making option D wrong as well). Option C is incorrect as it appears, on the face of it, that the claimant's contractual relationship is only with the defendant (therefore making this the only avenue of proceeding for the claimant). Finally, option E is not correct as a Part 20 claim cannot be issued without an accompanying defence, whether that defence admits, denies or submits non-admissions against the allegations the claimant is making.

Question 4:
The correct answer was E. As the last day on which the defendant could file the defence has passed, the defendant will need the permission of the court to make a counterclaim against the claimant. This makes option A incorrect. It is immaterial that the facts of the case are different to those in the original claim; the defendant is still entitled to bring a counterclaim against the claimant without needing to issue proceedings separately. This makes options B, C and D incorrect.

Question 5:
The correct answer was B. Under the Civil Procedure Rules 1998 (CPR), the claimant is entitled to request further information if a statement of case is not sufficiently clear to enable a proper response. This must be done in writing and must allow the defendant a reasonable timescale to provide their written response (making option D incorrect). Option A is not the best answer as it does not follow the appropriate process. Option C would only be correct if the claimant had already written to the

defendant for further information and the defendant had either ignored the request or failed to provide any clarity in their response. Finally, option E is incorrect as the defence is simply confusing; an application to strike out the defence would only be appropriate where it fails to plead a proper defence.

■ KEY CASES, RULES, STATUTES AND INSTRUMENTS

The SQE1 Assessment Specification does not require you to know any case names or statutory materials for the topic of statements of case. You must, however, be able to recall that the term 'Part 20' refers to Part 20 of the Civil Procedure Rules 1998 and you must be familiar with the principle underlying Part 20.

6

Interim applications

■ MAKE SURE YOU KNOW

This chapter will cover interim applications. It will consider the procedure for making interim applications, as well as the requirements for making applications for summary judgment, interim payments and interim injunctions. You are required to be able to apply these principles and rules appropriately and effectively to realistic client-based and ethical problems and situations for your SQE1 assessment.

■ SQE ASSESSMENT ADVICE

As you work through this chapter, remember to pay particular attention in your revision to:
- the correct procedure for making an interim application;
- the purpose, procedure and evidence required to make an application for summary judgment;
- the purpose, procedure and evidence required to make an application for interim payments;
- the purpose, procedure and evidence required to make an application for interim injunctions (including freezing injunctions and search orders).

■ WHAT DO YOU KNOW ALREADY?

Have a go at these questions before reading this chapter. If you find some difficult or cannot remember the answers, make a note to look more closely at that subtopic during your revision.
1) What is an interim application?
   [Introduction to interim applications, page 87]
2) True or false? Interim applications can only be made if the defendant has prior notice of the hearing and is able to attend to defend themselves.
   [Without notice applications, page 89]
3) What is the purpose of applying for an order for summary judgment?
   [Purpose of summary judgment, page 90]

4) What are the guidelines that the court considers when deciding whether to grant an application for an interim injunction?
  [The purpose, procedure and evidence required to make an application for interim injunctions, page 90]
5) True or false? If the applicant requests it, the court will always allow an application to be considered without notice.
  [Procedure for making an interim application, page 87]

INTRODUCTION TO INTERIM APPLICATIONS

Interim applications are applications made to the court by one of the parties to litigation after a claim has been commenced but before it has reached trial. This is why they are called interim (ie made during the intervening time between commencement and trial).

In making an application, the **applicant** is requesting that the court either makes an order or issues directions (see **Chapter 1, Table 1.5**). The **respondent** will be the party against whom the application is made.

The SQE1 Assessment Specification requires you to know the procedure for making interim applications in general, as well as the purpose, procedure and evidence required to make specific applications, such as for summary judgment, interim payments and interim injunctions. This chapter will cover each of these topics in turn.

Key term: applicant
The applicant is the party who makes an interim application during litigation proceedings.

Key term: respondent
The respondent is the party against whom the interim application is made.

PROCEDURE FOR MAKING AN INTERIM APPLICATION

In order to make an interim application, the applicant must prepare and file the following documents with the court:
- Application form (called form N244), which requests the court to make an order or direction and specifies what type of order or direction the applicant would like the court to make.
- Draft order, which is a draft of the order the applicant would like the court to make.

- Evidence, which is generally in the form of a witness statement. This should include details of why the order or direction is being requested and should include evidence to support the facts that are being relied upon.
- **Skeleton argument**, but only if the claim is in the High Court.

> **Key term: skeleton argument**
>
> This is a written document provided to the court in advance of a hearing, which summarises the factual and legal issues involved, the arguments that are being submitted in relation to those issues, and any legal authorities that the party will be relying upon.

What happens once the applicant has filed the relevant documents depends on whether the application has been made '**with notice**' or '**without notice**'. It is important to note that most interim applications are made 'with notice'.

> **Key term: with notice applications**
>
> These are applications where the applicant gives notice of the hearing to the respondent prior to the relevant court hearing.

> **Key term: without notice applications**
>
> These are applications where the applicant does not inform the respondent about the application or hearing until the court has already made an order.

With notice applications

Once the applicant has filed the relevant documents with the court, the court will then issue the application and send out a notice to the parties informing them of the time and date of the hearing. The following will then happen:
- The application notice, draft order and evidence (including witness statement) must then be served on the respondent at least three days before the hearing date.
- The respondent must then serve any evidence they wish to rely upon as soon as possible. There is no set timescale for the respondent to do this unless the court specifies one.
- The applicant is then permitted to serve any evidence in response to the respondent's evidence if they wish to do so.

The matter will then proceed to a hearing, where the court will decide whether to grant the application and make the order or direction being sought by the applicant or to reject the application.

Without notice applications

Without notice applications are only allowed in exceptional circumstances where urgency requires it. The most common without notice interim applications are freezing injunctions, where an applicant has genuine grounds to believe that a respondent will deliberately dispose of their assets to avoid paying a debt. In such cases, giving the respondent notice would defeat the point of the application as it would allow the respondent time to dispose of their assets before the hearing.

In a without notice application, the applicant must not only explain to the court in great detail and with evidence why notice was not given, but also provide the court with a witness statement setting out all of the facts, whether they are favourable to the application or not. The court will scrutinise the information and evidence they receive carefully before making an order, as the respondent does not have the opportunity to put forward their own arguments.

If the court grants the interim application and makes an order, the applicant must serve on the respondent the application notice, evidence, court order and a brief statement explaining the respondent's right to have the order set aside within seven days of it being granted. The court may also set a date for the matter to return to court for a full hearing with both parties, ordering that the injunction remains in place until the date of the next hearing, for example. Take a look at **Practice example 6.1** to test your knowledge of without notice applications.

Practice example 6.1

Rupert commences proceedings against David for breach of contract. The losses claimed are £145,000. After the defence is filed, Rupert is talking with a mutual friend who says that David is in the process of transferring his house (his only asset) to his sister. Rupert therefore decides to file an application for a freezing injunction against David's assets, but does not want him to know about it. What does Rupert need to do?

Rupert can issue an application without notice here. He must file an application notice (form N244) alongside a witness statement and any evidence he has of the steps David has taken to dispose of his assets. Rupert must give a substantial amount of detail in his witness statement, and it would also be appropriate to obtain and file a witness statement from the mutual friend as part of the evidence. If the court grants the injunction, Rupert will need to serve David with the application notice, witness statements, accompanying evidence and a notice explaining his right to apply to have the order set aside within seven days of the order being made.

THE PURPOSE, PROCEDURE AND EVIDENCE REQUIRED TO MAKE AN APPLICATION FOR SUMMARY JUDGMENT

As well as being aware of the general procedure relating to interim applications, the SQE also requires you to know the processes involved in applying for specific types of interim application that are regulated by different chapters of the Civil Procedure Rules 1998 (CPR; see **Chapter 1**). The first of these is **summary judgment**.

> **Key term: summary judgment**
> An application for summary judgment can be made by either party, and if successful has the effect of concluding a part of or an entire case before trial.

Purpose of summary judgment

Summary judgment under Part 24 of the CPR allows a party who is on the receiving end of a weak claim or defence to request the court to order that either part of or the whole of the relevant statement of case be disposed of. If an application for summary judgment is successful, the party against whom the order is made will not be allowed to continue with the part of their claim or defence that the order for summary judgment relates to. **Practice example 6.2** tests your ability to identify whether a summary judgment would be appropriate.

> **Practice example 6.2**
> Ashley commences proceedings against Adam for breach of contract. Adam files a defence to the claim but it fails to dispute either the claim's legal basis or any of the material facts contained within the particulars of claim. Ashley believes that Adam has filed the defence as a delaying tactic as he knows that the claim is valid and that he is simply trying to prolong matters to increase her legal costs. Ashley does not wish for the matter to proceed all the way to trial as this will simply increase her legal costs despite the fact that Adam has provided no legal or factual basis for him defending the claim. What can Ashley do?
>
> This would be a situation where an application for summary judgment against Adam would be appropriate. The purpose of Part 24 is to allow a party to ask the court to dismiss a claim or defence where there is no legal or factual basis for it, so as to save the parties costs, time and effort litigating a claim to which there is no valid defence.

Procedure and evidence required for an application for summary judgment

CPR 24.2 sets out the grounds that the applicant for summary judgment must meet to succeed. The grounds with an accompanying explanation are set out in **Table 6.1**.

Table 6.1: The grounds that the applicant for summary judgment must meet to succeed

Ground	Explanation
The respondent has no real prospect of succeeding with the claim or defence, and;	This is a high standard to meet. 'No real prospect' essentially means that that the respondent's prospect of success must be close to imaginary. Even if it is unlikely that the respondent will be successful, this will be enough for the court to refuse an application for summary judgment and allow the proceedings to continue.
. . . there must be no other compelling reason why the claim should proceed to trial.	Compelling reasons can include: • complex facts (the court will not allow summary judgment where the facts of the claim are overly complex or technical and require a full hearing); • the defendant requires more time to investigate the claim made; • expert or further witness evidence is required to make a proper determination on the claim.

Exam warning

Remember that to be successful in an application for summary judgment, the applicant must meet *both* of the criteria above. Meeting only one will not be sufficient for the court to make an order in the applicant's favour.

The procedure for an application for summary judgment is as follows:
- The applicant prepares and files an application notice (form N244) requesting an order for summary judgment to be made with an accompanying witness statement explaining why they believe the two-stage test laid out in Part 24 is met.
- The respondent must then be given at least 14 days' notice of the hearing date and is required to serve any written evidence at least seven days before the hearing.
- The applicant can then file and serve any further written evidence (this is usually evidence that shows the respondent's position to be factually or legally incorrect) no later than three days before the hearing.

Following the hearing, the court will then make any of the orders set out in **Table 6.2**.

Table 6.2: Orders that can be set out by the court in an application for summary judgment

Type of order	Explanation
Judgment on the claim	This is where the claimant has brought the application against the defendant. The court gives judgment in the claimant's favour as they have met both of the Part 24 criteria. The claim will therefore not proceed to trial.
Dismissal of the claim	This is where the defendant has brought the application against the claimant. The court gives judgment in the defendant's favour and dismisses the claimant's claim.
Dismissal of the application	This is where the applicant fails to meet the two-stage test set out in Part 24. The claim will then continue as if the application were never brought.
Conditional order	This is where the court orders that the claim can continue but subject to a particular condition being met. For example, where the claimant has brought an application on the basis that the defendant's defence has no real prospect of success and there is no other compelling reason why the claim should proceed to trial, the defendant may have persuaded the court that the prospects of their success *could be* more than imaginary at the hearing. If this is the case, the court will order that the claim can continue, but conditional on the defendant filing a proper defence setting out their legal and factual position within 14 days of the date of the hearing.
Costs order	Either one of four costs orders can be made by the court. They are: • One party pays the other party's costs of the application. This will usually be the losing party being ordered to pay the successful party's costs. • That costs be in the case. This means that the decision on costs is deferred until a later date. • No order as to costs. This means that each party will pay their own costs of the application. It is generally used where the applicant was justified in bringing the application and the defendant has been able to justifiably defend it (ie there is no clear winner or where the court is equally critical of both sides). • Wasted costs order. This is where the legal representatives have to pay the legal costs due to their own poor levels of conduct in dealing with the application.

> **Exam warning**
>
> The court does not need to give the applicant permission to make an application for summary judgment *unless* it is being made by the claimant prior to the defendant filing an acknowledgment of service and defence. Remember to pay close attention to the timing of the application in an SQE question where it is the claimant making the application.

THE PURPOSE, PROCEDURE AND EVIDENCE REQUIRED TO MAKE AN APPLICATION FOR INTERIM PAYMENTS

An interim payment is an amount paid by a defendant to a claimant 'on account' before the court has made its final decision at trial. This typically happens where the defendant admits liability for the claim (ie in personal injury claims) and understands that they will need to pay the claimant some money but the amount of the claim is still to be determined by the court. An interim payment enables the defendant to make a payment to the claimant earlier than trial, which is then offset against the amount the claimant is awarded.

Interim payments can be made on a voluntary basis by agreement between the claimant and defendant. It is only where the defendant has refused to make a voluntary interim payment that the claimant should consider making an application for the court to order an interim payment to be made by the defendant. **Practice example 6.3** shows how this can operate in practice.

> **Practice example 6.3**
>
> Emma is badly injured in an accident that is caused by the negligence of Zach. She commences proceedings against him. The matter is passed to Zach's insurance company who admit liability for the claim but dispute the amount claimed. Emma's solicitor agrees with Zach's insurance company that they will make a voluntary interim payment to Emma in the sum of £45,000, which they do. The matter proceeds to trial and Emma is awarded £75,000 in damages. How much does Zach's insurance company need to pay Emma?
>
> As the interim payment of £45,000 was made to Emma before trial, Zach's insurance company now owe her £30,000 plus any interest payments the court awards. The interest payments will be less than those that would have been payable had the insurance company not made the interim payment, as interest is only payable on sums outstanding.

Procedure and evidence required for an application for an interim payment

The grounds for an application for an interim payment are laid out in Part 25 of the CPR. The claimant must prove one of the following grounds for their application to be successful:
- the defendant has admitted liability to pay damages or some other sum of money to the claimant;
- the claimant has obtained judgment against that defendant for damages to be assessed or for a sum of money (other than costs) to be assessed;
- the court is satisfied that if the claim went to trial, the claimant would obtain judgment for a substantial amount of money (other than costs) against the defendant, from whom they are seeking an order for an interim payment.

Exam warning
The third ground described above is very difficult to prove. If an exam question arises where you are asked about the likelihood of an application for an interim payment succeeding where the claimant is applying based on this third ground, it is unlikely the claimant will be successful, unless they have a significant amount of evidence to show that they will win the case and that the damages they will be awarded will be substantial.

The procedure for making an application for an interim payment is as follows:
- The applicant prepares and files an application notice (form N244) requesting an order for an interim payment to be made with an accompanying witness statement explaining why they believe the grounds laid out in Part 25 are met.
- The respondent must then be given at least 14 days' notice of the hearing date and is required to serve any written evidence at least seven days before the hearing.
- The applicant can then file and serve any further written evidence (this is usually evidence that shows the respondent's position to be factually or legally incorrect) no later than three days before the hearing.

Once the court has heard the application, they will decide whether to order that the defendant makes an interim payment to the claimant, and if so how much that is to be. The court will also make one of the costs orders set out in **Table 6.2**.

THE PURPOSE, PROCEDURE AND EVIDENCE REQUIRED TO MAKE AN APPLICATION FOR INTERIM INJUNCTIONS

An interim injunction is an order that requires a party to either do something specific or refrain from doing something specific pending a full trial taking place. The SQE Assessment Specification requires you to know the guidelines that are applied by the court when deciding whether to grant an interim injunction generally.

Procedure and evidence required for an application for an interim injunction

The guidelines that the court applies when deciding to grant an application for an interim injunction, and an accompanying explanation of what they mean, are set out in **Table 6.3**.

Table 6.3: Guidelines applied by the court when deciding to grant an application for an interim injunction

Guideline	Explanation
Is there a serious issue to be tried?	The claimant needs to satisfy the court that the claim is not imaginary, frivolous or vexatious (ie where the action is being brought only to harass the defendant and does not have a legal or factual basis to it).
Would damages be an adequate remedy?	The court needs to consider whether damages alone would be a sufficient remedy for the claimant, and if awarded whether the respondent would be able to pay those damages.
Where does the balance of convenience lie?	The court must consider which party would suffer the biggest inconvenience: the claimant if the injunction was not granted, or the defendant if the injunction was granted.
Are there any other special factors?	The court looks at whether the facts of the case point to any particular factors that would either support granting an application for an injunction or refusing one.

The procedure for making an application for an interim injunction is dependent on whether it is made with notice or without notice:
- The procedure where the application is made with notice is set out on **page 88**.
- The procedure where the application is made without notice is set out on **page 89**.

Once the court has heard the application, they will decide whether to order that an interim injunction is put in place. If the application is on notice and the court awards the injunction, then the injunction will last until trial. If the application is without notice, the court will either:
- Grant the injunction temporarily but list the matter for a full hearing with both parties present. This allows the defendant the opportunity to argue that the injunction should be set aside.
- Grant the injunction but inform the defendant that they can make an application to set aside the order within seven days of the order being made.

The court will also make one of the costs orders set out in **Table 6.2**.

Applications for freezing injunctions and search orders

As well as the procedure to follow to apply for an interim injunction, the SQE Assessment Specification requires you to know about the purpose of specific types of interim injunctions: freezing injunctions and search orders. Each of these are considered in **Table 6.4**.

Table 6.4: Types of interim injunctions

Type of interim injunction	Description
Freezing injunction	An order that prevents the respondent of the application from disposing of their assets before trial. A respondent would usually do this if they were trying to protect their wealth and assets from being paid or transferred to the applicant in the event of a successful claim. The applicant must show that there is a real risk of the defendant dissipating their assets.
Search order	An order that allows an applicant to enter the premises of the respondent to search for and take copies of evidence required for a court case.

■ KEY POINT CHECKLIST

This chapter has covered the following key knowledge points. You can use these to structure your revision, ensuring you recall the key details for each point, as covered in this chapter.
- Interim applications are applications made to the court by one of the parties to litigation after a claim has been commenced but before it has reached trial.
- In order to make an interim application, the applicant must prepare and file with the court an application form, a draft order, evidence and a skeleton argument.
- Interim applications can either be made with notice or without notice.
- Without notice applications are only granted in exceptional circumstances. In a without notice application, the applicant must not only explain to the court in great detail and with evidence why notice was not given, but also provide the court with a witness statement setting out all of the facts, whether they are favourable to the application or not.
- Summary judgment allows a party who is on the receiving end of a weak claim or defence to request the court to order that either part of or the whole of the relevant statement of case be disposed of.
- In order to succeed in an application for summary judgment, the applicant must show that the respondent has no real prospect of succeeding with their claim or defence, and that there is no other compelling reason why the matter should proceed to trial.

- An interim payment is an amount paid by a defendant to a claimant 'on account' before the court has made its final decision at trial.

■ KEY TERMS AND CONCEPTS
- applicant (**page 87**)
- respondent (**page 87**)
- skeleton argument (**page 88**)
- with notice applications (**page 88**)
- without notice applications (**page 88**)
- summary judgment (**page 90**)

■ SQE1-STYLE QUESTIONS

QUESTION 1

A claimant commences a claim in the County Court for recovery of £68,000 following the defendant's alleged breach of contract. The defendant files a defence that does not explain the legal or factual basis for them defending the claim. The claimant therefore proceeds with making an application for summary judgment.

Which of the following best reflects the documents that the claimant will need to prepare and file with the court to make the application?

A. The claimant needs to complete and file an application form, a draft order, and a witness statement with accompanying evidence.

B. The claimant needs to complete and file an application form, a draft order, a witness statement with accompanying evidence, and a skeleton argument.

C. The claimant needs to complete and file an application form and a draft order, with a witness statement to follow seven days before the hearing date.

E. The claimant needs to complete and file an application form and a witness statement with accompanying evidence, alongside a skeleton argument.

E. The claimant needs to complete and file an application form and accompanying evidence.

QUESTION 2

A claimant company commences proceedings against a defendant company for breach of contract. The claimant's particulars of claim sets out concise

98 Interim applications

details of the events leading up to the contract being agreed, the terms of the contract, the way in which the defendant breached the contract, and the losses that the defendant suffered. The claimant also attached a copy of the written contract to the particulars of claim. The defendant files a defence to the claim, simply saying, *'We did not breach the contract and we did not cause the losses the claimant is claiming. The goods we supplied were suitable for the purpose they were used for, and we will get an expert to look at them if necessary to prove it.'* The claimant makes an application for summary judgment against the defendant.

Which of the following best represents the likely outcome?

A. It is likely that the claimant will be successful in their application. The defence does not show that the defendant has a real prospect of successfully defending the claim, nor is there any compelling reason why the case should proceed to trial.

B. It is likely that the claimant will be successful in their application. The requirement for expert evidence is a compelling reason why the case should proceed to trial, but the defendant has not shown a real prospect of being able to successfully defend the claim, and this will outweigh the need for expert evidence.

C. It is likely that the claimant will be successful in their application. The defence does show that the defendant has a real prospect of successfully defending the claim, but there is no compelling reason why the claim should proceed to trial.

D. It is likely that the defendant will successfully defend the application. They have said enough to prove that they have a real prospect of successfully defending the claim at trial.

E. It is likely that the defendant will successfully defend the application. The court will regard expert evidence being required to determine an issue as a compelling reason why the claim should proceed to trial.

QUESTION 3

A claimant is successful in an application for summary judgment. The court is highly critical of the defendant's defence and accepts the claimant's arguments that the defendant had only entered a defence to waste the claimant's time and money.

Which of the following best describes how the court will deal with the parties' legal costs?

A. The court will not make an order as to legal costs as the matter has not proceeded to a full trial.

B. The court will make a conditional costs order in favour of the claimant.

C. The court will order that the defendant pays the claimant's costs. The claimant's application was strong when compared to the defendant's response and so the court will recognise this in the costs order they make.

D. The court will make no order as to costs. Parties are required to cover their own costs unless the matter goes to trial.

E. The court will order wasted costs against the defendant on the basis that the defendant has wasted the court's time.

QUESTION 4

A claimant commences proceedings against a defendant for negligence. The specified damages claimed are £165,000 and the defendant admits liability for the claim in her defence. The claimant makes an application for an interim payment of £145,000.

Which of the following best reflects the likely outcome?

A. The claimant's application may not be successful as they have not attempted to negotiate a voluntary interim payment from the defendant.

B. The claimant's application will fail because the defendant has already admitted liability. The court will therefore insist on deciding on the value of the claim at a final hearing.

C. The claimant's application will succeed as the defendant has already admitted liability and the damages claimed are higher than the value of the interim payment requested.

D. The claimant's application will succeed as the court will be satisfied that if the claim went to trial, the claimant would obtain judgment for a substantial amount of money (other than costs) against the defendant.

E. The claimant's application will fail. The defendant has admitted liability but no judgment on either liability or value of the claim has yet been given. The court will therefore not grant an interim payment.

QUESTION 5

A claimant commences proceedings against a defendant. Shortly after receiving a defence, the claimant is made aware that the defendant's home has a 'sold' sign outside of it. The claimant is aware that this is the defendant's only asset. When the claimant contacts the estate agent, they tell him that the house was sold for substantially under its current value.

Which of the following best describes how the claimant should proceed?

A. The claimant should make an application for a freezing injunction against the defendant without notice immediately. It is clear that the defendant

is seeking to dispose and reduce the value of his assets to avoid paying any judgment ordered against him.
B. The claimant should make an application for a search order against the defendant with notice immediately. This will determine whether or not the defendant is seeking to dispose and reduce the value of his assets to avoid paying any judgment ordered against him.
C. The claimant should make an application for a search order against the defendant without notice immediately. This will determine whether or not the defendant is seeking to dispose and reduce the value of his assets to avoid paying any judgment ordered against him.
D. The claimant should make an application for a freezing injunction against the defendant with notice immediately. It is clear that the defendant is seeking to dispose and reduce the value of his assets to avoid paying any judgment ordered against him.
E. The claimant should proceed with the claim without making an application, as the basis of the claimant's suspicion is weak and the court will not make an order unless they are persuaded as to the defendant's intentions.

■ ANSWERS TO QUESTIONS

Answers to 'What do you know already?' questions at the start of the chapter

1) An interim application is made to the court by one of the parties to litigation after a claim has been commenced but before it has reached trial.
2) False. Certain applications can be made without notice, which means that the respondent does not know about them until the court has made a decision on the application.
3) The purpose of an application for an order for summary judgment is that it allows a party who is on the receiving end of a weak claim or defence to request the court to order that either part of or the whole of the relevant statement of case be disposed of.
4) The guidelines that the court considers when deciding whether to grant an application for an interim injunction are whether there is a serious issue to be tried, whether damages are an adequate remedy, where the balance of convenience lies, and whether there are any other special factors.
5) False. The court will only hear an application without notice in exceptional circumstances.

Answers to end-of-chapter SQE1-style questions

Question 1:
The correct answer was A. The claimant needs to complete and file an application form, a draft order for the court, and a witness statement with accompanying evidence, if appropriate. A skeleton argument would only be relevant if the claim was being heard in the High Court and we are told it is in the County Court (making options B and D incorrect). A witness statement needs to be filed at the same time as the application, making option C incorrect, and an applicant must always include both a draft order and a witness statement, making option E wrong.

Question 2:
The correct answer was E. The court regards the need for expert evidence as a compelling reason for the case proceeding to trial, and the claimant must prove that it would not be needed to be successful in an application for summary judgment (making options A, B and C incorrect). Option D is not correct as it is the need for expert evidence that is likely to persuade the court to dismiss the application.

Question 3:
The correct answer was C. When there is a clear winner of an application such as this, the court will generally go with the principle that the loser pays the winner's costs (making option D incorrect). The court has full discretion to make a costs order in an interim application hearing, making option A incorrect. The court will only make a conditional costs order where it also imposes a condition on the defendant, which in this case it has not (option B is therefore incorrect). Option E is wrong as the court only makes a wasted costs order against the legal representative of a party if their conduct of proceedings has fallen substantially short, not because the defendant has wasted the court's time.

Question 4:
The correct answer was A. It is possible that the application will be unsuccessful as the court expects attempts to be made between the parties to agree a voluntary interim payment prior to an application being made. The court will always be in a position where the value of the claim has not yet been decided, so this is not a reason for the application to fail (making options B and E incorrect). Option C is incorrect as this is not one of the criteria that the court takes into account when making a decision on whether to grant an application for an interim payment, and option D is incorrect as this would only be a ground of application where liability had not already been admitted.

Question 5:
The correct answer was A. There is sufficient evidence for the claimant to suspect that the defendant is seeking to reduce their assets in order to potentially avoid settling any judgment. The application would be made without notice, as giving the defendant notice would defeat the point

102 Interim applications

of the application, and this makes option D incorrect. A search order would not be appropriate here as the defendant is not trying to withhold information, which discards options B and C. Option E is incorrect as the claimant has enough to suspect the defendant of seeking to dissipate their assets, and so warrants making an application for a freezing injunction.

■ KEY CASES, RULES, STATUTES AND INSTRUMENTS

The SQE1 Assessment Specification does not require you to know any case names or statutory materials for the topic of interim applications.

7

Case management

■ MAKE SURE YOU KNOW

This chapter will cover case management and the overriding objective, track allocation, case management for cases proceeding on the fast or multi-tracks, non-compliance with orders, sanctions and reliefs, and case management conferences. You are required to be able to apply these principles and rules appropriately and effectively to realistic client-based and ethical problems and situations for your SQE1 assessment.

■ SQE ASSESSMENT ADVICE

As you work through this chapter, remember to pay particular attention in your revision to:
- the overriding objective and how it is used;
- how the courts actively manage the procedural steps and timetables in litigated cases, and the expectations they have on parties and their representatives to assist with this;
- the three tracks, their characteristics and the criteria used to determine which one is the most suitable for an individual claim;
- the guidance contained in the Civil Procedure Rules 1998 (CPR) and their accompanying Practice Directions on management of fast and multi-track cases;
- what sanctions can be imposed upon a party for missing a court-imposed deadline, and what a party should do if they want to avoid sanctions being ordered against them.

■ WHAT DO YOU KNOW ALREADY?

Have a go at these questions before reading this chapter. If you find some difficult or cannot remember the answers, make a note to look more closely at that subtopic during your revision.

1) Which of the Civil Procedure Rules (CPR) contains the overriding objective of civil litigation?
   [Case management and the overriding objective, page 104]

2) True or false? The judge sets the procedural steps and the timetable for a civil claim to follow with no assistance from the litigating parties or their representatives.
[Case management and the overriding objective, page 104]
3) What are the three tracks to which a claim can be allocated in civil proceedings?
[Tracks and track allocation, page 107]
4) What is a case management conference?
[Case management directions for cases proceeding on the fast or multi-tracks, page 110]
5) True or false? If a party fails to comply with a deadline in a court order, they cannot avoid being subject to a penalty from the court.
[Non-compliance with orders, sanctions and relief, page 113]

CASE MANAGEMENT AND THE OVERRIDING OBJECTIVE

Case management is the term used to describe the active role the court takes in managing the timetable that a case will follow from commencement to conclusion. When a defence is filed, this triggers the need for the court to make an order setting down a series of procedural steps, such as exchanging witness statements or filing an expert's report, and a timetable for those steps that the parties to the case must follow. The procedural steps and their timetable will be determined by which **track** a claim is allocated to at allocation to track stage (for more detail on tracks and track allocation, see **page 107**).

Key term: case management
This is the process carried out by the court that progresses a case towards a final trial.

Key term: track
When a case is allocated to a track, this determines the type of directions and timetable that the court will attach to a particular claim. There are three tracks: small claims track, fast track and multi-track.

Once a decision has been taken about which track the claim has been allocated to, the claimant and defendant parties, or their representatives, should work together to present to the court a proposed set of procedural steps and a timetable for those steps to comply with. These are called **directions**. Upon the proposed directions being presented to the court, a judge will either agree with them, and therefore make an order incorporating them, or disagree, and therefore alter them. The Civil Procedure Rule (CPR; see **Chapter 1**) that applies to the appropriate track and the Practice Direction which accompanies it set out generic suggested directions and timetables for a claim that has been allocated to that particular track. Parties will base their proposed directions and timetable for their specific claim on the framework contained within the appropriate CPR and Practice Direction.

Revision tip
Although the claimant and defendant parties, or their representatives, will propose directions to the court, it is the court that makes the final decision and order about how the case will be managed, the procedural steps which will be set down, and the timetable that the parties must follow.

Key term: directions
Directions are a list of instructions given by the court to the parties to litigation that set out the steps which each party needs to take to prepare for trial, and the deadlines by which each of those steps needs to be completed (eg when witness statements are to be exchanged). Parties to litigation often propose directions to the court, but the final decision rests with the court to make an appropriate order.

Exam warning
Do not confuse directions and Practice Directions. Remember that Practice Directions are supplementary guidance chapters to the CPR themselves.

The overriding objective
The court will manage litigation in accordance with the **overriding objective** of CPR 1.1.

Key term: overriding objective
The overriding objective is the principle that guides the civil courts in any action they take. It is contained within CPR 1.1 and enables the courts to deal with cases justly and at proportionate cost.

CPR 1.1(2) offers some further guidance on how the overriding objective is to be applied:

Dealing with a case justly and at proportionate cost includes, so far as is practicable –
(a) ensuring that the parties are on an equal footing;
(b) saving expense;
(c) dealing with the case in ways which are proportionate –
 (i) to the amount of money involved;
 (ii) to the importance of the case;
 (iii) to the complexity of the issues; and
 (iv) to the financial position of each party;
(d) ensuring that it is dealt with expeditiously and fairly;
(e) allotting to it an appropriate share of the court's resources, while taking into account the need to allot resources to other cases; and
(f) enforcing compliance with rules, practice directions and orders.

Practice example 7.1 demonstrates how the overriding objective could be applied in practice.

> **Practice example 7.1**
>
> Two parties are involved in a dispute over the quality of some leaflets. The value of the claim is £500. The claimant argues that the defendant did not follow their express instructions regarding the colour scheme of the leaflets and that they are 'a little tatty'; the defendant argues that the claimant was not specific about their desired colour scheme. The claimant wants to rely on the reports of three experts at a cost of £600 each and disclose 650 pages of emails that cover every piece of correspondence exchanged between the parties. If you are the claimant's solicitor, is this just and at proportionate cost, and therefore consistent with the overriding objective?
>
> **The answer is no; the time and cost involved are not proportionate to the value of the claim, and are therefore not consistent with the overriding objective and CPR 1.1.**

How does the court manage cases?

A key feature of the CPR is that cases will be closely monitored and controlled by the court. The court is therefore directly involved with the following key steps:
1. identifying disputed issues at an early stage;
2. deciding how those issues are to be presented and proved;
3. fixing the timetable for the claim to follow;
4. controlling costs;
5. disposing of cases by summary judgment (see **Chapter 6**);

6. dealing with matters without the parties having to attend court, and giving directions to ensure the progress of the case is efficient.

Judges manage cases based on the overriding objective. To accommodate this, fixed or standardised management decisions and timetables are used as much as possible. In fast track and multi-track cases, it will be for the parties to seek directions and case management decisions that better their cases (see **page 105**). Any requests for case management decisions that fall outside standardised directions and timetables will need to be justified.

TRACKS AND TRACK ALLOCATION

Civil proceedings are allocated to one of three 'tracks' designed to deal with cases of different value and complexity. Track allocation is the process of determining which track a case should follow.

Upon the defendant filing a defence, a court officer will provisionally decide which track appears most suitable for the claim. There are three tracks: small claims, fast track and multi-track. Each of these tracks has their own individual CPR that contains general criteria about the management of a case which has been allocated to that specific track (for more details about the criteria for track allocation, see **Table 7.1**).

The court officer will serve a notice on each party that:
- states the proposed track;
- requires the parties to complete a directions questionnaire, file it at court and serve copies on all of the parties.

If the claim appears to be suitable for fast track or multi-track, the notice requires the parties to file proposed directions with the court and gives a specified date for filing a directions questionnaire and, where appropriate, proposed directions. Those directions can include dates for exchange of witness statements, provision for the use of expert evidence (which will be covered in more detail in **Chapter 8**) and the date by which **disclosure** and **inspection** of evidence (see **Chapter 9**) must take place.

> **Key term: disclosure**
> This is the term used to describe the listing of documents that are in a party's possession.

> **Key term: inspection**
> This is where the opposing party asks for and inspects copies of the documents that have been disclosed to them.

The court decides which of the three tracks the case will be allocated to. It does this by matching the specifics of the individual case with the criteria laid out in CPR 26.8.1:

(a) the financial value, if any, of the claim;
(b) the nature of the remedy sought;
(c) the likely complexity of the facts, law or evidence;
(d) the number of parties or likely parties;
(e) the value of any counterclaim or other Part 20 claim and the complexity of any matters relating to it;
(f) the amount of oral evidence which may be required;
(g) the importance of the claim to persons who are not parties to the proceedings;
(h) the views expressed by the parties; and
(i) the circumstances of the parties.

> **Revision tip**
>
> In SQE1, if you are asked to calculate the value of the claim that the court will take into account at allocation stage, the court does not take into account any amount not in dispute, such as any claim for interest, claim for costs or any contributory negligence. **Practice example 7.2** illustrates how this might work in practice.

> **Practice example 7.2**
>
> Say the value of the leaflets in **Practice example 7.1** was £9,645. Interest, at a rate of 8% over 200 days at a daily rate of £2.11 and continuing is £422, plus fixed costs on issue of £100, would equal £10,167. What would be the financial value of the claim taken into account by the court on allocation?
>
> The answer is £9,645. The additional sums would not be taken into consideration when the claim is being allocated under CPR 26.8(2).

Criteria for track allocation

We have talked about the tracks and that the court will allocate the claim to one of them. However, what criteria will the court apply to decide which of the tracks to allocate a claim to? The tracks and their relevant criteria for allocation are outlined in **Table 7.1**.

Table 7.1: Track type and criteria for allocation

Track type	CPR	Criteria for allocation

Small claims track
 	
Hearings in this track are substantially less formal, and parties can represent themselves if they wish. Cases are heard by deputy or full-time district judges and the strict rules of evidence do not apply.
	CPR 27	The small claims track is the normal track for:
		• any claim that has a value of not more than £10,000;
		• any claim for personal injuries where:
		   – the value of the claim is not more than £10,000;
		   – the value of any claim for damages for personal injuries is not more than £1,000;
		• any claim that includes a claim by a tenant of residential premises against a landlord where:
		   – the tenant is seeking an order requiring the landlord to carry out repairs or other work to the premises (whether or not the tenant is also seeking some other remedy);
		   – the cost of the repairs or other work to the premises is estimated to be not more than £1,000;
		   – the value of any other claim for damages is not more than £1,000.

Fast track
 	
Cases allocated to this track must follow a strict timetable. Allocation takes place based on the information in the directions questionnaires filed by both parties.
	CPR 28	The fast track is the normal track for any claim:
		• for which the small claims track is not the normal track;
		• which has a value:
		   – for proceedings issued on or after 6 April 2009, of not more than £25,000;
		   – for proceedings issued before 6 April 2009, of not more than £15,000.
		The fast track is the normal track for the claims referred to above only if the court considers that:
		• the trial is likely to last for no longer than one day;
		• oral expert evidence at trial will be limited to:
		   – one expert per party in relation to any expert field;
		   – expert evidence in two expert fields.

Table 7.1: (continued)

Track type	CPR	Criteria for allocation
Multi-track Due to the typical value and complexity of multi-track cases, the court uses case management conferences to identify issues as early as possible and to explore (and in some cases, try) specific issues before the final trial. The stages of litigation are much more actively controlled and managed by the trial judge, who will sometimes be allocated to the claim throughout its life to maintain consistency.	CPR 29	The multi-track is the normal track for any claim for which the small claims track or the fast track are not the normal tracks.

Disagreement with track allocations

You could be asked a question on whether the track can be changed once a claim has been allocated to it. The answer is yes: where there has been a change in circumstances since an order was made allocating the claim to a particular track, the court may reallocate the claim to a different track. This can be done if one or both parties make an application, or by the court independently.

CASE MANAGEMENT DIRECTIONS FOR CASES PROCEEDING ON THE FAST OR MULTI-TRACKS

This section covers directions in the fast or multi-tracks, as the SQE1 Assessment Specification does not require you to know about the small claims track.

Directions for cases proceeding on the fast or multi-tracks   111

The fast track

In fast track cases, parties will typically base their proposed directions on the suggested timetable contained in Practice Direction 28, which states as follows:

- Disclosure – to take place within 4 weeks of the parties filing the directions questionnaire.
- Inspection – to take place within 6 weeks of the parties filing the directions questionnaire.
- Exchange of witness statements – to take place within 10 weeks of the parties filing the directions questionnaire.
- Exchange of experts' reports – to take place within 14 weeks of the parties filing the directions questionnaire.
- Filing of pre-trial checklist – to take place within 22 weeks of the parties filing the directions questionnaire.
- Trial – to take place within 30 weeks of the parties filing the directions questionnaire.

The judge will stick as rigidly as possible to the suggested fast track timetable. However, remember that the directions and timetable are only suggestions, and the court can depart from them in certain circumstances. One of those circumstances is where one party is unrepresented. In that instance, the court is required to have regard for the fact that at least one party is unrepresented and act accordingly in line with the overriding objective. This can include amending standard directions as appropriate. **Practice example 7.3** illustrates how this could apply in practice.

Practice example 7.3

A customer of a bathroom supply company is engaged in a dispute with the company following the supply and installation of a new bathroom suite. The customer is arguing that the bathroom is not fit for purpose and has issued proceedings for a partial refund in the sum of £12,500. The matter has been provisionally allocated to the fast track. The customer is unrepresented but the bathroom company have instructed solicitors. Directions have not been agreed as the bathroom company's solicitors are arguing that standard fast track directions, without amendment, should be issued by the court. What is the court's likely approach?

The court is likely to account for the unrepresented status of the claimant, and order that the defendant prepare the case summary and file and serve the trial bundle (see Chapter 11).

The multi-track

Once a claim has been allocated to the multi-track, the court will fix either a **case management conference (CMC)** or a pre-trial review (see **Chapter 11**), or both. It is to be attended by a legal representative, but in some cases the court can demand that the client attends.

> **Key term: case management conference (CMC)**
>
> This is a meeting between the judge and the parties to highlight the significant issues in the case, narrow those issues down, and discuss and decide upon directions and a timetable for the case to follow.

The purpose of CMCs is to allow the court to:
- review the steps that the parties have taken in the preparation of the case, and in particular their compliance with any directions which the court may have given;
- decide and give directions about the steps that are to be taken to secure the progress of the claim in accordance with the overriding objective;
- ensure as far as it can that all agreements which can be reached between the parties about the matters in issue and the conduct of the claim are made and recorded.

Parties must submit either agreed directions or their own proposals to the court at least seven days before the CMC. At the CMC, the court will then typically consider:
- whether the claimant has made clear the claim they are bringing, in particular the amount they are claiming, so that the other party can understand the case they have to meet;
- whether any amendments are required to the claim, a statement of case or any other document;
- what disclosure of documents, if any, is necessary;
- what expert evidence is reasonably required, and how and when that evidence should be obtained and disclosed;
- what factual evidence should be disclosed;
- what arrangements should be made about the giving of clarification or further information and the putting of questions to experts;
- whether it will be just and will save costs to order a split trial (where liability and quantum, or amount of damages, are decided separately) or the trial of one or more preliminary issues.

Following the CMC, the court will then issue a set of directions tailored to that specific matter. Those directions will concern the same matters as those in the fast track (disclosure, inspection, exchange of witness statements, etc.). However, the court will also deal with costs budgets (for more detail, see **Chapter 10**) and build a realistic individualised timetable for compliance with the directions, depending on the case's needs.

NON-COMPLIANCE WITH ORDERS, SANCTIONS AND RELIEF

At times a party will fail to comply with a case management direction (eg not exchanging their witness statements by the deadline set in the directions). The first thing to do is try to agree an extension with the representative of the other side, up to 28 days in accordance with CPR 3.8. This can only be done if it does not put any hearing dates at risk. If the other party will not agree, or the extension is needed beyond 28 days, an application must be made to the court under CPR 3.8 and CPR 3.9. The rule is that the sanction (see **Chapter 1, Table 1.5**) will automatically take effect unless the defaulting party obtains relief. The court will also consider making a wasted costs order against a legal representative if they are at fault for the default (see **Chapter 6, Table 6.2**).

The types of sanctions, in order of severity, are outlined in **Table 7.2**.

Table 7.2: Sanctions for failing to comply with directions

Unless order	The most common type of order for non-compliance, this allows the party in default to rectify the breach. Common orders are worded, for example, *'Unless the claimant files their updated particulars by 22 September 2022, the claimant shall be debarred from relying upon those particulars at trial.'*
Interest	Either the defaulting party cannot recover interest on damages at trial or the innocent party can recover enhanced damages.
Payment in court	The defaulting party must pay a sum of money, to be held by court funds until conclusion of the case (CPR 3.1(5)).
Costs	The defaulting party must pay the innocent party's costs relating to the application.
Disallowing evidence	The defaulting party is prevented from citing and relying on evidence (either documentary or witness) that they failed to file or serve by a deadline. This can potentially be catastrophic for the claim, especially if it is heavily reliant upon such evidence being admitted.
Striking out	The defaulting party's claim is struck out, either in whole or in part. This is only used by the court in the most serious of cases, as it essentially hands victory to the opponent on a procedural technicality.

If a party to proceedings fails to comply with an order imposing a sanction, rule or Practice Direction, then it is upon them to apply to the court for **relief** from that sanction under CPR 3.8 and CPR 3.9.

Key term: relief

This applies where the court removes a sanction from a party who has breached a rule, court order or direction.

The court will weigh the overriding objective against all the circumstances of the case and apply the following guidelines:
(1) Identify the default and assess its 'seriousness or significance'; relief will usually be granted for breaches that are neither serious nor significant (and do not impact on any court hearing dates or disrupt the conduct of the litigation).
(2) Consider why the default occurred (ie whether there is a good reason for it).
(3) Consider 'all the circumstances of the case, so as to enable the court to deal justly with the application'. This includes balancing the need for litigation to be conducted efficiently and at proportionate cost with enforcing compliance with rules, practice directions and court orders, as well as the promptness of the application and other past or current breaches committed by the defaulting party.

There are therefore no guarantees that the court will allow a defaulting party to redeem themselves.

■ KEY POINT CHECKLIST

This chapter has covered the following key knowledge points. You can use these to structure your revision, ensuring you recall the key details for each point, as covered in this chapter.
- Case management is the process by which the court controls the timetable and procedural requirements of a specific defended claim.
- Both the court and the parties to litigation must act in compliance with the overriding objective at all times to deal with cases justly and at proportionate cost.
- The court will expect parties to have agreed an appropriate track to allocate the claim to and a set of proposed directions, which will in turn form the basis of the directions order issued by the court.
- Directions are a list of instructions given by the court to the parties to litigation that set out the steps which each party needs to take to prepare for trial and deadlines by which each of those steps needs to be completed.
- Fast track directions are generally standard in nature, whereas multi-track directions are bespoke to the needs of the claim itself.
- If a party misses a deadline imposed by the case management directions, they should try to seek an agreed extension with the other side in the first instance. This can be a maximum of 28 days under CPR 3.8. If agreement cannot be reached, the defaulting party must make an application for

relief from sanctions to the court under CPR 3.9 to avoid penalties being imposed.

■ KEY TERMS AND CONCEPTS

- case management (**page 104**)
- track (**page 104**)
- directions (**page 105**)
- overriding objective (**page 105**)
- disclosure (**page 107**)
- inspection (**page 107**)
- case management conference (CMC) (**page 112**)
- relief (**page 114**)

■ SQE1-STYLE QUESTIONS

QUESTION 1

A claimant has commenced proceedings against a defendant for the sum of £9,000. The amount relates to the claimant supplying a range of bedroom furniture to the defendant, for which the defendant has failed to make any payment. The defendant argues that the claimant's sales representative verbally agreed to deliver and build the bedroom furniture for him. The claimant claims that the contract was for delivery only. The written contract is silent on this point. The claimant has instructed their solicitors to take witness statement evidence from 16 employees who claim that they witnessed the verbal exchange between the sales representative and the defendant, and that they are to insist that those employees be allowed to give oral evidence at trial.

Are the company's instructions to their solicitors likely to be consistent with the overriding objective in the Civil Procedure Rules 1998 (CPR)?

A. No, because the overriding objective requires parties to assist the court in dealing with cases proportionately.

B. Yes, because the overriding objective requires parties to assist the court in dealing with cases proportionately.

C. No, because the overriding objective requires parties to assist the court in dealing with cases justly.

D. Yes, because the overriding objective requires parties to assist the court in dealing with cases justly.

E. Yes, because the overriding objective only applies to the court, not the parties to litigation.

QUESTION 2

A claimant commences proceedings against a defendant for the sum of £27,000. The amount relates to non-payment of an invoice for the building of an orangery at the back of the defendant's customer's house. The defendant argues that the work carried out is defective, as the floor is not level and the window on the north side leaks in heavy rain. The claimant maintains that the building is sound and that full payment is due. The parties have jointly agreed to instruct one single joint expert to provide a written report addressing the issues raised. The issue of allocation falls to the court to consider.

Which of the following best represents the position that the court will likely adopt when allocating the claim to an appropriate track?

A. The court is likely to allocate the claim to the fast track on the basis of its complexity.

B. The court is likely to allocate the claim to the multi-track on the basis of its value.

C. The court is likely to allocate the claim to the multi-track on the basis of its value and complexity.

D. The court is likely to allocate the claim to the fast track on the basis that the trial is unlikely to last more than one day and there is only one expert.

E. The court is likely to allocate the claim to the multi-track because even though the trial is unlikely to last more than one day, its value is too high to be considered in the fast track.

QUESTION 3

A claim has been allocated to the multi-track and the court has fixed a date for a case management conference (CMC). Solicitors on behalf of both the claimant and defendant have agreed directions on most issues, but are unable to agree a suitable direction on the scope and timing of disclosure of documents.

Which of the following statements best reflects the likely approach of the court during the CMC?

A. The court will adjourn the CMC and expect the parties to agree the scope and suitable dates for disclosure of documents by a fixed date, whereupon they will be required to return to the court for approval.

B. The court will adjourn the CMC and expect the parties to agree the scope and suitable dates for disclosure of documents by a fixed date, whereupon they will be required to return to the court for approval. The court will also penalise the parties for failing to agree a suitable direction between themselves.

C. The court will make an order relating to the directions agreed upon between the claimant's and defendant's solicitors, but will schedule a further CMC to discuss the appropriate directions for disclosure.

D. The court will consider the arguments by the parties following their submission of their own proposals for directions to the court. The court will then make an order relating to disclosure of documents, as well as the remaining directions, at the CMC. If this needs to be amended, then it will be considered further on application by one of the parties.

E. The court will consider the arguments by the parties following their submission of their own proposals for directions to the court. The court will then make an order relating to disclosure of documents, as well as the remaining directions, at the CMC. There will be no scope to amend this order.

QUESTION 4

A school makes a claim against a contractor for non-completion of roofing works. Both sides are represented. The claim is valued at £8,500. The court allocates the claim to the small claims track. The defendant indicates that they intend to defend the whole claim. In order to prove the claim, the claimant school seeks to rely on the oral evidence of four witnesses, all of whom witnessed the material facts but none of whom came forward when the claim was originally issued. The claimant's solicitors apply to the court to reallocate the claim. The defendant objects to the application.

Which of the following best reflects the court's likely approach to the claimant's application?

A. The court would be likely to allow the application and reallocate the claim to the fast track. The court is required to consider all of the relevant circumstances when allocating the claim, not just the financial value. Four witnesses would most likely mean that a full-day hearing would be required.

B. The court would be likely to allow the application and reallocate the claim to the fast track. The court is required to consider the likely complexity of the matter, and four witnesses would mean that the issue would become evidentially too complex to be heard in the small claims track.

C. The court would be likely to refuse the application and the claim would remain in the small claims track. Value is the primary consideration of the court, and this has not changed.

D. The court would be likely to refuse the application and the claim would remain in the small claims track. The four witnesses should have been disclosed when the claim was originally allocated.

E. The court would be likely to refuse the application and the claim would remain in the small claims track. Even with four witnesses, it is unlikely that the trial will last more than half a day.

QUESTION 5

A solicitor is acting for a client in a claim. As part of the directions, the court has ordered that witness statements need to be exchanged no later than 4.00 p.m. on 20 October. The solicitor drafts all of the witness statements and has them signed by the witnesses by 15 October, but forgets to deliver the copies by the deadline. The defendant's witness statements are delivered by hand to the solicitor's reception at 3.58 p.m. on 20 October, and the receptionist informs the solicitor at 4.05 p.m. In response, the solicitor hand-delivers the claimant's witness statement to the defendant at 4.45 p.m. He immediately telephones the defendant's representative to propose an extension under the Civil Procedure Rules 1998 (CPR), but this is rejected. The claimant's solicitor therefore issues an application to the court for relief from sanctions under the CPR on 21 October.

Which of the following statements best represents the position of the court in response to the application?

A. The court is likely to reject the claimant's application and refuse relief. The court's role is to enforce compliance with procedural rules and directions.

B. The court is likely to grant relief from sanctions on the basis that the breach is neither serious nor significant, but will order the claimant to pay both the claimant's and defendant's costs.

C. The court is likely to grant relief from sanctions on the basis that the breach is neither serious nor significant, but will make a wasted costs order against the claimant's solicitor for failure to comply with the court-ordered direction.

D. The court is likely to grant relief from sanctions on the basis that there was good reason for the breach and penalise the defendant's solicitor for unreasonably refusing to agree an extension of time.

E. The court is likely to grant relief from sanctions on the basis that there was good reason for the breach, but will insist that both parties pay their own costs in relation to the application.

■ ANSWERS TO QUESTIONS

Answers to 'What do you know already?' questions at the start of the chapter

1) CPR 1.1 contains the overriding objective of civil litigation.
2) False. While the judge does make the final decision, parties or their representatives are expected to agree or propose as much of the timetable as they reasonably are able to.

Answers to questions 119

3) The three tracks are small claims track (CPR 27), fast track (CPR 28) and multi-track (CPR 29).
4) A case management conference is a meeting between the judge and the parties to highlight the significant issues in the case, narrow those issues down, and discuss and decide upon directions and a timetable for the case to follow.
5) False. Making an application to the court under CPR 3.9 may lead to the court ordering relief from sanctions being imposed.

Answers to end-of-chapter SQE1-style questions

Question 1:
The correct answer was A. It would be disproportionate to allow 16 witnesses to give oral evidence in relation to a claim worth £9,000 (making option B incorrect). The number of witnesses does not affect whether the court can deal with matters justly (making options C and D incorrect), and the duty to further the overriding objective is on the court and the parties (making option E incorrect).

Question 2:
The correct answer was D. While value is a consideration, the court is likely to regard the fast track as the normal track as the issues are not complex, the parties have agreed the appointment of one expert who is unlikely to give oral evidence, and the trial is not likely to last longer than one day (making option A incorrect). Even though the value is slightly above the bracket that would ordinarily qualify a claim for the multi-track, this is outweighed by the likely length of the trial and its complexity (making options B, C and E incorrect).

Question 3:
The correct answer was D. Under the CPR, parties are required to submit their own proposals to the court no later than seven days before the CMC in the event that agreement on an appropriate set of directions cannot be reached. The court will then consider the competing arguments between the parties and take a decision on the most appropriate way forward. The court would not adjourn the CMC until a later date as this would cause unnecessary delay (meaning that options A and B are incorrect), nor would they decide on the agreed directions and schedule a further CMC for the ones that were not agreed, for the same reason (meaning that option C is incorrect). In the event that the order needed to be amended in some way, either party would be able to make an application to the court to have their position considered, making option E incorrect.

Question 4:
The correct answer was A. The claimant is perfectly entitled to make an application to reallocate the claim as new evidence has come to light (making option D incorrect). While value is the primary consideration

of the court on allocation, it does not take precedence over the fact that four witnesses will likely mean the trial will take a full day (making options C and E incorrect). Finally, option B is incorrect as it is unlikely that the evidential complexity will be affected by the number of witnesses; it is the time that the trial will take which is the issue.

Question 5:
The correct answer was C. Even though there is no good reason for the breach (making options D and E incorrect), a 45-minute delay is likely to be found to be trivial, and the breach did not impact on any future court hearings. The court therefore has discretion to move away from their duty to enforce rules under the overriding objective (making option A incorrect). However, given that the breach was the fault of the legal representative, it is likely that a wasted costs order would be made against the solicitor for breaching the deadline (making option B incorrect).

■ KEY CASES, RULES, STATUTES AND INSTRUMENTS

The SQE1 Assessment Specification does not require you to know any case names or statutory materials for the topic of case management.

Evidence

■ MAKE SURE YOU KNOW

This chapter will cover the rules surrounding civil evidence. It will cover the relevance of civil evidence and how witness and expert evidence are dealt with. You are required to be able to apply these principles and rules appropriately and effectively to realistic client-based and ethical problems and situations for your SQE1 assessment.

■ SQE ASSESSMENT ADVICE

As you work through this chapter, remember to pay particular attention in your revision to:
- how the relevance of a piece of evidence determines whether or not it is admissible;
- the general rules around hearsay and admissibility of evidence;
- how expert and opinion evidence are dealt with in civil proceedings;
- the general duties of experts in civil cases, including single joint experts and how discussions should take place between independently instructed experts;
- how witness evidence is produced and dealt with in civil proceedings.

■ WHAT DO YOU KNOW ALREADY?

Have a go at these questions before reading this chapter. If you find some difficult or cannot remember the answers, make a note to look more closely at that subtopic during your revision.

1) What is the standard of proof in civil proceedings and who bears the burden of proof?
   [Introduction to civil evidence, page 122]
2) True or false? Evidence in civil proceedings is admissible, provided that it is relevant to the facts of the case pleaded.
   [Relevance of evidence, page 123]
3) What is hearsay evidence and is it admissible?
   [Hearsay evidence, page 125]

4) True or false? If the court orders that expert evidence is needed in relation to a claim, each party must instruct their own expert to make it fair.
[**Expert evidence, page 129**]
5) What is a single joint expert?
[**Role and duties of experts, page 129**]

INTRODUCTION TO CIVIL EVIDENCE

In previous chapters, we have concentrated on the rules concerning the drafting, preparation, filing and service of statements of case. Once the parties have filed and served their statements of case, they must then move on to *proving* the legal and factual positions that they have put before the court. This is done by relying on evidence.

Evidence is used in civil proceedings to satisfy the civil **burden of proof** and **standard of proof**.

Key term: burden of proof
This refers to the obligation that the party making an allegation (generally the claimant) provides sufficient evidence to the court to prove the relevant legal criteria and factual allegations relating to their cause of action.

Key term: standard of proof
This is the degree to which a party must prove its case to succeed. In civil cases, the standard of proof is on the balance of probabilities. This means that the party making the allegation (again, usually the claimant) must persuade the court that their version of events is more likely than those put forward by the defendant.

Exam warning
Make sure you remember that the burden of proof is on the party *making* the allegation. While this is mainly the claimant, it could also be on the defendant if they allege contributory negligence or if they have issued a counterclaim under Part 20 (see **Chapter 5**).

The rules relating to evidence in civil proceedings are regulated by both the Civil Procedure Rules 1998 (CPR; see **Chapter 1**) and the Civil Evidence Acts 1972 and 1995. The SQE1 Assessment Specification requires that you are familiar with the key concepts of civil evidence, which are as follows:
- relevance of evidence;
- witness evidence;
- expert evidence.

Each of these will be considered in turn.

RELEVANCE OF EVIDENCE

The general principle in civil evidence is that if a piece of evidence is relevant to the proceedings, it is **admissible**. However, there are certain exceptions to this rule, which principally relate to **opinion evidence** and **hearsay evidence**.

> **Key term: admissible**
> Admissible evidence is evidence that a party is allowed to present to the court and which the court is allowed to consider. Its use cannot be objected to on the basis that it is either irrelevant or immaterial, or that it violates the rules relating to an exception, such as hearsay.

> **Key term: opinion evidence**
> This is evidence of the opinion of a particular witness, as opposed to a direct account of the facts.

> **Key term: hearsay evidence**
> This is a specific type of evidence where the person giving evidence tells the court about a statement which was originally made by somebody else.

The SQE1 Assessment Specification requires you to be aware of opinion evidence and hearsay evidence in the context of the admissibility of witness evidence in civil proceedings (see **Chapter 1**), as well as the purpose and content of witness statements.

WITNESS EVIDENCE

This section is separated into two distinct parts. First, we will consider the rules relating to the admissibility of witness evidence, including how opinion and hearsay evidence are dealt with. Second, we will look at how witness statements are drafted.

Admissibility of witness evidence

Provided that evidence is relevant to the case, it will be admissible unless it triggers one of the exceptions. The exceptions identified on the SQE1 Assessment Specification are opinion evidence and hearsay evidence.

Opinion evidence

Witnesses can only give evidence to the court that is based on the facts of the case and not on their own personal viewpoint. Most opinion evidence will therefore be inadmissible. However, there are two circumstances in which opinion evidence will be heard by the court, governed by section 3 Civil Evidence Act 1972. These are laid out in **Table 8.1**.

Table 8.1: Exceptions on admissibility of opinion evidence

Exception	Explanation
Evidence based on facts that are personally *perceived* by the witness	These are statements that are technically opinions, but only to the point that they give the witness's perception of a fact. For example, in a road traffic collision case, the witness may provide the court with their perception that, based on the events they witnessed first-hand, the defendant was travelling 'about 50 mph'. This is an opinion, but it is one that directly relates to one of the material facts of the case, so would be admissible under this exception. It is not the same as the witness saying that the defendant was 'travelling too fast for the conditions', which would be inadmissible.
Expert opinion evidence	Opinions that are given by an expert on any relevant matter on which the expert is qualified to give an opinion (so it must be within their qualified area of expertise) will be admissible. For example, a medical expert who specialises in orthopaedics will be entitled to give their opinion on the length of time that a bone fracture will take to heal.

Exam warning

If you are asked about whether opinion evidence based on a witness's perceived facts is admissible, look carefully at the wording. Does it give a perception on a fact (eg 'it was cold outside') or does it draw a conclusion based on the witness's values (eg 'it was too cold to even think about driving that day')? If the former, it is likely to be admissible. If the latter, it will be inadmissible.

Practice example 8.1 illustrates how this could apply in practice.

Practice example 8.1

During the course of proceedings against Lewis, James is asked to provide a witness statement recounting his version of events. When describing Lewis's state of intoxication on the night of the incident, James states that he was 'too drunk to ride his bike'. Is this admissible evidence?

No. This will be regarded as inadmissible as James is giving an opinion as opposed to a perception based on the facts. If James had said that Lewis had consumed six pints of beer, was slurring his speech and appeared drunk, this would be admissible as he is offering his perception of Lewis's behaviour based on the facts that he witnessed: that Lewis had consumed six pints of beer and was slurring. 'Too drunk to ride a bike' is imposing James's opinion on the conclusion that the court needs to reach, which means the opinion is inadmissible.

Hearsay evidence

Hearsay evidence is defined as being a statement made outside of court that is repeated in court by somebody who did not originally make the statement to prove the truth of a particular fact or matter stated. For understandable reasons, the court treats hearsay evidence with a huge degree of caution as it is evidence repeated to the court by somebody who does not personally know the fact to be true. The person giving evidence only knows that another person said the fact was true. To answer a question in SQE1 about whether hearsay evidence is admissible or inadmissible, you must ask yourself four questions:

- Does the evidence in question fall under the definition of hearsay?
- Is the hearsay evidence admissible according to the test?
- Have the procedural requirements to use hearsay evidence been complied with?
- What weight is the court likely to attach to the hearsay evidence?

The considerations to be taken into account for each question are set out in **Table 8.2**.

Table 8.2: Matters to consider to establish whether hearsay evidence is admissible

Consideration	Explanation
Does the evidence in question fall under the definition of hearsay?	The statement itself (not the person making it) must be related to a relevant fact or be an admissible opinion. Take the following statement: *'Joshua said at the scene that the car was travelling at approximately 50 mph.'* Then apply the definition as follows: • The statement is a statement made outside of court (at the scene); • repeated by somebody in court (the witness); • to prove the truth of the matter stated (that the car was travelling at 50 mph). The statement satisfies all three elements and is therefore hearsay.
Is the hearsay evidence admissible according to the test?	The evidence will be admissible under section 1 Civil Evidence Act 1995 where it: • relates to a relevant fact; • is not repetition of an opinion that is *not* a perception of the facts.

Table 8.2: (continued)

Consideration	Explanation
Have the procedural requirements to use hearsay evidence been complied with?	If a party wishes to rely on hearsay evidence, they must give notice to the other parties to the claim that they wish to rely on evidence of a hearsay nature. The notice requirements are dependent on whether or not the party is intending to call the witness to court to give oral evidence. If the party is intending to call the witness to court to give oral evidence: • the witness statement containing the hearsay evidence must be served on the other party. If the party is not intending to call the witness to court to give oral evidence: • the whole of that witness's statement becomes hearsay; • the party wishing to rely on the evidence must serve a separate formal notice with the witness statement identifying the hearsay evidence, confirming that they wish to rely on it at trial and giving reasons why the witness will not be called; • the party who has been served with the notice can then ask the court to order that the witness be called to court to be cross-examined on their evidence (see **Chapter 11**) or serve a **notice to attack credibility** within 14 days of being served with the hearsay notice. If notice is not served, then this will not make the evidence inadmissible, but it may affect the weighting that the court attaches to it at the final trial.
What weight is the court likely to attach to the hearsay evidence?	The court will take the following into consideration when deciding what weight to attach to the evidence: • the reason that the witness has not been able to attend to give oral evidence (unless it is a very good one, the court is unlikely to attach any weight to a statement given by somebody who is not prepared to come to court to be questioned on it); • whether the original statement was made at the same time as the relevant fact that it is being used to support; • whether the evidence involves **multiple hearsay**; • whether any person involved had any motive to conceal or misrepresent matters; • whether the original statement was an edited account, or was made in collaboration with somebody else or for a particular purpose;

Table 8.2: (continued)

	• whether the party seeking to rely on the statement has given proper notice to their opponent of its hearsay nature. Note that these are only suggested guidelines, but they do give a good idea of the key factors that the court will take into account when deciding the extent to which they can rely on the hearsay evidence.

Key term: notice to attack credibility

A document which notifies a party that the opponent wishes to challenge their witness testimony on the basis that the witness is unreliable, untrustworthy or biased.

Key term: multiple hearsay

This is where the information that is the subject of the evidence has been passed through multiple people. For example, Brian (giving evidence) states that Johnny told him that Billy said the car was travelling at approximately 50 mph.

Practice example 8.2 demonstrates how hearsay could apply in practice.

Practice example 8.2

Taking the same facts as **Practice example 8.1**, Lauren is also brought in as a witness to show Lewis's level of intoxication. She did not witness it directly but arrived at the pub five minutes after Lewis left. Her witness evidence is that she spoke to the barman, Ian, who told her that Lewis had consumed six pints of beer, was slurring his words and appeared drunk. Ian is unable to give evidence directly as he has since moved abroad. Lauren is happy to attend court to give oral evidence. Is Lauren's evidence admissible, and if so what does the legal representative need to do?

Lauren's evidence is admissible as hearsay. The statement itself is a repetition of a direct witness's perception of Lewis's level of intoxication at the time and is therefore admissible hearsay evidence. As Lauren intends on appearing in court to give oral evidence, the legal representative needs to serve a copy of Lauren's statement on the opposition, and they will then have the opportunity to cross-examine her.

Witness statements

For SQE1, you need to know what to consider when drafting a witness statement. **Table 8.3** sets out what a statement should include.

Table 8.3: Contents of a witness statement

Section of statement	Contents of section
Top of the first page	This section should include: • the party on whose behalf it is made; • the initials and surname of the witness; • the number of the statement in relation to that witness; • the identifying initials and number of each document referred to; • the date the statement was made; • the date of any translation.
Introduction to the main body of the witness statement	The witness statement must be drafted in the first person ('I did', 'I went', etc.) and be drafted in the witness's own words or style of language. It should also state: • the full name of the witness; • their place of residence or – if they are making the statement in their professional, business or other occupational capacity – the address at which they work, the position they hold, and the name of their firm or employer; • their occupation or, if they have none, their description; • that they are either a party to the proceedings or an employee of a party to the proceedings, if that is the case; • the process by which the witness statement has been prepared (eg face-to-face, over the telephone and/or through an interpreter).
Main body of the witness statement	The witness statement must indicate: • the facts and dates of the witness's story, told in chronological order with any material facts included, and in the witness's own words; • which of the statements in it are made from the witness's own knowledge and which are matters of information or belief; • the source for any matters of information or belief. Where a witness refers to an exhibit or exhibits, they should state, '*I refer to the (description of exhibit) marked "…".*' The statement should not include any irrelevant or inadmissible evidence (eg opinion evidence).
Final section/ statement of truth	To verify a witness statement, it should contain a statement of truth as follows: '*I believe that the facts stated in this witness statement are true. I understand that proceedings for contempt of court may be brought against anyone who makes, or causes to be made, a false statement in a document verified by a statement of truth without an honest belief in its truth.*'

Generally speaking, if a witness provides a witness statement, they will also attend trial. At trial, the witness will take the **oath** or affirm and confirm that the contents of their witness statement are true. This will be taken as their evidence-in-chief, which means that the written words will apply as if the witness had said them to the court on the day. The opposition will then be given the opportunity to cross-examine the witness.

> **Key term: oath**
> This is the pledge which a witness will make that the evidence they shall give shall be the whole truth and nothing but the truth.

EXPERT EVIDENCE

Parties are entitled to use expert evidence to prove an element of their case. Experts are very useful to the court as they bring specialist knowledge and judgment on areas that the court cannot be expected to assess, such as the quality of building work, the value of a particular piece of land, or the extent and prognosis of the injuries suffered by the victim of a road traffic accident. Opinion evidence from an expert is admissible, provided that it is on a matter relevant to their expertise.

It is important that you remember that a party cannot rely on expert evidence without the prior permission of the court. Permission is usually given when the court gives initial directions, but it can be applied for independently by the party seeking to rely on expert evidence at any point in proceedings.

For SQE1, you need to be aware of the role and duties of experts, as well as what they need to do in the context of the proceedings overall.

Role and duties of experts

The CPR make it clear that any expert evidence is to be restricted to what is reasonably required to resolve the proceedings. This prevents a party relying on multiple experts to give their opinion on matters that are not relevant to the claim in hand.

> **Exam warning**
> Although an expert is instructed by a party directly, their overriding duty is to assist the court. This means that an expert should not be tempted to amend their report to be more favourable to a party's case if they are asked to do so.

Where practical and in the interests of the overriding objective, parties should attempt to agree the appointment of a **single joint expert**. If the other party does not agree to the appointment of the proposed expert, the

court can still direct parties to obtain the evidence of a single joint expert, provided that they have taken into account the following:
- the amount in dispute;
- the importance to the parties;
- the complexity of the issues.

Cases allocated to the fast track are therefore more likely to be suitable for the instruction of a single joint expert. Cases allocated to the multi-track are more likely to be better suited to the instruction of multiple experts.

> **Key term: single joint expert**
> This is an expert who is instructed to prepare a report for the court on behalf of two or more of the parties (including the claimant) to the proceedings.

What is required of experts?
An expert who has been given permission to produce evidence must produce an expert report. The report should:
- give details of the expert's qualifications;
- give details of any literature or other material that has been relied on in making the report;
- contain a statement setting out the substance of all facts and instructions that have been received from the parties instructing the expert;
- make clear which of the facts stated in the report are within the expert's own knowledge;
- say who carried out any examination, measurement, test or experiment that the expert has used for the report, give the qualifications of that person, and say whether or not the test or experiment has been carried out under the expert's supervision;
- where there is a range of opinions on the matters dealt with in the report, summarise the range of opinions and give reasons for the expert's own opinion;
- contain a summary of the conclusions reached;
- state the qualification if the expert is not able to give an opinion without qualification;
- contain a statement that the expert understands their duty to the court, has complied with that duty, and is aware of the requirements of the CPR;
- be verified by a statement of truth.

Where an expert is a single joint expert, a copy of the report is produced for all parties. The parties can then consider it and raise questions or queries on the contents of the report with the expert if they need to do so. Once the report is finalised, it will be filed with the court by the deadline laid out in the directions.

Instances can arise where the report of a single joint expert is unfavourable to one of the parties who is instructing them. This can lead to a disagreement. In this case, the party who is unhappy with the report of the single joint expert has the following options:
- Instruct another expert; however, they would have to seek permission of the court to rely on it in proceedings.
- Cross-examine the single joint expert at trial to expose what the party believes are the weaknesses and inconsistencies in the report.
- Obtain a second report and send this to the single joint expert prior to trial. This may result in the single joint expert re-evaluating their initial conclusions; however, be aware that the second report would not be able to be produced for the court.

Where there are multiple experts (commonly in multi-track trials), things can get more complicated. The court will direct the parties to exchange their experts' reports as part of the directions issued. The parties must do this by the date set in the directions order. Once the reports have been exchanged, it may become apparent that there are substantial areas of overlap (or not), or the parties may have questions for the opposing expert. SQE1 requires you to be aware of the rules relating to those two eventualities. **Table 8.4** sets out what can happen following the exchange of experts' reports.

Table 8.4: What happens after experts' reports have been exchanged?

Step	What is involved?
Discussion between experts	Experts are encouraged to meet to discuss the contents of their reports with their opposition experts. The court has the power to order this if they feel it is appropriate. The purpose of the experts meeting is to: • identify the issues that the experts agree on so that they are not unnecessarily contested at trial; • identify the issues that they disagree on so that the court can see the main areas of dispute to focus attention on at trial.
Questions to experts	Parties are also allowed to ask their opposition expert questions on the contents of the report. This must be done within 28 days of the report being served on them. The expert will then respond; however, there is no defined timescale set out in the CPR for this.

Practice example 8.3 illustrates how this may apply in practice.

> **Practice example 8.3**
>
> Tech-no Limited issue proceedings against DVD Maker Limited on the basis that they have supplied 400 faulty DVD players to them. The DVD players were sold to customers of Tech-no Limited and the same fault has recurred. DVD Maker Limited defend proceedings on the basis that the fault was caused by repeated heavy impacts to the goods, which must have happened when they were in the possession of Tech-no Limited. The court orders that a single joint expert be appointed to assess the faulty machines and give their technical opinion on what caused the fault and when it occurred. The single joint expert concludes that the fault was caused by a heavy impact on the goods, which must have occurred on the claimant's premises. The claimant disagrees with this assessment on the basis that the expert has only examined four machines, which is not an appropriately large sample. What can the claimant do?
>
> The claimant has three options. First, they could instruct another expert; however, they would have to seek the permission of the court to rely on it in proceedings, which would increase their overall costs. Alternatively, they could ask their legal representative to cross-examine the single joint expert at trial to expose what the party believes are the weaknesses and inconsistencies in the report. Finally, they could obtain a second report and send this to the single joint expert prior to trial in the hope that they will alter their initial report. However, this is by no means guaranteed, and they would not be allowed to rely on this second report in court without permission.

■ KEY POINT CHECKLIST

This chapter has covered the following key knowledge points. You can use these to structure your revision, ensuring you recall the key details for each point, as covered in this chapter.
- If a piece of evidence is relevant to the proceedings, it is admissible.
- The burden of proof of an action lies on the party who makes the allegations.
- The standard of proof is on the balance of probabilities.
- There are certain exceptions to this rule that principally relate to opinion evidence and hearsay evidence.
- Opinion evidence is generally inadmissible unless it is evidence based on facts that are personally *perceived* by the witness or expert evidence.
- Hearsay evidence is admissible where it relates to a relevant fact and it is not repetition of an opinion that is *not* a perception of the facts.
- A party cannot rely on expert evidence without the prior permission of the court.

■ KEY TERMS AND CONCEPTS

- burden of proof (**page 123**)
- standard of proof (**page 123**)
- admissible (**page 124**)
- opinion evidence (**page 124**)
- hearsay evidence (**page 124**)
- notice to attack credibility (**page 127**)
- multiple hearsay (**page 127**)
- oath (**page 129**)
- single joint expert (**page 130**)

■ SQE1-STYLE QUESTIONS

QUESTION 1

A claimant is bringing a claim against a defendant for breach of contract. The claimant alleges that the parties verbally agreed to a term of the contract when they met to finalise matters. The defendant denies that any agreement on any such term was reached. There were no witnesses and the case rests on the claimant's word against the defendant's.

Which of the following best describes the burden of proof that the court will apply in deciding the issue?

A. The burden of proof lies with the claimant to prove the allegation on the balance of probabilities.

B. The burden of proof lies with the defendant to disprove the allegation on the balance of probabilities.

C. The burden of proof lies with neither party; the court will take a view on the facts as they present themselves on the balance of probabilities.

D. The burden of proof lies with the defendant to prove their defence on the balance of probabilities.

E. The burden of proof lies with the claimant to prove the allegation beyond reasonable doubt.

QUESTION 2

A witness provides a statement in relation to a road traffic accident claim. In the statement, the witness states that the vehicle being driven by the defendant was 'unroadworthy' and that the defendant had 'clearly let the car fall below the standard you would expect of a vehicle in England'.

Which of the following best describes the admissibility of this statement?

A. The statement is admissible as it is a statement based on the facts witnessed.
B. The statement is admissible as it is a perception of a relevant fact.
C. The statement is admissible. Even though it is an opinion, it relates to a material and relevant fact in issue.
D. The statement is inadmissible as it is merely an opinion.
E. The statement is inadmissible as the condition of the vehicle is not a relevant fact for the court to consider.

QUESTION 3

A claimant is required to file and serve witness statements on the defendant. The claimant consults their solicitor and instructs them to draft their witness statement using the facts given to the solicitor in the initial interview.

Which of the following best describes how the solicitor should proceed?

A. The solicitor should refuse to draft the client's statement, as any witness statement filed with the court and served on the opposing party needs to be drafted by the witness themselves to preserve its authenticity.
B. The solicitor should proceed to draft the claimant's statement, but this should be in the claimant's own words as much as possible.
C. The solicitor should proceed to draft the claimant's statement so that it uses the facts to support each of the criteria that the claimant needs to prove to be successful in their cause of action.
D. The solicitor should proceed to draft the claimant's statement by copying the notes from the initial interview and adding a statement of truth to ensure that the statement is compliant with procedural rules.
E. The solicitor should refuse to draft the client's statement unless the claimant attends a further interview in which the specifics of the case are discussed in greater depth.

QUESTION 4

A claimant issues proceedings against a defendant for damages relating to personal injury caused by the defendant's negligent driving. A witness provides a statement saying that they were told by an individual who was a witness to the road traffic accident that the driver was travelling at approximately 45 mph at the time of the collision. The witness who provided the witness statement will not be attending the trial to give oral evidence.

Which of the following best reflects the way that the court will view this witness statement?

A. The court will exclude the evidence on the basis that hearsay evidence is inadmissible.
B. The court will exclude the evidence on the basis that hearsay evidence is only admissible where the witness attends court to be cross-examined on it.
C. The court will regard the evidence as inadmissible, as the hearsay evidence must be in relation to a perception of a relevant fact to be admissible. The speed that the car was travelling at is simply an opinion.
D. The court will regard the evidence as inadmissible as the original provider of the statement has not provided a witness statement to support it.
E. The whole statement will be viewed as admissible hearsay evidence as the witness is not attending court to give oral evidence, but the statement itself does relate to a perception of a relevant fact.

QUESTION 5

A claimant company commences proceedings against a local authority for breach of contract. The claim relates to the local authority refusing to pay for an order of 100 headphones as the goods developed two faults – one with the earpieces and the other with the microphones. The damages claimed are in the region of £500. The claimant company would like to instruct two experts: one to assess the earpieces and the other to assess the microphones.

Which of the following best represents the likely position of the court?

A. The court will allow the instruction of two experts as they are needed to assist the trial judge with making a determination on the cause of action.
B. The court will allow the instruction of two experts, provided that they are instructed jointly between the claimant and defendant.
C. The court will not allow the instruction of two experts on a claim involving low value as it is incompatible with the overriding objective.
D. The court will not allow the instruction of any experts on a claim involving low value.
E. The court will allow the instruction of two experts, provided that the claimant pays for both of them.

■ ANSWERS TO QUESTIONS

Answers to 'What do you know already?' questions at the start of the chapter

1) The standard of proof is the balance of probabilities and the burden lies on the party making the allegation. This is often the claimant, unless there is a counterclaim (in which case the burden is on the defendant/counterclaimant) or if the defendant is alleging contributory negligence.
2) True. Provided that evidence is relevant to the facts of the claim pleaded and that it does not fall within an exception such as opinion evidence or inadmissible hearsay evidence.
3) Hearsay evidence is evidence that is the repetition of a perception of a relevant fact. It is admissible, provided that the statement is not a mere opinion and that it relates to the facts of the matter pleaded.
4) False. Particularly in fast track cases, the court will often order the appointment of a single joint expert who will prepare a report on the same issues on behalf of both parties. This furthers the overriding objective and ensures that costs are kept proportionate to the value and complexity of the claim.
5) A single joint expert is an expert who is instructed to prepare a report for the court on behalf of two or more of the parties (including the claimant) to the proceedings.

Answers to end-of-chapter SQE1-style questions

Question 1:
The correct answer was A. The correct standard of proof for civil claims is the balance of probabilities (this makes option E incorrect), and the burden of proof falls on the claimant to prove the allegations they are making, which makes options B, C and D incorrect.

Question 2:
The correct answer was D. The statement made is the opinion of the witness and is therefore inadmissible (making options A and B incorrect). Opinion evidence is only admissible where the statement is a perception of a relevant fact. The condition of the vehicle is a relevant fact (making option E incorrect), and option C is incorrect as the statement needs to be more than a mere opinion to be admissible.

Question 3:
The correct answer was B. The Civil Procedure Rules 1998 (CPR) make it clear that the witness statement should be in the witness's own words, but do not preclude a solicitor from assisting with drafting the statement based on the witness's account (making option A incorrect). Option C is incorrect as this would be the approach a solicitor would take drafting a

statement of case, not a witness statement. Option D is incorrect as it is not only non-CPR-compliant, but it is also a breach of privilege. Finally, option E is incorrect as a good initial interview should have given the solicitor a thorough and comprehensive version of the facts from the client's point of view.

Question 4:
The correct answer was E. Hearsay evidence is admissible where it recounts a perception made by another person about a relevant fact (making option A incorrect). The speed that the vehicle was travelling is a relevant fact (making option C incorrect) and the statement was made by another person, making it admissible hearsay evidence. Where the witness does not attend court, the court will view the whole statement as hearsay evidence, but they will not rule it as inadmissible; it will simply affect the weight that the court attaches to the statement (making option B incorrect). Option D is not right as the whole purpose of having admissible hearsay evidence is to account for where the original provider of the statement cannot or will not give their own witness account.

Question 5:
The correct answer was C. The overriding objective makes it clear that cases should be dealt with justly and at proportionate cost. With the value of the claim being so low, the appointment of two experts is not proportionate (which makes options A, B and E incorrect). Option D is incorrect as the court is likely to need some form of expert evidence to determine the issue, rather than none at all.

■ KEY CASES, RULES, STATUTES AND INSTRUMENTS

The SQE1 Assessment Specification does not require you to know any case names or statutory materials for the topic of evidence.

9

Disclosure and inspection

■ MAKE SURE YOU KNOW

This chapter will cover the rules surrounding disclosure and inspection. It will cover the principles of standard disclosure, orders for disclosure and specific disclosure, the operation of privilege, pre-action and non-party disclosure, and electronic disclosure. You are required to be able to apply these principles and rules appropriately and effectively to realistic client-based and ethical problems and situations for your SQE1 assessment.

■ SQE ASSESSMENT ADVICE

As you work through this chapter, remember to pay particular attention in your revision to:
- standard disclosure;
- orders for disclosure;
- specific disclosure;
- privilege and without prejudice communications;
- pre-action and non-party disclosure;
- electronic disclosure.

■ WHAT DO YOU KNOW ALREADY?

Have a go at these questions before reading this chapter. If you find some difficult or cannot remember the answers, make a note to look more closely at that subtopic during your revision.

1) What is the difference between disclosure and inspection?
   [Introduction to disclosure and inspection, page 139]
2) What is the extent of the duty that parties are under to search for documents for the purposes of disclosure?
   [Introduction to disclosure and inspection, page 139]
3) What is standard disclosure?
   [What is a party obliged to disclose?, page 140]
4) True or false? The standard direction in the fast track is for parties to file and serve all documents on which they intend to rely no later than 14 days prior to the trial date.
   [Court's approach to disclosure in each track, page 141]

5) What is pre-action disclosure?
   [Pre-action disclosure, page 145]

INTRODUCTION TO DISCLOSURE AND INSPECTION

Disclosure is the process by which a party informs another party that they possess a particular **document**. Parties are under a **duty to search** for documents, and the duty to disclose is limited to the documents which are in that party's control. Inspection refers to the right of the other party to read or receive copies of a document that has been disclosed.

> **Key term: document**
>
> A document is anything in which information of any description is recorded. This is deliberately defined very widely and could include an email, a USB stick, a photograph, a video or any information held on a hard drive.

> **Key term: duty to search**
>
> All parties are under a duty to make a reasonable search for all documents required under the appropriate basis for disclosure. Reasonable search means giving consideration to issues such as the overall number of documents involved, the nature and complexity of the proceedings, how significant an individual document will actually be in the context of the proceedings overall, and the ease and expense of finding any particular document. The extent of the search can be limited by a party, but only where it can be justified.

For SQE1, you need to have an understanding of the rules surrounding both disclosure and inspection, as well as the processes for disclosure and electronic disclosure and the types of orders that can be made by the court in the event that a party does not comply with their obligations. These key topics are covered in this chapter.

DISCLOSURE AND INSPECTION

In order to establish whether a document needs to be disclosed by one party to another, you need to consider the following:
- What is a party obliged to disclose?
- Is the document within the party's control?
- Does the party have the ability to prevent another party from inspecting the document?

Each of these will now be dealt with in turn.

What is a party obliged to disclose?

The court determines the basis of the disclosure of documents. The general position is that a party must disclose documents on which they intend to rely that adversely affect their own case, adversely affect another party's case, support another party's case or are required to be disclosed by a relevant Practice Direction. This is called **standard disclosure** or disclosure on the standard basis. If this is the basis of disclosure that the court requires, it will be specified in the directions order (given at the initial stage of case management, discussed in **Chapter 7**) as 'disclosure on the standard basis'. The only documents that need to form part of disclosure are those which are relevant to the matters in dispute. There is no requirement to disclose documents on elements of the dispute that have already been agreed upon by the parties.

> **Key term: standard disclosure**
>
> This is the most common type of disclosure, and is the default position unless the court orders otherwise.

Practice example 9.1 illustrates how the principles of standard disclosure work in practice.

> **Practice example 9.1**
>
> Denise commences proceedings against Johnny for recovery of money that she paid towards the renovation of his house. She argues that she paid in cash for all of the renovations between January 2016 and January 2019. Johnny defends the claim on the basis that he paid for at least 75% of the work. The court orders her to undertake disclosure on the standard basis. Having conducted a reasonable search, Denise finds a receipt from a builder which shows that the builder received cash from the property owner, accompanied by the signature of both the builder and Johnny. Does she need to disclose this?
>
> Yes. Disclosure on the standard basis includes disclosing any document that adversely affects the party's case. If Denise failed to disclose this document, she would be in breach of the order.

Depending on the matter type, and more specifically the track to which a matter is allocated (see **Chapter 7**), the court may make an order for disclosure to take place on a different basis to that of standard disclosure. **Table 9.1** summarises how the court generally approaches disclosure depending on which track the matter has been allocated to.

Table 9.1: The court's approach to disclosure in each track

Track	The court's approach to disclosure
Small claims track	The standard direction is that each party shall, at least 14 days before the date of the final hearing, file and serve on every other party copies of all documents (including any expert report) on which they intend to rely at that hearing. While the court has discretion to depart from this approach if they see fit, it seldom is necessary.
Fast track	The standard order is that disclosure will take place on the standard basis in line with the suggested fast track timetable for directions laid out in Practice Direction 28.
Multi-track	The court is most likely to depart from disclosure on the standard basis if the claim is allocated to the multi-track. This is because claims tend to be higher-value and more complex, and therefore the volume of documents needs to be carefully controlled so as to allow the court to only consider those that are relevant to the dispute. The court can make the following alternative disclosure orders: • an order dispensing with disclosure; • an order that a party disclose the documents on which it relies, and at the same time request any **specific disclosure** it requires from any other party; • an order which directs that the disclosure is given by each party on an issue-by-issue basis (where the overall litigation is so expansive that the areas in dispute need to be compartmentalised); • any other order in relation to disclosure that the court considers appropriate.

Key term: specific disclosure
This is where the disclosure of specific documents or classes of documents is specified in the court order. This is discussed in more detail on **page 144**.

The judge will decide what type of order in relation to disclosure to make, usually at the first case management conference. Any decision taken by the court will be guided by the overriding objective (ie what is necessary to deal with the case justly and at proportionate cost; see **Chapter 7**).

Is the document within the party's control?

The second question to consider is whether a document is classed as being in a party's control. A party only needs to disclose a document that is in their control. Under CPR 31.8, a document is in a party's control if:
• it is or was in the physical possession of the party;

142 Disclosure and inspection

- the party had or has had the right to inspect the document;
- the party has or has had the right to inspect or take a copy of the document.

Exam warning
An SQE1 question may ask you about what happens in circumstances in which a party no longer has physical possession of a document. If this is the case, the document will still need to be disclosed (remember that inspection is the stage where the other party receives a copy) but a detailed explanation of how the document was lost must be included on the disclosure form.

Does the party have the ability to prevent another party from inspecting the document?

CPR 31 sets out that a party to whom a document has been disclosed has a right to inspect it. This is the position unless an exception applies. For the purposes of SQE1, the only exception you need to be aware of is where the document is **privileged**.

Key term: privileged
If a document is privileged, then even though the opposing party will be aware of the existence of the document (it will still need to be disclosed), they are prevented from inspecting or seeing it.

There are three types of privilege. They are as follows:
- legal advice privilege;
- litigation privilege;
- without prejudice privilege.

Table 9.2 explains what each of these terms mean.

Table 9.2: Types of privilege

Type of privilege	Explanation
Legal advice privilege	This protects confidential communications between a legal representative and their client, but *not* communications with third parties (such as between the legal representative and an instructed expert). This is widely applied and *does not* need to be in relation to litigation that is either commenced or is being contemplated. In order to benefit from this privilege, the dominant purpose of the communication must be the seeking and receiving of legal advice. This means that general advice given (eg about the litigation process) will not be privileged, but a letter specifically advising a client on the merits of their claim certainly would be.

Table 9.2: (continued)

Type of privilege	Explanation
Litigation privilege	This protects confidential communications between a legal representative *and* a client *and* a third party, or between a client and a third party directly. A third party can be an expert, a witness or any other party consulted in connection with the litigation. This is narrower than legal advice privilege as the document must have been created for the sole or dominant purpose of obtaining information or advice in connection with the litigation itself, which either existed or was reasonably contemplated at the time the document was created.
Without prejudice privilege	This applies to documents that are typically written in the course of negotiations to settle with another party. Without prejudice communications are used generally where a party is seeking to make an offer during the course of litigation proceedings that it does not want to be seen by the court. The communication itself is generally marked 'without prejudice', although this is not a requirement. To establish whether the document benefits from without prejudice privilege, the substance of it must be looked at. Is it a genuine offer to settle on sensible terms by a party open to settlement? If so, the document is likely to be protected by without prejudice privilege whether it is marked 'without prejudice' or not.

The party who is withholding inspection of a document based on privilege is able to **waive** that privilege if they wish. This would generally occur where the party thought that the document would work favourably for them in proceedings. In order to waive privilege, the party would simply write to the opposition to indicate that they are not relying on the privilege, as well as inviting them to inspect the document in question if they wished to.

Key term: waive

This is where a party does not rely upon, insist upon or use their right. So, if a party waives privilege, they will allow the other party to inspect the document in question.

Revision tip

The topics of disclosure and inspection can be complicated; but provided you break them down and apply the questions set out above, you will be able to work out whether a document qualifies for disclosure, whether the basis of disclosure requires you to disclose it to the other party, and whether there is a way of you preventing inspection through application of one of the aspects of privilege.

Once you have established whether a document is disclosable, you then need to know how exactly you go about disclosing it to the opposing party. This and other important elements of disclosure are covered in the next section.

DISCLOSURE PROCEDURE, ORDERS, AND RULES RELATING TO ELECTRONIC DISCLOSURE

This section outlines the process that a party needs to follow for disclosure, as well as covering orders for disclosure, pre-action disclosure, non-party disclosure and electronic disclosure.

Disclosure and inspection process
While the rules relating to disclosure can be complicated, the procedure itself is not. The following is an outline of the procedure that a party must follow:
- Once a reasonable search has been carried out and the relevant documents have been identified, the party will prepare a numbered list of those documents using form N265.
- The list must also contain a disclosure statement, signed by the party, confirming the extent of the search made to locate documents and certifying that they understand their duty of disclosure.
- The N265 form must then be served on the other party by the deadline set out in the directions order.
- Upon receipt of the other party's N265 form, the opposition must prepare a written notice informing the party of the documents that they wish to inspect from the list. The party must allow inspection within seven days of receiving that notice.

Orders for disclosure
We will now consider the three types of orders in relation to disclosure.

Specific disclosure
There are circumstances that arise where a party may need to ask the court to intervene on a specific matter regarding disclosure. This is generally because they feel that the opposing party has not searched as extensively as their duty requires. If this is the case, the party who is dissatisfied should first write to the other party setting out their reasons for believing that the search has not been carried out as thoroughly as required, and including what they would like to be done to rectify matters. If the issue is not rectified, the party is entitled to apply to the court, using form N244 and an accompanying witness statement for specific disclosure.

If the court grants an order for specific disclosure, they will require the party against whom the order is made to do one or more of the following:
- disclose specific documents or classes of documents covered in the order (this would be where the party who has applied has identified that a particular document or documents exist that fall within the extent of the disclosure required and wish the court to specifically order the other party to disclose those documents);
- carry out an additional search;
- disclose any documents located as a result of that search.

If a party has an order for specific disclosure made against them, they must comply with it within the relevant timescale set out in the order.

Pre-action disclosure

As we know, the Practice Direction on Pre-Action Conduct and Protocols (PDPACP) requires parties to share information (see **Chapter 2**), but prior to a claim being commenced there is no fixed duty on either party to disclose documents on the standard basis or otherwise. This can lead to parties picking and choosing which documents to disclose and which benefit their claim the most, in a way that they cannot after proceedings have been issued.

Where a party feels that their opponent is deliberately withholding a document that could have a material impact on the chances of the matter being settled by negotiation, or whether the claim is suitable for being issued at all, an application for pre-action disclosure may be useful. It is as the name suggests: an application that asks the court to make an order requiring a party to disclose a particular document or class of document *before* proceedings are issued.

The party making the application must complete an N244 form and attach a witness statement that outlines:
- both the respondent and applicant are likely to be parties to the anticipated proceedings;
- the document or class of documents that the applicant would like to be disclosed;
- that if proceedings have already started, the respondent would be under a duty to disclose the document or documents in question;
- that disclosure prior to proceedings being commenced is desirable as it will save costs, assist with the dispute being resolved without proceedings, or is likely to enable the parties to dispose fairly of the anticipated proceedings (the emphasis therefore is that the document or documents must be capable of assisting the parties to avoid court).

Non-party disclosure

An application for non-party disclosure is appropriate where proceedings have been issued, disclosure has taken place, and a party has said that they are

no longer in possession of a relevant document but they know that somebody who is not a party to proceedings is in possession of it. An application for non-party disclosure can then be made using form N244 and an accompanying witness statement that explains:
- the documents are likely to support the case of the applicant or adversely affect the case of one of the other parties to proceedings;
- disclosure is necessary in order to dispose fairly of the claim or to save costs.

Electronic disclosure

Electronic disclosure (or e-disclosure) means any document that is in electronic form, and includes those available from servers, computer systems and hard drives. Due to the sheer volume of potential electronic documents that can be relevant to a claim, the CPR specifically require parties to agree between them how the volume of electronic disclosure can be limited, for instance, with reference to specific keywords, agreeing specific categories of documents to be disclosed, and the manner in which these documents will be inspected by the other party.

E-disclosure will typically arise more in multi-track claims between commercial entities where there is a huge volume of potentially relevant documents to disclose. The court will deal specifically with the limitations or boundaries that the parties have agreed at the case management conference, and will either make an order that specifies those limitations or boundaries, where appropriate, or list the matter for a separate hearing, where the court feels that e-disclosure requires more careful consideration.

■ KEY POINT CHECKLIST

This chapter has covered the following key knowledge points. You can use these to structure your revision, ensuring you recall the key details for each point, as covered in this chapter.
- Disclosure is the process by which a party informs another party that they possess a particular document. Parties are under a duty to search for documents, and the duty to disclose is limited to the documents which are in that party's control.
- Inspection refers to the right of the other party to read or receive copies of a document that has been disclosed.
- The general position is that a party must disclose documents on which they intend to rely that adversely affect their own case, adversely affect another party's case, support another party's case or are required to be disclosed by a relevant practice direction. This is called standard disclosure.
- A document is in a party's control if it is or was in the physical possession of the party, the party had or has had the right to inspect the document, or the party has or has had the right to inspect or take a copy of the document.

- If a document is privileged, then even though the opposing party will be aware of the existence of the document (it will still need to be disclosed), they are prevented from inspecting or seeing it. There are three types of privilege: legal advice privilege, litigation privilege and without prejudice privilege.
- The court has the power to make orders for disclosure. These are for specific disclosure, pre-action disclosure and non-party disclosure.

■ KEY TERMS AND CONCEPTS
- document (**page 139**)
- duty to search (**page 139**)
- standard disclosure (**page 140**)
- specific disclosure (**page 141**)
- privileged (**page 142**)
- waive (**page 143**)

■ SQE1-STYLE QUESTIONS

QUESTION 1

A claimant is bringing an action against a defendant for breach of contract. The court orders that disclosure take place on the standard basis.

Which of the following best describes the duty to search for documents that the parties are under?

A. The parties are under a duty to make an adequate search for all documents required under the appropriate basis for disclosure. The extent of the search should be limited to only documents that are directly relevant to the claim.

B. The parties are under a duty to make an extensive search for all documents required under the appropriate basis for disclosure. The extent of the search should be anything remotely related to proceedings, however minimal.

C. The parties are under a duty to make a reasonable search for all documents required under the appropriate basis for disclosure. The extent of the search should be proportionate in line with the overriding objective.

D. The parties are under a duty to make a reasonable search for all documents required under the appropriate basis for disclosure. The extent of the search should be anything remotely related to proceedings, however minimal.

E. The parties are under a duty to make an extensive search for all documents required under the appropriate basis for disclosure. The extent of the search should be proportionate in line with the overriding objective.

QUESTION 2

A company is a defendant in an action for breach of contract against them. The claimant is arguing that the defendant took the wrong details for an order, and instead of supplying 100 brochures in fact supplied and invoiced for 1,000 brochures. Disclosure is ordered on the standard basis as part of the directions order. During the defendant's search for documents, they come across a written letter from the claimant which specifies that she would like the defendant to supply 100 brochures.

Which of the following best describes the defendant's position?

A. The defendant does not have to disclose the document as it is clearly adverse to their case.

B. The defendant must disclose the document as even though it is clearly adverse to their case, the document falls within the test for standard disclosure.

C. The defendant must disclose the document as it has been discovered as part of a reasonable search.

D. The defendant must disclose the document but can withhold inspection on the basis that the document is privileged.

E. The defendant does not have to disclose the document on the basis that the document is privileged.

QUESTION 3

A claimant commences proceedings against a defendant for breach of contract. Shortly after the proceedings were issued, the claimant's solicitor wrote to the defendant stating that it was clearly not in any of the parties' interests for the matter to proceed to court, that the claimant recognised that both parties could have conducted themselves more appropriately, and that the claimant therefore wished to negotiate. The letter included an offer to settle but was not marked 'without prejudice'. The defendant did not accept the offer to settle and refused to negotiate further, and so the litigation continued.

Which of the following best describes whether the claimant is entitled to withhold inspection from the defendant?

A. The claimant cannot withhold inspection. The letter was sent to the defendant and they have therefore already seen it.

B. The claimant cannot withhold inspection. It was not marked 'without prejudice' and therefore cannot benefit from without prejudice privilege.

C. The claimant can withhold inspection. The letter contains an offer to settle and is therefore by its very nature privileged.

D. The claimant can withhold inspection. Although the letter was not marked 'without prejudice', it can still benefit from being covered by without prejudice privilege if it is clearly a genuine attempt to settle.

E. The claimant can withhold inspection. It has resulted from advice given to the claimant by his solicitor and therefore can benefit from legal advice privilege.

QUESTION 4

A claimant issues proceedings against a defendant for damages relating to a personal injury caused by the defendant's negligent driving in failing to stop in time to prevent a collision. The defendant defends the action on the basis that the brakes of the car did not seem to function as well as they should, increasing the vehicle's stopping distance. As part of the disclosure list, the defendant references a checklist and report that was conducted internally by a local garage on the condition of the car following its most recent vehicle safety test. The defendant states that the document cannot be inspected as the garage has told them that it is private and the garage will not release it.

Which of the following best reflects the way that the claimant should proceed?

A. The claimant should ignore the document. It is unlikely that the document is relevant as the action is focused on the defendant's standard of driving.

B. The claimant should proceed and make an application for specific disclosure against the defendant immediately.

C. The claimant should write to the garage and request that the document be handed over, failing which they should make an application to the court for specific disclosure against the defendant.

D. The claimant should write to the garage and request that the document be handed over, failing which they should make an application to the court for specific disclosure against the garage.

E. The claimant should write to the garage and request that the document be handed over, failing which they should make an application to the court for non-party disclosure against the garage.

QUESTION 5

A claimant company commences proceedings against a defendant for breach of contract. The court has ordered that disclosure takes place on the standard basis, and the claimant company has conducted a reasonable search and has identified the documents that are appropriate for disclosure. The claimant company has acted up to this point on their own but has decided to instruct a solicitor to advise them on the disclosure process that they need to comply with.

Which of the following best represents the way in which the claimant company should proceed?

A. The claimant company should prepare a list of the documents for disclosure on the standard form and sign a disclosure statement before filing the list with the court.

B. The claimant company should prepare a list of the documents for disclosure on the standard form and sign a disclosure statement before serving the list on the other parties to the claim.

C. The claimant company should prepare a list of the documents for disclosure on the standard form and serve the list on the other parties to the claim.

D. The claimant company should simply write to the defendant with a numbered list of the documents for disclosure. Although the standard form is available, it is not a prescribed form, so alternative means can be used.

E. The claimant company should simply write to the court with a numbered list of the documents for disclosure. Although the standard form is available, it is not a prescribed form, so alternative means can be used.

■ ANSWERS TO QUESTIONS

Answers to 'What do you know already?' questions at the start of the chapter

1) Disclosure is the process by which a party to a claim tells another party that they are in possession or control of a particular document. Inspection is the process by which the other party requests to look at that document.

2) The duty is to conduct a reasonable search. Reasonable search means giving consideration to issues such as the overall number of documents involved, the nature and complexity of the proceedings, how significant an individual document will actually be in the context of the proceedings overall, and the ease and expense of finding any particular document.

3) Standard disclosure is the most common basis on which the court will order that disclosure is made. A party must disclose documents on which they intend to rely that adversely affect their own case, adversely affect another party's case, support another party's case or are required to be disclosed by a relevant practice direction.

4) False. This is the standard direction for the small claims track. The standard directions in the fast track are laid out in Practice Direction 28.

5) Pre-action disclosure is a type of order that the court can make which specifies documents that a likely party to anticipated proceedings should disclose to another likely party to anticipated proceedings before proceedings are issued.

Answers to end-of-chapter SQE1-style questions

Question 1:
The correct answer was C. Parties are under a duty on the standard basis to conduct a reasonable search for documents. Nowhere in the Civil Procedure Rules 1998 (CPR) does it mention that the search must be either extensive (making options B and E incorrect) or adequate (making option A incorrect). The CPR also recognise that the extent of the search must be proportionate to the value and complexity of the claim to save parties from expending huge amounts of energy, time and money on finding documents that are limited in their relevance to the matter overall, making option D incorrect.

Question 2:
The correct answer was B. The defendant must disclose the document in this case, as the test for standard disclosure specifically states that documents which adversely affect a party's own case must be disclosed. This makes options A and E incorrect. Option C is incorrect as even though the document was found as part of a reasonable search, this is not the basis on which it must be disclosed. Option D is incorrect as the document will not be protected by privilege and is therefore able to be inspected.

Question 3:
The correct answer was D. Without prejudice privilege can be used even where the document is not marked 'without prejudice' (making option B wrong) where the correspondence makes a genuine attempt to settle matters in dispute, which is the case here. Option A is incorrect as it is immaterial whether or not the claimant has already seen the document; inspection relates to the right of the other party to view and use the document as a part of the proceedings. An offer to settle in and of itself is not a privileged document, as it is perfectly possible for an open letter offering to settle proceedings to be sent, which makes option C incorrect. Option E is wrong as legal advice privilege is only over correspondence containing advice that has passed between a solicitor and their client, which this is not.

Question 4:
The correct answer was E. The most appropriate initial step would be to write to the garage prior to making any application in the hope that the costs of applying to the court could be saved (making option B incorrect). In the absence of a response from the garage, or a refusal to disclose the document in question, an application for non-party disclosure should be made, as the garage is not a party to proceedings

and the document is clearly helpful to the claim being made. Applications for specific disclosure can only be made against parties to proceedings (making option D incorrect), and there is little point in applying for specific disclosure against the defendant as it is clear that they are not in possession of the document (making option C incorrect). Option A is incorrect as the state of the vehicle is clearly a material issue that requires consideration by the court, and the document itself is relevant to that.

Question 5:

The correct answer was B. The claimant company needs to complete the standard form with a numbered list of the documents for disclosure and sign the disclosure statement. That document must then be served on every other party to the claim, not the court (making options A and E incorrect). A disclosure statement must be included, making option C incorrect, and the standard form is prescribed and not optional, which makes option D incorrect.

■ KEY CASES, RULES, STATUTES AND INSTRUMENTS

The SQE1 Assessment Specification does not require you to know any case names or statutory materials for the topic of disclosure and inspection.

Costs and funding

■ MAKE SURE YOU KNOW
This chapter will cover the rules surrounding costs. It will cover how costs management and budgeting work, as well as the variety of costs orders that the court can make and the basis of those orders. Finally, we will look at Part 36 offers and the different options that a party has for funding litigation. You are required to be able to apply these principles and rules appropriately and effectively to realistic client-based and ethical problems and situations for your SQE1 assessment.

■ SQE ASSESSMENT ADVICE
As you work through this chapter, remember to pay particular attention in your revision to:
- fixed and assessed costs;
- costs management and budgeting;
- inter-partes costs orders;
- non-party costs;
- qualified one-way costs shifting;
- Part 36 and other offers;
- security for costs;
- options for funding litigation:
  - conditional fee agreements;
  - damages-based agreements;
  - fixed fees;
  - third-party funding.

■ WHAT DO YOU KNOW ALREADY?
Have a go at these questions before reading this chapter. If you find some difficult or cannot remember the answers, make a note to look more closely at that subtopic during your revision.
1) How does the court generally deal with costs in fast track cases?
   [Fixed and assessed costs, page 155]

2) True or false? If a costs budget is approved by the court, then the party is guaranteed to recover those costs.
   [Costs management and budgeting, page 157]
3) What is the difference between the standard basis and the indemnity basis?
   [Are costs to be assessed on the standard basis or the indemnity basis?, page 159]
4) What is qualified one-way costs shifting?
   [Qualified one-way costs shifting, page 162]
5) What is a Part 36 offer?
   [Part 36 offers, page 163]

INTRODUCTION TO COSTS AND FUNDING

One of the most important areas to have a good and thorough understanding of in litigation practice is that of **costs**. An incorrect piece of advice or a poor use of a tactic could mean that your client can be left facing significant adverse consequences. Matters concerning costs can crop up at a range of different stages in the litigation process. For example, after an interim application (covered in **Chapter 6**), the court will usually also make a costs order following determination of the issues that are the subject of the application. However, costs are most commonly dealt with by the court after trial or judgment.

> **Key term: costs**
>
> This umbrella term generally includes solicitors' fees and disbursements (other costs that are incurred during the life of a litigated matter, such as court fees, barristers' fees, experts' fees, etc.).

The first key difference to understand is between how the court views and deals with costs compared with the costs that a client actually pays to their solicitor. They are not the same thing. A client's agreement with their solicitor (called a retainer) is contractual; they are liable to pay the costs properly incurred for the work done by their solicitor in line with the retainer signed. If the court is not able or decides not to award the full value of costs claimed to a party, then that party will still need to pay any shortfall to their solicitor. The court focuses on two key areas:
- Which party should pay the other's costs (or should the parties simply pay their own)?
- How much or what proportion of the costs incurred should the paying party be liable for?

SQE1 requires you to be able to assess what the court is likely to order in specific circumstances. This chapter summarises how costs are likely to be dealt with in a variety of different scenarios.

FIXED AND ASSESSED COSTS, AND COSTS MANAGEMENT AND BUDGETING

The general principle is that the loser pays the winner's costs. However, this is only the starting point. There are many exceptions and variations to this rule, some of which are at the court's discretion and some that the Civil Procedure Rules 1998 (CPR; see **Chapter 1**) specifically govern. The first issue to consider is how the level of costs awarded is to be assessed.

Fixed and assessed costs

Much of how costs are dealt with by the court after the final hearing depends on the track to which they were allocated (see **Chapter 7**). Table 10.1 explains how costs are generally dealt with on each track.

Table 10.1: How costs are dealt with on each track

Track	How costs are dealt with
Small claims track	Generally, costs awarded are limited to **fixed commencement costs** and third-party costs, such as court fees and experts' fees.
Fast track	Legal costs and disbursements are recoverable from the other party; however, they are generally **summarily assessed**.
Multi-track	Legal costs and disbursements are recoverable from the other party; however, they are generally subject to **detailed assessment**.

> **Key term: fixed commencement costs**
>
> CPR 45.2 allows a successful claimant or applicant to recover very limited fixed costs. The amount depends on the value of the claim and the way in which the claim was served on the defendant. It is worthwhile looking up CPR 45 to see how this operates.

> **Key term: summarily assessed**
>
> Summary assessment is where the court takes an instant view on the value of the costs that are to be paid by one party to another. If costs are assessed summarily, the court will make its decision based on a costs summary (called a statement of costs) provided to them by the party at least 24 hours in advance of the hearing or trial. The court should make a summary assessment of costs at the conclusion of a fast track trial or at the conclusion of any other hearing that does not last for more than one day.

Key term: detailed assessment

Detailed assessment generally occurs where summary assessment is not possible. It is the procedure by which the amount of costs is decided by the court on the basis of a detailed bill of costs, which is a full breakdown of the legal charges and expenses incurred by a party throughout the litigation.

If the court orders that costs are to be subject to detailed assessment, the parties will need to comply with the following procedure:
- The party in whose favour the costs order has been made must serve on the paying party a notice of commencement (a formal document that commences the process) within three months of the date of judgment or order.
- The paying party must then serve any points of dispute within 21 days.
  - If no points of dispute are served, the receiving party can then apply for a default costs certificate entitling them to payment of the full amount in the bill of costs (the legal expenses incurred) plus fixed costs and the court fees.
  - If only minor points are in dispute, then the receiving party can apply for an interim certificate entitling them to the costs that are not in dispute.
- If there is no agreement on costs, the receiving party must serve any reply within a further 21 days.
- The paying party must then file a request for a hearing within three months of the expiry of the initial three-month period. This hearing is called an 'assessment hearing', the format of which depends on the criteria set out below.

How the court then proceeds depends on whether the bill of costs totals more than or less than £75,000.
- If the amount is less than £75,000, the court will carry out a provisional assessment where the judge will consider the documents submitted by the parties without a hearing and without the parties present. A decision on the appropriate amount will be taken based on the bill of costs, points of dispute and reply, and any supporting evidence filed.
- If the costs claimed are more than £75,000, then the matter will proceed to a hearing in front of a Costs Judge or a District Judge to debate the points that are in dispute.

Detailed assessment is significantly more expensive than assessing costs on a summary basis, which is why it is generally only used in high-value cases.

Practice example 10.1 sets out how this might apply in practice.

Practice example 10.1

Andy is successful in a multi-track breach of contract action against Phil. The court orders that Phil pays Andy's costs subject to detailed assessment. Andy serves a notice of commencement on Phil and Phil serves minor points of dispute on Andy; however, the bulk of the costs are agreed. Is there anything that Andy can do to be paid at least a proportion of his costs pending resolution of the issues in dispute?

Andy can apply to the court for an interim certificate, which will entitle him to the costs that are not in dispute. It is then for the court to settle the outstanding points of dispute.

Costs management and budgeting

In multi-track cases, the court actively manages costs. This is to try to ensure two things: first, that the costs which are incurred by the legal representatives of each party are done so in proportion to the value and complexity of the matter in hand; and second, to ensure consistent application of the overriding objective. This is designed to prevent cases where one side's solicitor runs up huge legal costs that vastly eclipse the value of the claim overall, in expectation that they can simply recover those costs from the other side. The first stage of this is the preparation and filing of a **costs budget**.

Key term: costs budget

This is a document that provides an estimate of the reasonable and proportionate costs which a party is intending to incur throughout the life of the litigation.

Costs budgets must be prepared, filed with the court, and exchanged with the other parties at the same time as the directions questionnaire (see **Chapter 7**) if the claim is valued at under £50,000, and no later than 21 days before the first case management conference if the claim is valued at over £50,000. The court will then consider both parties' budgets and approve all or part of them at the hearing accordingly.

The costs budget is a key document because if the court approves it, it is highly likely that the party will be able to recover the full value of the costs set out in their budget if they are successful in their claim and the court makes a costs award in their favour. The following summarises additional key points in relation to costs budgets:
- Approval of the budget from the court will come in the form of a costs management order, in which the court will set out whether they approve all or part of a party's budget.
- If the court only approves part of a budget, the costs management order will specify which parts.

- If a costs budget is approved and later in proceedings a party wishes to revise it by either increasing or decreasing the estimate, this must be done either by agreement between the parties or by approval from the court. If the court does not find the revision to be reasonable and proportionate, they will reject it.

> **Revision tip**
>
> If the court does not approve part of a costs budget, then this does not mean that those costs cannot be incurred by the legal representative; it simply means that they are unlikely to be recovered from the other side in the event of a successful claim.

If a party fails to file their costs budget on time, the party will be limited to recovering court fees alone. This is potentially very serious, as court fees will generally represent a tiny proportion of the legal costs that will be claimed overall.

> **Exam warning**
>
> Remember that a costs budget is only an estimate. Even if approved, it is only one of the factors that the court will take into account when determining the amount of costs to award when the matter reaches a final hearing or after judgment or order has been made. If an SQE question asks whether an approved costs budget is the same as a final costs order made by the court, it is not.

COSTS ORDERS

The court can make a variety of costs orders following either an interim hearing or a final judgment or order being made. The SQE requires you to know about the following types of orders:
- inter-partes costs orders;
- non-party costs orders;
- security for costs orders.

Each of these will be considered in turn.

Inter-partes costs orders

This simply means costs that are awarded by the court in favour of one party against another. Such orders are given either at the conclusion of an interim hearing or after the final judgment or order. For SQE1, it is important that you know how the court will assess the appropriate amount of costs which are payable from one party to another.

The process that the court will apply is as follows:
- Are costs to be assessed on the standard basis or the indemnity basis?
- Are there any other factors that the court needs to take into consideration?

Are costs to be assessed on the standard basis or the indemnity basis?

The standard basis and the indemnity basis are the two methods that are used to calculate the amount of costs which an unsuccessful party will pay to a successful party. The operation of the standard basis and the indemnity basis are explained in **Table 10.2**.

Table 10.2: Operation of the standard basis and the indemnity basis

Basis	How it operates
Standard basis	The court will consider every item of costs claimed and decide if they were: • proportionately and reasonably incurred; • proportionate and reasonable in amount. If an item is not reasonably incurred, it will be disallowed completely. If an item is not reasonable in amount, it will be reduced. If the total of the items in the relevant section claimed (eg time spent on drafting documents) is not found to be proportionate, the court will either disallow or reduce the amount claimed for that category accordingly. In instances where the court is in doubt over whether to disallow, reduce or award the full value of an item or category of costs claimed, this will be resolved in favour of the *paying* party. The standard basis is therefore more advantageous to the party who has had a costs order made against them.
Indemnity basis	The court will look at whether the costs were: • reasonably incurred; • reasonable in amount. If an item is not reasonably incurred, it will be disallowed completely. If an item is not reasonable in amount, it will be reduced. In instances where the court is in doubt over whether to disallow, reduce or award the full value of an item or category of costs claimed, this will be resolved in favour of the *receiving* party. The indemnity basis is therefore more advantageous to the party who has had a costs order made in favour of them.

Therefore, the main differences between the standard basis and the indemnity basis are whether proportionality needs to be taken into account and in whose favour any doubt will be resolved. From a practical perspective, this generally means that costs which are awarded on the indemnity basis

160   Costs and funding

are higher than they would have been if they had been awarded on the standard basis.

Are there any other factors that the court needs to take into consideration?
Under CPR 44.4, the court will also have regard to:
- the conduct of all the parties, including in particular their conduct before as well as during the proceedings, and the efforts made, if any, before and during the proceedings in order to try to resolve the dispute;
- the amount or value of any money or property involved;
- the importance of the matter to all of the parties;
- the particular complexity of the matter;
- the skill, effort, specialised knowledge and responsibility involved;
- the time spent on the case;
- the place where and the circumstances in which work or any part of it was done;
- the receiving party's last approved or agreed upon budget.

Once the court has determined the basis on which the amount of costs will be awarded and then applied any additional factors, it will be in a position to take a decision on the amount of costs to award.

Practice example 10.2 demonstrates how the criteria under CPR 44.4 can be applied.

Practice example 10.2
Ben is successful in a breach of contract multi-track claim valued at £275,000 against Chris. The parties both filed their costs budgets on time before the directions hearing, and the court approved those costs budgets. Ben's costs budget totalled £110,000. At trial, the court makes a costs order in Ben's favour, with such costs to be assessed on the standard basis. Ben submits a costs claim in the sum of £235,000, arguing that the litigation has proved more costly than predicted. Is Ben likely to recover the full value of his costs?

First, the court will look at the basis on which costs have been awarded: the standard basis. This means that they must take proportionality into consideration when making their award. With the value of the claim being £275,000, his claim for £235,000 is therefore likely to be viewed as being disproportionate, and the trial judge will consider each item in the costs breakdown to see whether it was reasonably incurred (if not, it will be disallowed) and reasonable in amount (if not, it will be reduced). With the claim being a multi-track high-value matter, the parties have already submitted and had approved a costs budget, which the trial judge must take into consideration under CPR 44.4. Proportionality of the costs budget is also considered by the judge in the directions

> hearing, and so it is highly likely that Ben will recover the costs that were submitted as part of the costs budget (£110,000) but not the full value he has claimed (£235,000).

Non-party costs orders

A non-party costs order is where the court makes a costs order against or in favour of somebody who is not party to proceedings. It is extremely rare and generally only occurs where a third party (ie somebody who is not named as either the claimant or defendant) is:
* substantially controlling the course of the litigation;
* stands to benefit from the successful outcome of proceedings.

Therefore, a friend or family member who simply funds litigation for a claimant or defendant and has no interest in the outcome is not at risk of having a non-party costs order made against them. However, a private individual who is the sole director and shareholder of an insolvent claimant company and who would benefit exclusively from the action being successful would be at risk of a non-party costs order being made against them.

Security for costs orders

Security for costs orders are made by defendants, and are designed to make sure that the claimant can meet any possible future costs orders which are made against that claimant. If the defendant's application is successful, the claimant will be ordered to pay a specified sum either into court or to the defendant's solicitor. If no costs order is made, the court or the defendant's solicitor will pay the claimant's money back to them.

In order to be successful in an application for security for costs, the applicant must prove that:
* it is just in the circumstances for the court to make an order, and;
* one of the following conditions applies:
  - the claimant is resident outside of England and Wales;
  - the claimant is a company and there is reason to believe that it will be unable to pay the defendant's costs if ordered to do so;
  - the claimant has taken steps in relation to their assets that would make enforcement of a costs order more difficult (eg transferring property).

Therefore, the application must centre around the risk that the claimant's circumstances or actions will make it more difficult or impossible for the defendant to recover costs from them if they are successful in defending the claim.

If the defendant decides to make an application for security for costs, they should first try to agree a voluntary payment with the claimant. If this is unsuccessful, the defendant should file and serve an N244 application notice with accompanying witness statement that sets out the grounds and evidence for the application. The court has complete discretion on whether to make a security for costs order; even if the applicants meet both of the grounds, this does not necessarily mean that the court will make the order.

QUALIFIED ONE-WAY COSTS SHIFTING

Qualified one-way costs shifting applies to personal injury claims only. It is extremely advantageous to claimants, as it operates as follows:
- If the claimant is successful and the court also makes a costs order in their favour, the defendant will have to pay the claimant's costs on the basis ordered.
- If the defendant is successful in defending the claim, they will not be able to successfully recover their costs of doing so from the claimant.

The only circumstances in which the defendant could successfully recover their costs from the claim are as follows:
- The claim is found on the balance of probabilities to be 'fundamentally dishonest'.
- The claim is struck out as disclosing no reasonable grounds for bringing the proceedings, or because the claimant has unfairly or unreasonably used proceedings to pursue a vexatious agenda (abuse of process), or for conduct likely to prevent the court from making a just decision in relation to the proceedings overall.
- The claimant has failed to beat a defendant's Part 36 offer to settle (for more details on this, see **page 163**).

Practice example 10.3 illustrates how this could apply in practice.

Practice example 10.3

Nusrat is injured in a car accident caused by the alleged negligent driving of Graham. Graham is insured and the matter is therefore passed to his insurance company, Springtime Insurers Limited. Nusrat consults a solicitor and asks whether he will be liable to pay for Graham or his insurer's costs if he is unsuccessful in his claim. What is the position?

Nusrat can issue proceedings here and be reassured that provided his claim is not fundamentally dishonest and he has a legal basis to bring the claim, he will be protected from having to pay Graham or his insurer's costs in the event that he loses the claim. He is protected due to the qualified one-way costs shifting rule.

PART 36 OFFERS

A Part 36 offer (as it is generally known) is a very specific type of offer that can be made by any party to proceedings. Once made, the response (or lack of response) from the other party may lead to certain consequences regarding their liability for costs. Part 36 and its rules are considered by candidates to be one of the most complex areas of civil procedure. To enable you to understand Part 36 properly, you must first understand its purpose and the procedural requirements associated with making a proper Part 36 offer. You can then move on to consider how it operates in two specific circumstances:
- where an offer under Part 36 is made and accepted by the other party before trial;
- where an offer under Part 36 is made but not accepted by the other party before trial.

This section will cover each of these in turn.

Purpose of Part 36 and procedural requirements

The simple purpose of Part 36 is to incentivise parties to make or accept offers to settle. They are marked *'without prejudice save as to costs'*, which means that they will not be seen by the court until the trial of the substantive matters has concluded and the court is considering what costs order to make.

In order to make a valid Part 36 offer, the following criteria need to be met:
- the offer must be in writing;
- it must be clear that it is made pursuant to Part 36;
- it must state whether it relates to the whole or part of the claim;
- it must state whether it includes any counterclaim;
- it must state a relevant period.

Part 36 offers are typically very confusing; so to ensure that it makes sense to you, it is important that you understand the significance of the term **relevant period** before you begin to consider the potential consequences.

> **Key term: relevant period**
>
> The relevant period is the time period from the date on which a Part 36 offer is served and within which a party can accept the offer without any penalty consequences being applied to them. The relevant period must be 21 days or more (if specified by the offeror) from the date that the Part 36 offer is made. It is very important as the expiry of the relevant period is the date from which any Part 36 costs consequences will begin to apply.

The key to understanding a Part 36 offer is to break it down into sections. If you are asked a question on Part 36 in SQE1, remember to ask yourself the following questions:
- Who made the offer? (This is key as different rules apply depending on whether the claimant or the defendant made the offer.)
- Was it accepted, rejected or ignored by the other party? (This is key as the impact on costs differs depending on the other party's reaction to the offer.)
  - If it was accepted, was it accepted within or outside the relevant period?
  - If it was ignored or rejected, when did the relevant period expire, and was the offer beaten, equalled or not beaten at trial?

Once you have answered these questions, you can map the impact on costs. The different eventualities are covered in the following sections.

Where an offer under Part 36 is made and accepted by the other party before trial

Procedurally, what the party who wants to accept a Part 36 offer needs to do is serve a notice of acceptance on the party who has made the offer. From the date of acceptance, proceedings are then stayed (or paused) and the defendant must pay the claimant the sum agreed within 14 days. If the defendant fails to pay the claimant within 14 days, the claimant has the right to apply for judgment against the defendant.

The position on costs then needs to be finalised, and this is largely dependent on whether the offer was accepted inside or outside the relevant period. **Tables 10.3** and **10.4** set out the position for each scenario, depending on whether the offer was made by the claimant or the defendant.

Table 10.3: Where the offer is made by the claimant to the defendant

Timing of acceptance	Effect
Acceptance within the relevant period	The defendant will pay the claimant's costs of the proceedings to the date of the *notice of acceptance* on the standard basis.
Acceptance outside the relevant period	The defendant will pay the claimant's costs of the proceedings to the date of the *notice of acceptance* on the standard basis.

No matter what the eventuality here, the result is therefore the same.

Table 10.4: Where the offer is made by the defendant to the claimant

Timing of acceptance	Effect
Acceptance within the relevant period	The defendant will pay the claimant's costs of the proceedings to the date of the *notice of acceptance* on the standard basis.
Acceptance outside the relevant period	The defendant will pay the claimant's costs of the proceedings to the date of the *expiry of the relevant period* on the standard basis. THEN The claimant will pay the defendant's costs from the date of the expiry of the relevant period to the date of the notice of acceptance on the standard basis.

We can therefore see where the incentive lies for the defendant in making a Part 36 offer that is subsequently accepted by the claimant. **Practice example 10.4** illustrates how this works.

Practice example 10.4

Green Grains Limited issue proceedings against Syed for recovery of an unpaid invoice. Syed makes a Part 36 offer and the relevant period expires on 1 July. Green Grains Limited serve a notice of acceptance of the offer on 30 July. What is the position on costs?

Syed is the defendant, so the rules set out in Table 10.4 apply. Green Grains Limited accepted the offer outside the relevant period, so therefore Syed will pay Green Grains Limited's costs of the proceedings on the standard basis until 1 July (date of expiry of the relevant period) and Green Grains Limited will pay Syed's costs on the standard basis from 1 July to 30 July (date of notice of acceptance).

Where an offer under Part 36 is made but not accepted or rejected by the other party before trial

Now that we have considered the position where a party accepts a Part 36 offer, we now need to consider what happens where the other party either rejects or ignores it. The consequences here depend on who made the offer to whom and what the result at trial was. **Tables 10.5** and **10.6** set out the respective positions.

Table 10.5: Where the offer is made by the claimant to the defendant

Outcome	Effect
The claimant is successful at trial and is awarded a sum that is equal to or beats the value of their offer	The court has discretion to award the claimant: • an additional sum for damages of up to 10% for damages up to £500,000 and up to 5% for damages above £500,000, up to a maximum of £75,000 (this is designed to penalise the defendant significantly for failing to accept the claimant's offer); • up to the expiry of the *relevant period*, interest on damages awarded, plus the defendant will pay the claimant's costs on the standard basis; • from the expiry of the relevant period to the *date of judgment*, the defendant could be liable to pay interest on damages awarded, will pay the claimant's costs on the *indemnity basis* (so removing the requirement for proportionality), and will pay interest on the costs. It is important to recognise that these are the maximum penalties which the court can apply, but you can clearly see why Part 36 offers need to be taken very seriously by a defendant who receives one. The CPR state that any penalty imposed by the court must be 'just'.
The claimant is successful at trial but is awarded a sum that is less than the value of their offer	The Part 36 offer will not have any effect and there will be no penalties imposed on either party. It is likely that the defendant will be ordered to pay the claimant's costs on the standard basis, but this is because of the general rules relating to costs as opposed to any impact that the Part 36 offer has had.
The claimant loses at trial	The Part 36 offer will not have any effect and there will be no penalties imposed on either party. It is likely that the claimant will be ordered to pay the defendant's costs on the standard basis, but this is because of the general rules relating to costs as opposed to any impact that the Part 36 offer has had.

Therefore, from the claimant's perspective, if they make a Part 36 offer, then they have everything to gain and nothing to lose. **Practice example 10.5** illustrates how this works.

Practice example 10.5

Karen issues proceedings against Jim for recovery of an unpaid invoice of £98,000. Karen makes a Part 36 offer to Jim in the sum of £90,000, which Jim rejects. The relevant period expires on 1 January. Karen is awarded judgment for the full value of her claim (£98,000) on 30 July. What is Jim potentially liable for following the judgment?

Karen has made the offer and is the claimant, so the rules set out in Table 10.5 apply. In this case, Karen has been successful at trial and recovered damages that beat the value of her offer. Jim therefore potentially faces the full range of penalties available to the court. They could be:
- damages of £98,000;
- additional damages of 10% (£9,800);
- to pay Karen's costs of proceedings to 1 January (the date of expiry of the relevant period) on the standard basis, plus interest on those costs;
- to pay Karen's costs of proceedings from 2 January (the day after expiry of the relevant period) to 30 July (the date of judgment) on the indemnity basis, plus interest on those costs.

Table 10.6: Where the offer is made by the defendant to the claimant

Outcome	Impact
The claimant is successful at trial and is awarded a sum that beats the value of the defendant's offer	The Part 36 offer will not have any effect and there will be no penalties imposed on either party. It is likely that the defendant will be ordered to pay the claimant's costs on the standard basis, but this is because of the general rules relating to costs as opposed to any impact that the Part 36 offer has had.
The claimant is successful at trial but is awarded a sum that is less than the value of the defendant's offer	Up to the expiry of the *relevant period*, the defendant will pay the claimant's costs on the standard basis. From the expiry of the relevant period to the *date of judgment*, the claimant will pay the defendant's costs on the *standard basis* and will pay interest on those costs.
The claimant loses at trial (no judgment is awarded against the defendant)	It is likely that the claimant will be ordered to pay the defendant's costs on the standard basis, plus interest on those costs, as they have failed to accept the defendant's Part 36 offer.

Therefore, while the consequences for the claimant are much less significant, there is still a good incentive for the defendant to make an early and reasonable Part 36 offer, as if the claimant wins but does not beat the offer, then the claimant will pay the defendant's costs from the date of expiry of the relevant period to the date of judgment.

Where both parties have made an offer

Where both parties have made a Part 36 offer and neither offer has been accepted, it is necessary to work out which one takes effect for the purposes of costs. **Table 10.7** sets this out.

Table 10.7: Which Part 36 offer takes effect?

Circumstance	Which offer takes effect?
Where the claimant is successful and the damages awarded beat the Part 36 offer that the claimant made	The claimant's Part 36 offer will take effect here and the defendant would face the consequences set out in **Table 10.5**.
Where the claimant is unsuccessful in the action, or where the claimant is successful but is not awarded damages higher than the defendant's offer	The defendant's offer will take effect here and the claimant would face the consequences set out in **Table 10.6**.
Where the claimant wins less than their own offer but more than the defendant's offer	Neither offer will take effect here and the court will award costs in the usual way, without taking either Part 36 offer into consideration.

Withdrawing or amending a Part 36 offer

A party can only withdraw or amend a Part 36 offer if it has not already been accepted. Procedurally, the offeror must serve a notice of withdrawal or notice of amendment on the other party. Whether they can do this or not depends on whether the party wants to withdraw or amend the offer before the end of the relevant period or after the expiry of the relevant period.

Where the party wants to withdraw or amend the offer before the expiry of the relevant period

- If the offeror wants to amend the offer to make it more advantageous to the other party, they can do this, and a new relevant period would commence.
- If the offeror wants to withdraw the offer or amend it to make it less advantageous to the other party, then it depends on whether the other party accepts the original offer between receipt of the notice of withdrawal/notice of amendment and expiry of the relevant period.
  - If the other party accepts the original offer between receipt of the notice of withdrawal/notice of amendment and expiry of the relevant period, then the offeror needs the permission of the court to withdraw or amend the offer.
  - If the other party does not accept the original offer between receipt of the notice of withdrawal/notice of amendment and expiry of the relevant period, then the new offer or the withdrawal takes effect from the date of expiry of the original relevant period.

FUNDING OPTIONS

For SQE1, you need to understand the range of funding options that may be available to a client to pay for litigation. They are:
- conditional fee agreements;
- damages-based agreements;
- fixed fees;
- third-party funding.

For a detailed explanation of each of these funding options, see *Revise SQE: The Legal System and Services of England and Wales,* Chapter 8.

■ KEY POINT CHECKLIST

This chapter has covered the following key knowledge points. You can use these to structure your revision, ensuring you recall the key details for each point, as covered in this chapter.
- Decisions concerning costs are generally dealt with after the trial of the legal issues in the case has finished. The way in which the court deals with costs is generally determined by the track to which the claim has been allocated.
- Costs are either limited to fixed commencement costs, subject to summary assessment or subject to detailed assessment.
- In multi-track issues, parties are subjected to the costs budgeting regime.
- The court is also able to make inter-partes costs orders, non-party costs orders and security for costs orders.
- Qualified one-way costs shifting applies to personal injury claims only, and means that if the claimant is successful and the court also makes a costs order in their favour, the defendant will have to pay the claimant's costs on the basis ordered. Furthermore, if the defendant is successful in defending the claim, they will not be able to successfully recover their costs of doing so from the claimant.
- A Part 36 offer is designed to incentivise parties to make or accept offers to settle. In order to make a valid Part 36 offer, the offer must be in writing, it must be clear that it is made pursuant to Part 36, it must state whether it relates to the whole or part of the claim, it must state whether it includes any counterclaim, and it must state a relevant period.

■ KEY TERMS AND CONCEPTS

- costs (**page 154**)
- fixed commencement costs (**page 155**)
- summarily assessed (**page 155**)
- detailed assessment (**page 156**)
- costs budget (**page 157**)
- relevant period (**page 163**)

170 Costs and funding

■ SQE1-STYLE QUESTIONS

QUESTION 1

A claimant is bringing a small claim against a defendant for breach of contract, with the damages claimed being valued at £3,400. The claimant is successful in the action and seeks to recover their legal costs from the defendant.

Which of the following best describes the claimant's legal position?

A. The claimant will only be entitled to fixed commencement costs and third-party fees, such as court fees.
B. The claimant will only be entitled to fixed commencement costs.
C. The claimant will be entitled to their legal costs, which will be summarily assessed.
D. The claimant will be entitled to their legal costs, which will be subjected to detailed assessment.
E. The claimant will not be entitled to any of their costs as they are not recoverable in the small claims track.

QUESTION 2

A claimant is ordered to file and serve a costs budget no later than 4.00 p.m. on 3 June. They fail to do so, and instead send the defendant a copy of a costs budget three days before the trial is due to begin. The claimant is successful at trial and the defendant is ordered to pay the full value of the damages claimed.

Which of the following best describes the position on costs?

A. The claimant will be able to recover a small portion of their legal costs, reduced to reflect their failure to file and serve a costs budget.
B. The claimant will be able to recover all of their legal costs. Being successful in the action overall will override their failure to file and serve a costs budget.
C. The claimant will be limited to recovering court fees only.
D. The claimant will be limited to recovering fixed commencement costs and court fees only.
E. The claimant will not be able to recover anything at all due to their failure to comply with the relevant court direction.

QUESTION 3

A claimant commences proceedings against a defendant building company following allegedly negligent work being carried out on the claimant's property. The defendant company is run by a sole director and shareholder, who is also the sole employee. The claimant is successful in the action and is awarded the full damages claimed, and the defendant company is ordered to pay the claimant's costs on the standard basis. The claimant is concerned that the company may not be able to afford to pay the costs.

Which of the following best describes how the claimant should proceed?

A. The claimant should raise their concerns with the judge at trial and request that the costs order be made against the sole director, shareholder and employee of the defendant company.

B. The claimant should make an application for a security for costs order against the sole director, shareholder and employee, as the claimant has suspicions that they are going to attempt to avoid payment.

C. The claimant has been awarded a costs order against the defendant company and should therefore expect to receive payment imminently.

D. The claimant should make an application for a security for costs order against the defendant company as the claimant has suspicions that they are going to attempt to avoid payment.

E. The claimant should make an application for a non-party costs order against the sole director, shareholder and employee of the defendant company, as it is clear that he is both controlling the litigation and has a personal interest in the outcome.

QUESTION 4

A claimant commences proceedings against a defendant for damages relating to personal injury caused by the defendant's alleged negligent driving. At trial, the defendant successfully defends the claim on the basis that their driving did not fall below the standard reasonably expected, and therefore did not cause the claimant's injuries.

Which of the following best reflects the claimant's liability for the defendant's costs?

A. The general principle is that the loser pays the winner's costs, and therefore the claimant is likely to be ordered to pay the defendant's costs on the standard basis.

B. The general principle is that the loser pays the winner's costs, and therefore the claimant is likely to be ordered to pay the defendant's costs on the indemnity basis.

C. The claimant is unlikely to be ordered to pay the defendant's costs.

D. The claimant is likely to be ordered to pay the defendant's costs as their cause of action was defeated by the defendant at trial.

E. The claimant is likely to be ordered to pay the defendant's costs as they have brought the claim dishonestly.

QUESTION 5

A claimant makes a Part 36 offer to a defendant in the sum of £73,000. The relevant period expires on 1 April. The defendant does not respond to the offer and the claimant is successful in the action at trial on 16 November, but only recovers £64,000.

Which of the following best represents the likely position regarding the applicability of the Part 36 offer?

A. The Part 36 offer will not apply. The defendant did not respond to the offer, so it is not relevant.

B. The Part 36 offer will not apply. The claimant's failure to beat the offer at trial is not relevant.

C. The Part 36 offer will apply. The claimant is likely to be ordered to pay the defendant's costs on the standard basis from the date of expiry of the relevant period to the date of judgment.

D. The Part 36 offer will apply. The defendant is likely to be ordered to pay the claimant's costs on the standard basis from the date of expiry of the relevant period to the date of judgment as they failed to respond to the offer.

E. The Part 36 offer will apply. The claimant is likely to be ordered to pay the defendant's costs on the indemnity basis from the date of expiry of the relevant period to the date of judgment.

■ ANSWERS TO QUESTIONS

Answers to 'What do you know already?' questions at the start of the chapter

1) Costs in the fast track are generally dealt with by summary assessment, which means that the judge will make an instant decision on the day of the trial on how much to award.
2) False. The costs budget is merely an estimate; and although court approval of a previously submitted budget is one of the factors that the final trial judge has to take into consideration under CPR 44.4, they can depart from this if they feel it is appropriate.
3) The difference is that the court must consider the proportionality of the costs claimed when using the standard basis, whereas proportionality is not a consideration when costs are awarded on the indemnity basis. This generally means that costs awarded on the indemnity basis end up being considerably higher than those awarded on the standard basis.
4) Qualified one-way costs shifting applies to personal injury claims only. If the claimant is successful and the court also makes a costs order in their

favour, the defendant will have to pay the claimant's costs on the basis ordered. If the defendant is successful in defending the claim, they will not be able to successfully recover their costs of doing so from the claimant.

5) A Part 36 offer is a special type of offer that is designed to incentivise a party into making or accepting an offer to settle proceedings. Failure to accept a reasonable Part 36 offer can lead to significant consequences for the party who fails to accept it, in particular circumstances.

Answers to end-of-chapter SQE1-style questions

Question 1:
The correct answer was A. On the small claims track, the claimant is entitled to claim limited costs (making option E incorrect). However, they are only entitled to claim fixed commencement costs under the Civil Procedure Rules 1998 (CPR), as well as third-party fees such as court fees and experts' fees (making option B incorrect). The level of costs recoverable is fixed, and so is not assessed either summarily (making option C incorrect) or on a detailed basis (making option D incorrect).

Question 2:
The correct answer was C. The CPR make it clear that failure to file and serve a costs budget is a serious breach which will lead to a party being limited to recovering their court fees only (making option E incorrect). The fact that the party has been successful in the action overall is immaterial, making option B incorrect. Fixed commencement costs are only applicable in the small claims track, making option D incorrect. Option A is incorrect as the court would not arbitrarily reduce the recoverable costs in such a situation.

Question 3:
The correct answer was E. An application for a non-party costs order is appropriate where it is clear that there is an individual who is not named as party to proceedings who is controlling the litigation (which the sole director would be) and stands to benefit personally from defending the litigation successfully (which the sole shareholder would do). Security for costs would not be appropriate here, as such an application would be made before trial where there is a genuine reason to believe that the defendant company is taking steps to make it more difficult for the claimant to recover their costs from them once judgment has been given (making options B and D incorrect). The trial judge will not simply make a costs order against a non-party upon verbal request from the claimant, which makes option A incorrect, and the claimant believes that the defendant company will simply not pay the costs order, making option C incorrect.

Question 4:
The correct answer was C. Qualified one-way costs shifting applies here, which means that a claimant is protected from paying the defendant's costs in personal injury claims where the claim is not fundamentally

174 Costs and funding

dishonest (the claimant lost on the basis that they did not prove that the defendant drove negligently, which makes option E incorrect) and where the claim is brought using a proper cause of action (it has been brought under the tort of negligence, which is a proper cause of action, rendering option D incorrect). As qualified one-way costs shifting applies, the general principle on costs is overridden, making options A and B incorrect.

Question 5:
The correct answer was B. Where the claimant has made a Part 36 offer and been successful in the overall action, but failed to recover damages equal to or more than the amount in the offer, the Part 36 offer is disregarded (making options C, D and E incorrect) and the court will apply the usual rules on costs when deciding on an appropriate costs order to make. The defendant's failure to respond to the offer is also irrelevant (making option A incorrect).

■ KEY CASES, RULES, STATUTES AND INSTRUMENTS

The SQE1 Assessment Specification does not require you to know any case names or statutory materials for the topic of costs and funding. You must, however, be able to recall that the term 'Part 36' refers to Part 36 of the Civil Procedure Rules 1998 (CPR) and you must be familiar with the principle underlying Part 36.

Trial, appeals and enforcement of money judgments

■ MAKE SURE YOU KNOW

This chapter will cover the trial itself, how and where to appeal, if appropriate, and the various options for enforcing money judgments. It will cover the way in which witnesses can be summoned and how the Civil Procedure Rules 1998 (CPR) require parties to prepare for trial. We will also look at the destination, grounds and time limits for appeals and the methods of enforcing a money judgment if the claimant is successful. You are required to be able to apply these principles and rules appropriately and effectively to realistic client-based and ethical problems and situations for your SQE1 assessment.

■ SQE ASSESSMENT ADVICE

As you work through this chapter, remember to pay particular attention in your revision to:
- summoning witnesses for trial;
- preparations for trial, specifically pre-trial hearings, what to include in trial bundles and how a trial is conducted;
- destination of appeal, grounds for appeal and time limits for appeal;
- the various options that a claimant has to enforce money judgments.

■ WHAT DO YOU KNOW ALREADY?

Have a go at these questions before reading this chapter. If you find some difficult or cannot remember the answers, make a note to look more closely at that subtopic during your revision.

1) What, if anything, can a party do if they are concerned that a witness may not attend court?
   [Summoning witnesses, page 176]
2) What is the purpose of a pre-trial hearing?
   [Pre-trial checklists and hearings, page 177]
3) What are the grounds for appealing a judgment?
   [Grounds of appeal and permission to appeal, page 180]

4) In what circumstances would an application for an attachment of earnings order be appropriate to enforce a money judgment?
[Attachment of earnings orders, page 185]
5) True or false? The court will enforce a judgment given in a party's favour on its own motion.
[Enforcement of money judgments, page 182]

INTRODUCTION TO TRIALS, APPEALS AND ENFORCEMENT OF MONEY JUDGMENTS

Few claims actually reach trial as the majority settle at some point during the litigation process. However, you need to be aware of what happens to those claims that do reach trial, what needs to happen if there is a need to appeal against a decision taken at trial, and how a successful claimant party can proceed in the event that the defendant does not comply with the terms of an order made against them.

TRIALS

The SQE1 Assessment Specification states that, particularly relating to trials, you should know about summoning witnesses, pre-trial hearings, trial bundles and how a trial is conducted. Each of these will be considered in turn.

Summoning witnesses

Sometimes one of the parties may have concerns over whether a witness is going to attend court to give evidence. If this is the case, that party can apply to the court for a **witness summons**.

Key term: witness summons
A witness summons either requires a witness to attend court or to produce documents for the court's benefit. If the court accepts the application, they will serve the witness with a summons, alongside an offer for the party requiring the witness's attendance to pay that witness's expenses to attend court or compensation for loss of working time.

Exam warning
If a witness summons is served by the court but is not accompanied by an offer to compensate for expenses or lost time, the summons is invalid.

A witness summons must be served at least seven days before the court date. If the witness fails to attend, they could face a fine or even be held in contempt of court, which means that someone has unfairly influenced a court case (if the proceedings are being heard in the High Court).

Pre-trial checklists and hearings

As part of the court's general commitment to active case management, in fast track and multi-track trials (see **Chapter 7**) parties are required to complete and file a pre-trial checklist document. This is filed by all parties eight weeks prior to the trial date and provides the court with an overview of:
- whether the parties have complied with all of the directions issued by the court;
- whether there is a need for any additional last-minute directions;
- who will be giving oral, witness and expert evidence (for further discussion, see **Chapter 8**);
- whether any expert evidence is being relied upon, and if so whether there is more than one expert;
- whether the party themselves, a solicitor or a barrister will be presenting the case at trial;
- whether the time estimate for the trial (ie the number of days it is listed for) is still accurate.

Once the court has reviewed the checklist document, the judge will decide whether any further directions are necessary, or whether the matter requires listing for a **pre-trial review**.

Key term: pre-trial review
This is a specific hearing that takes place around 10 weeks prior to the trial in multi-track trials that are scheduled to take place over a number of days. The court will check that the parties have complied with all orders and directions, issue a direction for all parties to file a trial bundle, and set the **trial timetable**.

Key term: trial timetable
This is a detailed schedule for a trial that sets out time limits for each party to set out their case and for the examination and cross-examination of witnesses.

The parties will then proceed to prepare and file the trial bundle, which is considered below.

Trial bundles
A trial bundle is an indexed and paginated file of documents that contains all documents which are to be referred to by *any* party at trial. It is important to

note that there is only one trial bundle for the whole matter, so it essentially contains all documents on which every party to proceedings is seeking to rely. Generally, the contents of the bundle are agreed between the parties and are placed in order of the oldest documents first and the most recent documents at the bottom. Classes of documents are typically separated from one another for ease of reference; so, for example, sections could include the chronology (see **Chapter 5, page 74**) and skeleton arguments (see **Chapter 6, page 88**), witness statements for the claimant, witness statements for the defendant, correspondence, etc.

The claimant is responsible for preparing the trial bundle and must also make sufficient copies for the court, all parties and all witnesses (including experts). The claimant should also ensure that all original copies of the documents are available if needed during the trial.

The contents of the trial bundle are prescribed by the Civil Procedure Rules 1998 (CPR; see **Chapter 1**), and should include:
- the claim form and all statements of case (see **Chapter 5**);
- an agreed case summary/chronology of key events in the matter/skeleton arguments;
- any requests for further information and replies;
- any witness statements;
- any notices of intention to rely on hearsay evidence;
- experts' reports and any responses to questions raised with those experts;
- directions orders;
- any other necessary documents.

The claimant must ensure that the trial bundle is filed with the court no earlier than seven days before the trial but no later than three days before the trial.

Practice example 11.1 demonstrates how this could apply in practice.

Practice example 11.1

Nafisa is in the final stages of a claim against Blue Rock Limited over an alleged breach of contract, with the value of the damages claimed being £178,000. Blue Rock Limited write to Nafisa with a list of documents that they require to be included in the trial bundle. Nafisa writes back and tells Blue Rock Limited that they must prepare and file their own bundle and she will do hers. Is this correct?

No. Nafisa, as the claimant, must agree the contents of the trial bundle with Blue Rock Limited and deal with the preparation of the bundle, including making sufficient copies for the court, all parties and all witnesses. The trial bundle must contain all documents on which all parties are intending to rely in the trial.

How a trial is conducted

Table 11.1 sets out the stages of a typical civil trial, along with an explanation of each stage.

Table 11.1: Stages of a typical trial

Stage	Explanation
Opening speeches	Where the court permits it (which is rare as the judge will already have read the trial bundle), the claimant's representative may be allowed to give a brief opening speech outlining the facts and the outstanding issues in dispute.
Witnesses	The claimant and their witnesses will generally be called first. You will remember from **Chapter 8** that the witness statement stands as the witness's evidence-in-chief. Each witness will be subject to: • **examination-in-chief**; • **cross-examination**; • **re-examination**. For examination-in-chief, lawyers will generally only ask open and **non-leading questions**, with **leading questions** being reserved for cross-examination.
Closing speeches	Each party representative will then sum up their case. The defendant will go first, followed by the claimant.
Judgment	The judge will then either make their judgment immediately or (if the issue is complex) reserve judgment being made until a later date if they feel that they are unable to make a decision so quickly. Once judgment on the substantive issues has been given, the court will then turn its attention to the award that the claimant should receive (if the claimant has been successful in proving their cause of action), plus interest and costs (ie which party should pay the other's costs; see **Chapter 10**). If the defendant is successful, then the proceedings will come to an end and the judge will decide whether the claimant should make a contribution to the defendant's costs.

> **Key term: examination-in-chief**
>
> This is where the party who has called the witness questions them in support of the case that is being made.

180   Trial, appeals and enforcement of money judgments

> **Key term: cross-examination**
> This is where the opposition representative asks the witness a series of questions to try to highlight gaps or inconsistencies in the evidence given.

> **Key term: re-examination**
> This is where the witness is asked some follow-up questions by the party who has called the witness.

> **Key term: non-leading questions**
> These are open questions that do not lead the witness to an answer (eg *'What is your occupation?'*).

> **Key term: leading questions**
> These are closed questions that lead the witness to a particular answer (eg *'You're a solicitor, aren't you?'*).

Advocates must remember to address the judge correctly. For the correct modes of address, see **Revise SQE: The Legal System and Services of England and Wales**.

At the conclusion of the trial, it could be that a party feels very strongly that a wrong decision has been taken. In such circumstances, we now need to consider the rules relating to appeals.

APPEALS

SQE1 requires you to know three key areas relating to civil appeals. They are:
- grounds of appeal and permission to appeal;
- time limits to appeal;
- destination of appeal (ie which court to appeal to).

Each of these will be considered in turn.

Grounds of appeal and permission to appeal

There is not an automatic right to appeal a decision made by the court. Permission must be sought from the court by the party looking to make the appeal. Permission to appeal will only be granted where:
- the decision of the lower court was wrong, or;
- the decision was unjust because of a serious procedural or other irregularity in proceedings.

> **Exam warning**
>
> Permission to appeal will not be given where a party simply disagrees with the way in which a judge has exercised their discretion. They need to demonstrate that the judge made a serious mistake or that the court did not follow the proper procedural steps.

The test for whether permission is to be granted by the court is laid out in the CPR, which set out that the court must consider that:
- the appeal has a real prospect of success, or;
- there is some other compelling reason why the appeal should be heard.

Practice example 11.2 illustrates how appeals can work in practice.

> **Practice example 11.2**
>
> Neil is unsuccessful in a personal injury claim against Kimi in the final trial. The judge set out in the judgment that she found Neil's account to be unsatisfactory and Neil's witnesses inconsistent in their accounts of Kimi's alleged negligent driving. As a result, the judge did not find that Kimi was negligent. Neil would now like to appeal the judgment. Can he do this?
>
> No. Neil would only be able to appeal where the judgment was wrong or there had been a serious procedural irregularity that resulted in the judgment being unjust – neither of which has happened here. The witnesses for Neil have given inconsistent evidence (which is acknowledged), and the judgment therefore appears correct on the facts presented.

Time limits to appeal

An application for permission to appeal a decision must be made within *21 days* of the original decision if the decision was taken in the County Court or High Court, and *28 days* if the decision was taken in the Court of Appeal.

Destination of appeal

When considering which court will hear the appeal, you must consider the following:
- which court made the decision that is being appealed;
- which level of judge made the decision.

Table 11.2 sets out the correct destination depending on which court and which level of judge made the decision that is being appealed.

182 Trial, appeals and enforcement of money judgments

Table 11.2: Where to appeal

Where and by whom the appeal decision was made	Where to appeal
District Judge in the County Court	Circuit Judge in the County Court
Circuit Judge in the County Court	High Court Judge in the High Court
Master in the High Court	High Court Judge in the High Court
High Court Judge in the High Court	Court of Appeal

ENFORCEMENT OF MONEY JUDGMENTS

Enforcement is the process by which a successful claimant can recover the amount(s) due to them under a court order from a defendant who has failed to pay within the time specified by the court.

Revision tip

The court does not automatically enforce a judgment; it is for the claimant to apply to the court for an order forcing the defendant to pay.

For SQE1, you need to know about:
- oral examination;
- methods of enforcement;
- mechanisms of enforcement in other countries.

Each of these will be considered in turn.

Oral examination

The term 'oral examination' that appears on the SQE1 Assessment Specification is in fact now outdated. It is now referred to in the CPR as an 'order to obtain information'. Put simply, this is designed as a way for a claimant to work out whether it is worthwhile taking enforcement action, and if so what method of enforcement would be most suitable against the specific defendant.

The procedure involves the claimant completing a notice of application accompanied by the order, which is the subject of the enforcement and the amount owed. The defendant is then ordered to attend the court to be questioned, on oath, by a court officer. Examples of the information the court officer will ask the defendant to confirm are as follows:
- employment status and income;
- details of any property owned;
- details of any other assets of financial value (eg cars, other property);
- details of bank accounts and the amounts that are contained in them.

The information obtained will then be passed back to the claimant, who can make a decision on how to proceed.

Methods of enforcement

If the claimant decides to proceed with enforcement, they have several options open to them. This section will cover the following:
- taking control of goods orders;
- third-party debt orders;
- charging orders;
- attachment of earnings orders.

Taking control of goods orders

This type of order allows a defendant's goods or assets to be seized then sold at auction to pay the debt owed to the claimant. It is only suitable in circumstances where the defendant owns assets that are moveable and can therefore be picked up by an enforcement officer and sold off later. The claimant must apply to the correct court for either a writ of control (in the High Court) or a warrant of control (in the County Court). Once granted, an enforcement officer will take steps to attend the defendant's premises and seize goods.

The correct court to which the claimant should apply is as follows:
- For debts of up to £600, apply to the County Court.
- For debts of between £600 and £5,000, apply to either the County Court or the High Court.
- For debts of over £5,000, apply to the High Court.

Third-party debt orders

A third-party debt order is an order made against a third party, such as a bank or building society or a trade debtor (if the defendant is a company), to pay the debt owed by the defendant. For example, if the obtaining information stage reveals that the defendant has, in their sole name, savings of £11,500 and the amount owed to the claimant is £2,400, the court can order the bank in which the savings are held to pay the amount of the judgment to the claimant.

Exam warning

A third-party debt order can only be given where the source of the funds is owed to the defendant and the defendant alone. So, for example, if the defendant shares a bank account with a partner or spouse but the judgment debt is in their name alone, the court cannot make a third-party debt order in that instance as the defendant is not solely entitled to the money in that bank account.

Charging orders

A charging order effectively secures the amount of the judgment debt against land held by the defendant. If the claimant is granted a charging order, this means that when the defendant sells that particular asset, the judgment debt will be paid to the claimant out of the proceeds of sale.

There are three stages to securing payment for a judgment debt through a charging order:
- Interim charging order
  - The claimant files an application for charging order with supporting evidence and a draft interim charging order.
  - Provided that documentation is in order, a court officer will grant an interim charging order without a hearing.
  - The claimant must then serve the interim charging order, the application and any supporting evidence on the defendant within 21 days.
  - The defendant has 14 days to respond and request that the matter be referred for an in-person hearing. If the defendant does not respond, the court will automatically make a final charging order.
- Final charging order
  - If the defendant objects to the interim charging order and requests a hearing, they must file and serve a statement explaining their reasons for objection within 28 days of the date of the interim charging order.
  - The matter is then referred to a judge who will hold an in-person hearing where both parties will submit their arguments. The judge will then make a decision on whether to grant a final charging order or dismiss the interim charging order.
- Order for sale
  - If the claimant secures a final charging order, they can then make a further application for an order that forces the defendant to sell the property which has the final charge attached to it. If the court makes an order for sale, the defendant must sell the property, with the proceeds of sale being used to settle any charges against the title of the land in date order, earliest first.

Exam warning

Charging orders are only suitable where the land does not already have multiple charges registered against it. Charges are paid from the proceeds of sale in the order of the date they were registered (earliest first); so, if a piece of land already has two charges registered against it, they will be paid before the claimant's charge. It is imperative to check whether there is likely to be enough money left to pay the claimant once the other charges are settled. When obtaining information about the defendant's financial position, copies of the Land Registry titles to all pieces of land owned by the defendant either jointly or solely should be obtained, and the defendant should be asked to produce documentation showing the balance outstanding on each of those charges, as well as the value of the property itself. This is to avoid a situation where a charging order is obtained but the proceeds of sale are insufficient to cover the balance owed to the claimant.

Attachment of earnings orders

An attachment of earnings order is only available through the County Court and is only applicable where the defendant is employed (not self-employed). If granted, it requires the defendant's employer to pay a specific sum from the defendant's wages directly to the court, which then passes this on to the claimant in part satisfaction of the judgment debt until it is paid in full.

Consideration should be given by the claimant as to the security of the defendant's position before embarking on this route. If they are likely to lose their job at any point, payments will stop and the claimant will need to return to court to enforce the amount outstanding on the judgment.

Mechanisms of enforcement in other countries

If the defendant holds assets in a different country, enforcement is made more complicated. Various rules apply, and it would be for the claimant to check the specifics of the methods of enforcement in that particular country. The SQE1 requires you to know the basic procedure under CPR 74 in differing jurisdictions. This involves first registering the judgment with the country in which the defendant holds their assets, then using one of the country's local methods to enforce it. In this section, we will cover Scotland and Northern Ireland, the Commonwealth countries, and the EU.

Scotland and Northern Ireland

The procedure involves:
- obtaining a certificate of a High Court or a County Court money judgment;
- within six months of the date of issue of the certificate, the claimant must make an application to the foreign court to register the judgment;
- the judgment will then be registered in the jurisdiction and can be enforced using one of the methods allowed by either Scottish or Northern Irish law.

Commonwealth countries

Enforcing a judgment against one of the Commonwealth countries is governed by either the Administration of Justice Act 1920 (AJA 1920), for High Court judgments, or the Foreign Judgment (Reciprocal Enforcement) Act 1933 (FJ(RE)A 1933), for County Court judgments.

In order to be enforced in a Commonwealth country, the judgment must be:
- final (ie not subject to appeal);
- for a specific sum;
- registered within six months if using FJ(RE)A 1933;
- registered within 12 months if using AJA 1920.

If the above criteria are not complied with, then the claimant will lose the right to enforce against the defendant in the relevant Commonwealth country.

EU

Since the UK's withdrawal from the EU, the claimant will have to register the judgment with the relevant country and then enforce it using one of the methods available in that particular country.

■ KEY POINT CHECKLIST

This chapter has covered the following key knowledge points. You can use these to structure your revision, ensuring you recall the key details for each point, as covered in this chapter.

- If a party has concerns that a witness may fail to attend trial, they can apply to the court for a witness summons.
- In fast and multi-track cases, parties are required to complete and file a pre-trial checklist.
- A trial bundle is an indexed and paginated file of documents that contains all documents which are to be referred to by any party at the trial.
- The structure of a typical civil trial is opening speeches, witnesses, closing speeches, and judgment.
- There is not an automatic right to appeal a decision made by the court. Permission must be sought from the court by the party looking to make the appeal. Permission to appeal will only be granted where the decision of the lower court was wrong, or the decision was unjust because of a serious procedural or other irregularity in proceedings.
- An application for permission to appeal a decision must be made within *21 days* of the original decision if the decision was taken in the County Court or High Court, and *28 days* if the decision was taken in the Court of Appeal.
- The court does not automatically enforce a judgment; it is for the claimant to apply to the court for an order forcing the defendant to pay.
- There are various methods of enforcement, including taking control of goods orders, third-party debt orders, charging orders and attachment of earnings orders.
- If the defendant holds assets in a different country, enforcement involves first registering the judgment with the country in which the defendant holds their assets, then using one of that country's local methods to enforce it.

■ KEY TERMS AND CONCEPTS

- witness summons (**page 176**)
- pre-trial review (**page 177**)
- trial timetable (**page 177**)
- examination-in-chief (**page 179**)
- cross-examination (**page 180**)
- re-examination (**page 180**)
- non-leading questions (**page 180**)
- leading questions (**page 180**)

■ SQE1-STYLE QUESTIONS

QUESTION 1

A claimant is bringing a small claim against a defendant for breach of contract, with the damages claimed being valued at £44,000. The claimant has obtained a witness statement from a key witness but is aware of a rumour that the witness is not going to attend trial.

Which of the following best describes the claimant's position?

A. The claimant should apply to the court for a witness summons with an offer to pay the witness's expenses for attending trial and to reimburse them for any money lost for missing work.

B. The claimant should apply to the court for a witness summons, which will require the witness to attend court. If the witness claims lost expenses after the trial, the claimant should reimburse the witness for those.

C. The claimant should apply to the court for a witness summons, which will require the witness to attend court. If the witness claims lost expenses after the trial, the claimant is under no obligation to reimburse them.

D. The claimant should apply to the court for a witness summons, which will require the witness to attend court. If the witness does not attend, the claimant cannot do anything about this.

E. The claimant should apply to the court for a witness summons, which will require the witness to attend court. If the witness does not attend, the witness could face penalties for failing to do so.

QUESTION 2

A trial is listed to take place between a claimant and a defendant in 21 days. The claimant has prepared all of the documentation on which they intend to rely at trial for the trial bundle.

Which of the following best describes what the claimant should do next?

A. The claimant should incorporate all documents on which they intend to rely at trial into a trial bundle and file the bundle with the court no later than three days and no earlier than seven days before the trial.

B. The claimant should contact the defendant to agree which documents the defendant would like included in the trial bundle, incorporate them into the bundle, and file the bundle with the court immediately.

C. The claimant should incorporate all documents on which they intend to rely at trial into a trial bundle and file the bundle with the court immediately.

188 Trial, appeals and enforcement of money judgments

D. The claimant should contact the defendant to agree which documents the defendant would like included in the trial bundle, incorporate them into the bundle, and file the bundle with the court no later than seven days before the trial.

E. The claimant should contact the defendant to agree which documents the defendant would like included in the trial bundle, incorporate them into the bundle, and file the bundle with the court no later than three days and no earlier than seven days before the trial.

QUESTION 3

A claimant is unsuccessful in their claim against a defendant in the County Court. The matter was heard by a District Judge. The claimant disagrees with the decision made by the trial judge and wishes to appeal it.

Which of the following best describes how the claimant should proceed?

A. The claimant should appeal to the High Court to be heard by a District Judge within 21 days of the date of the judgment.

B. The claimant should appeal to the County Court to be heard by a Circuit Judge within 21 days of the date of the judgment.

C. The claimant should appeal to the High Court to be heard by a High Court Judge within 28 days of the date of the judgment.

D. The claimant should appeal to the County Court to be heard by a Circuit Judge within 28 days of the date of the judgment.

E. The claimant should appeal to the County Court to be heard by a High Court Judge within 21 days of the date of the judgment.

QUESTION 4

A claimant is successful in a breach of contract claim against a self-employed defendant valued at £4,000. The defendant fails to settle the judgment debt within the time frame ordered by the court. Following an order to obtain information, the defendant discloses that they own property worth £140,000, which has a single charge with £25,000 outstanding on it, and two bank accounts in their sole name – one containing £6,750 and the other containing £500.

Which of the following is the best way for the claimant to proceed with enforcing the debt?

A. The claimant should apply for an attachment of earnings order.

B. The claimant should apply for a third-party debt order against the defendant's two bank accounts.

C. The claimant should apply for a third-party debt order against the defendant's bank account that contains £6,750.

D. The claimant should apply for a charging order against the defendant's property.
E. The claimant should apply for a taking control of goods order.

QUESTION 5

A claimant company is successful in a breach of contract claim against a defendant in the sum of £68,000. The defendant fails to settle the judgment debt within the time frame ordered by the court.

Which of the following represents the best way for the claimant company to proceed?

A. The claimant company should write to the defendant demanding payment from the defendant within 14 days, failing which an application for a taking control of goods order should be made to the court.
B. The claimant company should write to the defendant requesting details of the defendant's assets, income and liabilities.
C. The claimant company should make an application to the court for an order to obtain information from the defendant.
D. The claimant company should write to the defendant demanding payment from the defendant within 14 days, failing which an application for an attachment of earnings order should be made to the court.
E. The claimant company should write to the defendant demanding that the defendant provides details of their assets, income and liabilities within 14 days, failing which an application for a taking control of goods order should be made to the court.

■ ANSWERS TO QUESTIONS

Answers to 'What do you know already?' questions at the start of the chapter

1) A party who is concerned that a witness will not attend trial can make an application to the court for the witness to be summoned. This means that they must attend trial and will face penalties if they fail to do so.
2) A pre-trial hearing is an opportunity for the court to consider whether the matter is ready for trial, to ensure that all of the relevant directions have been complied with, and to check whether any additional directions are necessary.
3) The only grounds for appealing a judgment are either that the decision of the lower court was wrong or the decision was unjust because of a serious procedural or other irregularity in proceedings.

4) An application for an attachment of earning order would be suitable where the defendant is in employment and there is no imminent risk that they will lose their job.
5) False. A party must make a separate application to enforce the terms of a judgment.

Answers to end-of-chapter SQE1-style questions

Question 1:
The correct answer was A. An application for a witness summons will not be valid unless it is accompanied by an offer from the claimant to reimburse the witness for their expenses for attending trial and for any money lost due to work being missed. The witness would not make a standalone claim for expenses, making options B and C incorrect. If the witness does not attend, then they could face penalties (making option D incorrect); but without an accompanying offer to reimburse the witness, the application would not be valid anyway, which makes option E incorrect.

Question 2:
The correct answer was E. The claimant is responsible for filing an agreed trial bundle containing all parties' evidence within three and seven days before the trial (making options B, C and D incorrect). The claimant cannot simply file a bundle with just their own evidence (making option A incorrect).

Question 3:
The correct answer was B. The original judgment was made by a District Judge in the County Court, which means that any appeal will go to a Circuit Judge in the County Court (making options A, C and E incorrect). As the hearing took place in the County Court, the relevant time limit for appeal is 21 days, therefore making option D incorrect.

Question 4:
The correct answer was C. The best way for the claimant to proceed here is to apply for a third-party debt order specifying the account that has £6,750 in it (as this is enough to clear the judgment debt against the defendant). This makes option B incorrect. Although the claimant could apply for a charging order, and there is sufficient equity in the property to mean that the claimant could be repaid, it would be much simpler and quicker to apply for a third-party debt order in this case (making option D incorrect). The defendant is self-employed, meaning that an attachment of earnings order could not be made, making option A incorrect. A taking control of goods order would not be the best option as we are not told anything about the value of the defendant's goods, making option E incorrect.

Question 5:
The correct answer was C. The claimant company should make an application to the court for an order to obtain information, following

which the claimant company will be in a much better position to assess which method of enforcement is the most appropriate. Although the claimant company could write to the defendant to ask for this information, it is best for the court to obtain the details from the defendant, making option B incorrect. We are given no details about the nature of the defendant's employment status or assets, therefore making options A, D and E incorrect.

■ KEY CASES, RULES, STATUTES AND INSTRUMENTS

The SQE1 Assessment Specification does not require you to know any case names or statutory materials for the topic of trial, appeals and enforcement of money judgments.

Index

absolute defence, limitation period 23, 24, 33, 34
acknowledgment of service 53, 54, 56, 57–8, 59, 63–4, 67, 93
adding/removing/substituting parties 36, 45–7, 51
Administrative Court 38
Admiralty Court 38
admissible evidence 121–9, 132–3, 134–7
admission form 55–6, 63, 65, 68, 76, 81, 83, 84, 93–4
admit claim/liability 53, 54, 55–6, 63, 65, 67, 68–9, 76, 81, 83, 84, 93–4, 99, 101
adverse costs order 1, 2, 4–5, 14–15, 16, 18, 19
aggravated (additional) damages 73, 80, 167
alternative dispute resolution (ADR) 1–10, 13, 14–15, 18–19, 21–2, 25, 27–9, 34; advantages/disadvantages 6, 8–10, 16, 18–19, 21–2; costs 3, 4–5, 6, 7; Halsey-justified-refusal considerations 3–4; limitation period extensions 25; reasonable-refusal circumstances 3–4, 5, 13, 14–16, 18–19; sanctions/penalties 1, 2–3, 4–5, 14–16, 18–19, 29–30; without prejudice (confidential) aspects 2, 6, 143, *see also* adverse costs order; arbitration; mediation
appeals 9, 11–12, 14, 17, 18, 19, 175–6, 180–2, 186, 188, 190; arbitration 9, 17, 18, 19; destination of appeal 175, 180, 181–2; grounds 175, 180–1, 186, 189; permission (leave) to appeal 11–12, 180–1, 186; time limits 175, 180, 181–2, 186, 188, 190
applications 45–6, 51, 58–61, 64, 66–7, 68–9, 86–102
appropriate place of service, claim form 41–2, 48–9, 51–2
arbitration 1–3, 4, 7–10, 14–15, 17, 18–19
assessed costs 29, 30, 62, 64, 153–4, 155–69, 172–4, 179
attachment-of-earnings enforcement orders 176, 183, 185, 186, 190

bankruptcy/company searches 26, 46
breach of contract 4–5, 30–7, 48–52, 73–8, 89–90, 97–8, 115, 133–7, 147–8, 170, 187–90
breach of duty element of negligence 24, 75
budgets, costs 112, 153–4, 157–8, 160, 169, 170, 172, 173
burden of proof 77, 81, 84, 106, 121–2, 132–3, 136

capacity issues 26, 32–3, 34, 74, 77
case management conferences (CMCs) 103–4, 110, 112, 115, 116–17, 119
case management litigation stage 11, 14, 103–20, 140–1, 157–8, 177; extension to deadlines 113–14, 118, 120; non-compliance with directions 11, 103–4, 105, 113–14, 118, 120; overriding objective of litigation 103–7, 112, 114–15, 118, 119–20, 135, 137, 141; procedural steps and timetables 103–7, 109–14, 118, 120, 141, 157, 177–8, 186; proportionality requirements

Index

105-6, 114, 115, 119, 141, 151; sanctions/penalties 103-4, 113-14, 118, 120; time limits 111-14, 141, 157-8; track allocation 103-5, 107-12, 114-15, 116, 117, 119-20, 141, 157-8; unrepresented parties 109, 111
Chancery Division of the High Court 37-8
charges, land 184, 190
charging enforcement orders 183-4, 186, 190
Circuit Judges 182, 188, 190
civil court process 2, 4, 6, 8, 10-15, 35-52
claim amounts, commencement litigation stage 35, 36-9, 47, 48, 51, 72-5, 80, 83-4; interest payments 4, 29, 59, 72-5, 80, 83-4, 93, 108, 113, 166-9, 179-80; track allocation criteria 109-10, 116, 117, 119-20, 141
claim form 14, 23, 35-6, 39-52, 54, 57-60, 63-4, 68, 70-3, 79-84, 178; adding/removing/substituting parties 45-7, 51; appropriate place of service 41-2, 48-9, 51-2; contents' list 39-40, 70, 71-3, 178; day-count CPR rules 42-4; deemed dates of service 35, 43-5, 47, 49, 52; definition 14, 36, 39-40, 47, 51-2, 54, 70-3, 79; outside jurisdictions 36, 46-7, 50-2, 57-8; sealing the claim form 39, 47; service methods/requirements 35-6, 39-45, 47, 48-9, 51-2, 72; time limits 35, 39-40, 42-5, 46-7, 50, 51, 52, 54, 60
claim number 39, 47, 77
claimant, adding/removing/substituting parties 36, 45-7, 51; admit the claim 55-6; case management 104-20; definition 11, 14, 22, 26, 39, 71-3; discontinuance of a claim 53, 54, 61-4, 68; enforcement 9, 11, 12, 14, 63, 175-6, 182-6, 188, 190; financial circumstances of the parties 22, 26; identification needs 22, 26, 71-5; interim applications 86-102, 106; judgment in default 53-4, 57, 58-61, 64, 66-7, 68-9; jurisdiction and governing law 20, 22-3, 32, 33, 34, 35-9, 46-7, 50-2, 57-8, 185-6; letters between claimant and defendant 27-8, 32, 34, 36, 41-5, 47, 49, 51, 52, 72-3, 79, 83; offers from the defendant 56, 59, 63, 65, 68, 143, 148-9, 151, 163-9, 173; offers to the defendant 163-9, 172, 173, 174; other additional claims 78-80; Part 36 offers 153-4, 162, 163-9, 172, 174; reply to defence 77, 79; security for costs orders 153, 158, 161-2, 169; settlement of a claim 59, 61, 62-4, 67, 69, 163-9; summary judgment 59, 64, 86-7, 90-3, 96-9, 101, 106; trial bundle 175, 177-9, 186, 187-8, 190
clinical disputes 27
closing speeches stage of a trial 179-80, 186
commencement litigation stage, adding/removing/substituting parties 36, 45-7, 51; claim amounts 35, 36-9, 47, 48, 51, 72-5, 80, 83-4; court selection 35, 36-9, 48, 51, 72, 75, 77; deemed dates of service 35-6, 39-45, 47, 49, 52, 69; definition 14, 35-47, 51-2, 70-3, 79, 83; outside jurisdictions 36, 46-7, 50-2, 57-8; time limits 35, 39-40, 42-5, 46-7, 50, 51, 52, 57-8, *see also* claim form; particulars of claim
Commercial Court 38
Commonwealth country enforcement mechanisms 185
companies registered in England and Wales, claim forms 40, 42, 44, 71
compliance with case management directions 11, 103-4, 105, 112, 113-14, 140
conditional fee funding agreement 153, 169
conditional orders, summary judgment 92, 101

Index 195

confidential schedule, Tomlin order 62-3, 67, 69
consent order 62-3, 64, 69
contempt of court 177
contract law 4-5, 30-7, 48-52, 73-8, 89-90, 97-8, 115, 133-7, 147-8, 170, 187-90; jurisdiction and governing law 22-4, 29, 32, 33, 34, 50-2; limitation period 24, 30, 33-4
contributory negligence 37, 108, 122
copies of documents 139, 141, 146
corporations incorporated in England and Wales, claim forms 40, 42
costs 1-19, 28-30, 61-4, 78, 90-9, 101, 105-8, 112-13, 141, 153-74, 179-80; adverse costs order 1, 2, 4-5, 14-15, 16, 18, 19; alternative dispute resolution (ADR) 3, 4-5, 6, 7; arbitration 9; assessed costs 29, 30, 62, 64, 153-4, 155-69, 172-4, 179; budgets 112, 153-4, 157-8, 160, 169, 170, 172, 173; definition 11, 13, 29, 30, 62, 64, 92, 94-5, 153-69, 172-4, 179-80; discontinuance of a claim 62; fixed commencement costs 153-4, 155-7, 169, 170, 173; indemnity basis assessment method 29, 30, 154, 158-60, 167, 172; interim applications 92, 94-5, 154; multi-track allocation 155-7, 160-1, 169; non-party costs orders 153, 158, 161, 169, 171, 173; orders 1-5, 14-19, 92-5, 98-101, 113, 118-20, 153, 158-62, 169, 171-3; Part 36 offers 153-4, 162, 163-9, 172, 174; proportionate/reasonable requirements 157-8, 159-61, 172; security for costs orders 153, 158, 161-2, 169; standard basis assessment method 62, 64, 154, 158-61, 164-7, 172; summary judgment 92, 98-9, 101; track allocation 153-7, 160-1, 169, 170, 172, 173; types 11, 13, 28, 62-3, 153-69, 172-4
Costs judges 156
counterclaims 27, 37, 47, 55-7, 63, 70, 77-83, 84, 108, 122, 136, 163, 169;

defence 79; definition 37, 47, 55-7, 63, 77-8, 80, 83, 84, 122, 136; time limits 57, 78-9, 82, 84, see also Part 20 CPR claim
County Court 35-7, 39, 47, 48, 51, 72, 75, 101, 182-6, 188, 190
Court of Appeal 3, 182, 186
court fees 11, 13, 154-6, 158, 170, 173
court records 11, 58-9
court selection 35-9, 48, 51, 72, 75, 77, 103-12, 114-15, 117, 119-20
cross-examination of witnesses 8, 126-7, 129, 131, 132, 179-80, 186

damages, definition 72-5, 79-80, 179-80
damages-based funding agreement 153, 169
date of judgment, Part 36 offers 166-7
day-count CPR rules, documents 42-4, 69
deemed dates of service 35, 43-5, 47, 49, 52, 62, 69
defamation 27
defence form 55, 57-8, 76, 77, 107
defendant, acknowledgment of service 53, 54, 56, 57-8, 59, 63-4, 67, 93; admission form 55-6, 63, 65, 68, 76, 81, 83, 84, 93-4; admit claim/liability 53, 54, 55-6, 63, 65, 67, 68-9, 76, 81, 83, 84, 93-4, 99, 101; case management 104-20; counterclaims 27, 37, 47, 55, 57, 63, 70, 77-83, 84, 108, 122, 136, 163, 169; definition 11, 14, 22, 26, 39, 54, 72-3, 76-7; denial of the allegations 76-80, 81, 83, 84, 98, 101, 122, 136; disputing the court's jurisdiction 57-8; enforcement 9, 11, 12, 14, 63, 175-6, 182-6, 188, 190; filing a counterclaim 57, 63, 77-81, 82-3, 84, 108, 122, 136; filing a defence 53, 54, 57, 58, 59, 63-4, 66, 67, 68, 76-81, 84, 90, 98, 104-5, 107; financial circumstances of the parties 22, 26; identification needs 22, 26, 51, 71-5; ignoring the claim

196 Index

53–4, 57, 58–61, 63, 64, 67; interim applications 86–102, 106; interim payments 86, 93–4, 97, 99, 101; jurisdiction and governing law 20, 22–3, 32, 33, 34, 35–9, 46–7, 50–2, 53, 57–8, 185–6; letters between claimant and defendant 27–8, 32, 34, 36, 41–5, 47, 49, 51, 52, 72–3, 79, 83; non-admission 76, 80, 81, 83, 84; offers from the claimant 163–9, 172, 173, 174; offers to the claimant 56, 59, 63, 65, 68, 143, 148–9, 151, 163–9, 173; oral examination (order to obtain information) 182–3, 188, 189, 190–1; other additional claims 78–80; Part 36 offers 153–4, 162, 163–9, 172, 174; response pack 55–8, 65, 68, 76, 77, 107; security for costs orders 153, 158, 161–2, 169; set aside the judgment in default 53–4, 58, 59–61, 64, 66–7, 68–9; settlement of a claim 59, 61, 62–4, 67, 69, 163–9; summary judgment 59, 64, 86–7, 90–3, 96–9, 101, 106, *see also* claim form; trial
defending litigation stage 14, 27, 53–4, 63–4, 71, 76–84, *see also* defendant; responding
denial of the allegations 76–80, 81, 83, 84, 98, 101, 122, 136
destination of appeal 175, 180, 181–2
detailed assessment of costs 155–6, 169
directions 11, 87, 103–5, 107–8, 111–12, 114–15, 140–1, 157–8, 178, 189; non-compliance with case management directions 11, 103–4, 105, 113–14, 118, 120; questionnaire 107–8, 111–12, 157–8; track allocation 110–17, 119, 130–1, 136, 141, 146, 150, 157, 160–1, 177
disallowed evidence sanction 113
disclosure 5–17, 27, 28–9, 107, 111–12, 115, 138–52; control issues 139, 141–2, 146, 150; definition 11, 12, 14, 27, 28–9, 107, 111–12, 115, 138–47, 150–2; mediation 5–6, 7; non-party order for disclosure 138, 145–6, 147, 149, 151–2; obligations to disclose 139–42; orders for disclosure 12, 28–9, 138–9, 140–1, 144–7, 150–1; pre-action order for disclosure 12, 28–9, 138–9, 145, 147, 151; procedures, orders and rules 144–7, 149–52; time limits 111–12, 116–17, 119, 141; track allocation 111–12, 138, 140–1, 146, 150, *see also* documents; evidence; inspection
discontinuance of a claim 53, 54, 61–2, 64, 68
discretionary grounds to set aside the judgment in default 59, 60–1, 66–7, 68–9
dismissal orders, summary judgment 92, 106
disposal hearing 55–6, 63
dispute resolution options 1–15, 18–19, 27, *see also* alternative dispute resolution; litigation
disputing the court's jurisdiction 57–8
District Judges 109, 156, 182, 188, 190
Document Exchange 41, 47
documents 11, 12, 14, 27–9, 87–9, 96, 107, 111–12, 115, 138–52, 175–9, 186; copies 139, 141, 146; deemed dates of service 35, 43–5, 47, 49, 52, 62, 69; definition 139, 146–7; duty to search documents 138, 139, 144–5, 146, 147, 150, 151; privileged documents 138, 142–4, 147, 149, 151, 163; service methods/requirements 35–6, 39–45, 47, 48–9, 51–2, 69, 72; trial bundle 175, 177–9, 186, 187–8, 190, *see also* claim form; disclosure; inspection; particulars of claim
draft order 87–8, 96, 97, 101
duty of care 24, 75
duty to search documents 138, 139, 144–5, 146, 147, 150, 151

early neutral evaluation 2
electronic disclosure (e-disclosure) 138, 139, 144, 146
emails 41, 44, 139, 146

Index 197

employer's liability 26, 28
enforcement 9, 11, 12, 14, 63, 175-6, 182-6, 188, 190; methods 175, 182, 183-6, 188, 190; oral examination (order to obtain information) 182-3, 188, 189, 190-1; in other countries 185-6
ethics vi, 1, 20, 35, 53, 70, 86, 103, 121, 138, 153, 175
EU 20, 22-3, 34, 46-7, 50-2, 186
evidence 108-9, 115, 119, 121-33, 134-7, 175-91; disallowed evidence sanction 113; interim applications 86-97, 101; relevance 121-3, 136-7; strict rules of evidence 109; summary judgment 90-3, 96; types 108, 115, 119, 121-33, 136-7
examination-in-chief, definition 179-80, 186
exemplary (punitive) damages 73, 80
expenses 62, 64, 154-7, 158-61, 164-7, 172, 176-7, 187, 190
experts 11, 13, 28, 129-33, 136, 154-5, 173-8; fees 11, 13, 28, 154-5, 173; multiple experts 131-2; permission of the court 129, 131, 132; single joint expert 28, 121-2, 129-31, 132, 133, 136; time limits 111-12, 141
extensions to time periods 24-5, 33, 113-14, 118, 120

Family Division of the High Court 37
fast track allocation 103-11, 114-20, 130, 136, 138, 150, 153, 155-7, 172, 177, 186; costs 153, 155-7, 172; directions 110-11, 114, 130, 136, 141, 150, 177; disclosure approach 111, 141, 150
fax 41, 44, 47
fees 11, 13, 18, 28, 61, 62, 64, 104-5, 154-7, 170, 173
file a document, definition 11, 14, 39
financial circumstances of the parties 22, 26
fixed commencement costs 153-4, 155-7, 169, 170, 173

fixed fees funding agreement 153, 169
freezing interim injunctions 86, 89, 96, 99-100, 101-2
funding options 153, 169

grounds of appeal 175, 180-1, 186, 189

Halsey-justified refusal considerations for ADR 3-4
hearsay evidence 121-2, 123, 125-7, 132-3, 135-7, 178
High Court 9, 17, 19, 35, 36-9, 47, 75, 88, 101, 177, 182-3, 185-6; structure 37-9, *see also* Chancery Division; Queen's Bench Division
High Court Judges 182

ignoring the claim, judgment in default 53-4, 57, 58-61, 63, 64, 67
indemnity basis method of assessing costs 29, 30, 154, 158-60, 167, 172
injunctions 86-7, 89, 94-6, 99-100, 101-2
Insolvency and Companies Court 38
inspection 107, 111-12, 115, 138-52; privileged documents 138, 142-4, 147, 149, 151; procedures, orders and rules 144-7; time limits 111-12, 141, *see also* disclosure; documents; evidence
instalment figures/time-periods, admit the claim 55, 69
Intellectual Property Enterprise Court 38
inter-partes costs orders 153, 158-9, 169
interest payments 4, 29, 59, 72-5, 80, 83-4, 93, 108, 113, 166-9, 179-80
interim applications 86-102, 106, 144-6, 154; costs 92, 94-5, 154; documents 87-9, 91, 96; draft order 87-8, 96, 97, 101; N244 form 87, 89, 91, 94, 144-6; with notice interim applications 88-9, 95, 96-7; procedures 87-9, 96, 97, 101, 144; set aside the interim application order 89, 95; skeleton

argument 88, 96–7, 101, 178; without notice interim applications 88–9, 95, 96–7, 99–100, 101–2
interim certificates 156–7
interim charging orders 184
interim injunctions 86–7, 89, 94–6, 99–100, 101–2
interim payments 86, 93–4, 97, 99, 101
'issue protectively' circumstances, limitation period extensions 25
issuing proceedings 37, 39, 43, 44, 47

joinder of parties 35, 45–7, 51
judges 104–12, 118–20, 156, 179–82; destination of appeals 181–2; modes of address 180; stages of a trial 179–80
judgment in default 53–4, 57, 58–61, 64, 66–7, 68–9
judgment stage of a trial 179–80
judicial precedent 12, 88
judicial review 27
jurisdiction and governing law 20, 22–3, 29, 32, 33, 34–9, 46–7, 50–3, 57–8, 185–6; commencement in outside jurisdictions 36, 46–7, 50–2, 57–8; disputing the court's jurisdiction 57–8; enforcement in other countries 185–6

land law 22, 38, 109, 183–4
landlords, tenants 109
last-resort guidelines of litigation 2, 10, 14, 18, 19
latent damage cases 24, 25, 30, 33
leading questions 179–80, 186
leave (permission) to appeal *see* permission (leave) to appeal
leaving the claim form at a specified place 41
legal advice privilege 142–3, 147
legal authorities 88
legal cause of action 22–4, 26–8, 30, 35, 46, 49–52, 75, 77, 79, 112, 122

letters between claimant and defendant 27–8, 32, 34, 36, 41–5, 47, 49, 51, 52, 72–3, 79, 83
liability, definition 14
limitation date 20, 22, 23–6, 29–31, 33–4, 36, 39, 45–6
limitation period 20, 22, 23–6, 29–31, 33–4, 36, 39, 45–6, 49
limited liability partnerships 42
listed, definition 11, 13
litigation 1–6, 10–15, 18, 35–47, 51–2, 62–9, 103–7, 118–20; advantages 12; adversarial aspects 6, 13; backlogs 13; binding aspects 2, 12; costs 9, 10, 11, 13, 14, 18, 28–9, 61–3, 78, 90, 92, 105–8, 112–13, 141; definition 1–2, 10–15, 18, 35–47, 51–2, 103–5, 118–20; disadvantages 6, 8, 10, 12, 13, 18; judicial precedent 12, 88; key terms 10–11; last-resort guidelines 2, 10, 14, 18, 19; need for solicitors/barristers 13; stages' overview 10–11, 13–15, 35–6, 103–7, *see also* appeals; case management; commencement; costs; defending; enforcement; interim applications; pre-action; responding; *separate Table of statutes*; trial
litigation friend 26, 30, 33, 34, 74, 75, 77
litigation privilege 142–3, 147

mandatory grounds to set aside the judgment in default 59–60, 67
Master in the High Court 182
mediation 1–2, 4–7, 8, 9, 10, 14–17, 18–19
Mercantile Court 38
minors 26, 32–3, 34
multi-track allocation 103–7, 110–19, 130–1, 141, 146, 155–7, 160–1, 169, 177, 186; costs 155–7, 160–1, 169, 177; directions 110, 112, 114, 116–17, 119, 130–1, 141, 146, 157, 160–1, 177; disclosure approach 112, 141, 146
multiple hearsay evidence 126, 133

N1 form *see* claim form
N244 form, interim applications 87, 89, 91, 94, 144–6
N265 form, disclosure and inspection process 144
negligence, contributory negligence 37, 108, 122; definition 24, 75
'no other compelling reason' criteria, summary judgment 91, 96, 98, 101
'no real prospect' criteria, summary judgment 91–2, 96
non-admission 76, 80, 81, 83, 84
non-compliance with case management directions 11, 103–4, 105, 113–14, 118, 120
non-leading questions 179–80, 186
non-party costs orders 153, 158, 161, 169, 171, 173
non-party order for disclosure 138, 145–6, 147, 149, 151–2
notice of acceptance 164–5
notice of application 182, 189, 190–1
notice of commencement 156–7
notice to attack credibility document 126, 127, 133

oath 129, 133, 182
offers, from the claimant 163–9; from the defendant 56, 59, 63, 65, 68, 143, 148–9, 151, 163–9
opening speeches stage of a trial 179–80, 186
opinion evidence 121, 123–4, 132–3, 134, 136
options for dispute resolution 1–15, 18–19, 27
oral evidence 108, 115, 119, 126–7, 129, 177–80
oral examination (order to obtain information) 182–3, 188, 189, 190–1
order for sale 184
orders for costs 1–5, 14–19, 92–5, 98–101, 113, 118–20, 153, 158–62, 169, 171–3
orders for disclosure 12, 28–9, 138–9, 140–1, 144–7, 150–1

other additional claims 78–80
the other side, definition 11
overriding objective of litigation 103–7, 112, 114–15, 118, 119–20, 135, 137, 141

Part 20 CPR claim 70–1, 77–80, 81, 84–5, 108, 122
Part 36 offers 153–4, 162, 163–9, 172, 173, 174
particulars of claim 36, 39–40, 47, 54, 60, 63–4, 68, 70–2, 73–5, 76–84; adding/removing/substituting parties 45–6; content' list 39, 73–5, 79–80, 83–4; contract law 73–4; deemed dates of service 35, 43–4, 47, 69; definition 36, 39–40, 47, 54, 70–1, 72, 73–5, 79, 83; time limits 43, 46–7, 54, 58, 60; tort law 73, 75
partnerships 38, 40, 42, 48–9, 51–2, 71
Patents Court 38
payment-in-court sanction 113
permission (leave) to appeal 11–12, 175, 180–1, 186
personal injury cases 24–8, 31–4, 37, 93, 109, 134–5, 153–4, 162, 169, 171–4, 181; claim amounts 37, 93, 109; limitation period extensions 25; qualified one-way costs shifting 153–4, 162, 169, 172–4
personal service of documents 40, 44, 47, 48–9, 51–2
phone calls 36, 51
photographs 139
position statements, mediation 5–6
post-trial litigation stage, definition 14, 186
postal service 27–8, 32, 34, 36, 41–5, 47, 49, 51, 52, 69, 72–3
Practice Direction 10–11, 13, 20, 21, 26–30, 73, 103, 105, 141, 145, 150
Practice Direction on Pre-Action Conduct and Protocols (PDPACP) 20, 21, 26–7, 28–30, 33, 34, 145; definition 21, 26–7, 28–30, 33, 145; guidance-only aspects 21, 28, 33, 145; key requirements 28–9, 34, 145

pre-action conduct litigation stage 12, 13, 17, 20-1, 26-30, 34, 138, 145, 151
pre-action order for disclosure 12, 28-9, 138-9, 145, 147, 151
pre-action protocols 27-30, 33, 34
pre-trial checklist 111-12, 175-6, 177-8, 186
pre-trial hearings 111-12, 175-6, 177-8, 186, 189
pre-trial review 112, 175, 177-8, 186
privileged documents 138, 142-4, 147, 149, 151, 163
probate 38
procedural steps and timetables 103-5, 106-7, 109-12, 113-14, 118, 120, 141, 157, 177-8, 186
proceedings, definition 11
proportionality requirements 28-9, 105-6, 114, 115, 119, 137, 141, 151, 157-61, 172
public interest 37

qualified one-way costs shifting 153-4, 162, 169, 172-4
quantum definition 14, 112
Queen's Bench Division of the High Court 37-9

re-examination of witnesses 179-80, 186
reasonable-refusal circumstances for ADR 3-4, 5, 13, 14-16, 18-19
relevant period of the Part 36 offer 163-9, 172, 174
reliefs 103, 113-15, 118, 119, 120
remedies 6, 9, 14, 72, 86, 95, 100, 108-9, see also claim amounts; damages; enforcement; injunctions
reply to defence 70-1, 77, 79
requests for further information 70-1, 76, 79-80, 83, 84-5, 112
reserve judgment 179
resolving disputes through civil claims 20-34, 45-6

respondent against whom an interim application is made 87-97
responding to a claim, definition 14, 27, 53-64, 67-9, 76-7; time limits 53-4, 56, 57-60, 63, 66, 68, 78-9, 84, see also defendant; defending
response pack 55-8, 76
retainer (client agreement) 154
road traffic accident claims 23, 28, 32-3, 34, 75, 93, 124, 133, 137, 149, 151-2, 162, 181

sanctions/penalties 1-5, 10, 11-30, 33, 103-4, 113-14, 118, 120, 189; alternative dispute resolution (ADR) 1, 2-3, 4-5, 14-16, 18-19; case management 103-4, 113-14, 118, 120; definition 11-12, 14, 16, 18, 19, 113; reliefs 103, 113-15, 118, 119, 120
Scotland and Northern Ireland enforcement mechanisms 185
sealing the claim form 39, 47
search orders, interim injunctions 86, 96
security for costs orders 153, 158, 161-2, 169
serve a document 11, 35-45, 47-9, 51-4, 58-64, 72, 79, 107, 122, 126, 141
service methods/requirements, claim form 35-6, 39-45, 47, 48-9, 51-2, 72
set aside the interim application order 89, 95
set aside the judgment in default 53-4, 58, 59-61, 64, 66-7, 68-9
settlement of a claim 59, 61, 62-3, 64, 67, 69, 163-9, 176; definition 62-3, 67, 69; Part 36 offers 153-4, 162, 163-9, 172, 173, 174
single joint expert 28, 121-2, 129-31, 132, 133, 136
skeleton argument 88, 96-7, 101, 178
small claims track allocation 104, 107-10, 117, 119, 141, 150, 155, 170, 173
specialist courts 35, 38-9
specific disclosure 138, 141, 144-5, 147
specified claim 53, 55-6, 63-4, 67, 75
split trials 112

Index 201

standard basis method of assessing costs/fees/expenses 62, 64, 154, 158-61, 164-7, 172
standard disclosure 138, 140-2, 146-8, 150-2
standard of proof 121-2, 132-3, 136
statement of truth 39, 72, 74-5, 77, 128, 130
statements of case 5-6, 11, 46, 49-50, 52, 70-85, 112, 178; requests for further information 70-1, 76, 79, 80, 83, 84-5, 112, see also claim form; defending; Part 20 CPR claim; particulars of claim; reply to defence
statute barred 23-4, 30
statutes see separate Table of statutes
stayed (paused) litigation matters 4, 62, 63, 65, 67-9
strict liability torts 75
strict rules of evidence 109
striking out sanction 113
struck out 59, 64, 72, 162
summarily assessed costs, definition 155-6, 169, 172
summary judgment 59, 64, 86-7, 90-3, 96-9, 100, 101, 106; costs orders 92, 98-9, 101; definition 59, 64, 86-7, 90-1, 96-7, 100, 101; dismissal orders 92, 106; 'no other compelling reason' criteria 91, 96, 98, 101; 'no real prospect' criteria 91-2, 96; purpose, procedure and evidence required 90-3, 97, 100, 101; wasted costs order 92, 99, 101, 113
supporting evidence 39, 58, 60-1

taking-control-of-goods enforcement orders 183, 186, 190
Technology and Construction Court 38-9
tenants, landlords 109
text messages 36, 41, 51
third-party debt enforcement orders 183, 186, 188, 190
third-party funding 153, 169

timetables, case management 103-7, 109-14, 118, 120, 141, 157, 177-8, 186; trial 177-8, 186
Tomlin order 54, 62-3, 64, 67-8, 69
tort law vii, 22-3, 24, 31, 34, 73, 75, 153-4, 162, 169, 172-4
track allocation 103-5, 107-12, 114-15, 117, 119-20, 140-1, 155, 177-8; claim amounts 108, 109-10, 116, 117, 119-20; costs 153-7, 160-1, 169, 170, 172, 173; criteria 107, 108-10, 116, 117, 119-20, 141; directions 110-17, 119, 130-1, 136, 141, 146, 150, 157, 160-1, 177; disagreements 110; disclosure 111-12, 138, 140-1; pre-trial checklist 111-12, 177-8; time limits 107-8, 111-12, 141, see also fast; multi; small claims
trial 11-14, 87, 95-6, 100, 104-13, 119-20, 126-37, 154-5, 160-9, 172-91; definition 11-12, 14, 175-80, 186; oath 129, 133; split trials 112; structure 179-80, 186; time limits 111-12, 177-8, 180-1, 186, 188, 190; timetables 177-8, 186
trial bundle 175, 177-9, 186, 187-8, 190

unless orders 113
unreasonable-party ADR sanctions/penalties 1, 2-5, 13, 14-16, 18-19, 29-30
unrepresented parties 109, 111
unspecified claim 53, 55-6, 59, 63-4, 65, 67, 68, 75

verbal agreements 7, 115, 133, 136
vicarious liability 26, 28

waived privilege 143, 147
wasted costs order 92, 99, 101, 113, 118, 120
with notice interim applications 88-9, 95, 96-7
without notice interim applications 88-9, 95, 96-7, 99-100, 101-2
without prejudice (confidential) aspects of ADR 2, 6, 143

without prejudice privilege 142-3, 147, 149, 151, 163
witness evidence 91, 121-2, 123-9, 133, 175-7, 179-80, 186, 187-91
witness statements, contents' list 127-9, 134, 136-7, 178; definition 127-9, 134, 136-7, 179-80; time limits 111-12, 113, 118, 120
witness summons 175, 176-7, 186, 187, 189, 190
writs/warrants of control 183

Ingram Content Group UK Ltd.
Milton Keynes UK
UKHW022053120523
421667UK00012B/259